DATE DUE

05 16			

DEMCO 38-296

Textile Coloration
and
Finishing

R

Textile Coloration
and
Finishing

Warren S. Perkins

Carolina Academic Press
Durham, North Carolina

Carolina Academic Press
700 Kent Street
Durham, North Carolina 27701
Telephone (919) 489-7486
Fax (919) 493-5668

Library of Congress Cataloging in Publication Data

Perkins, Warren S.
    Textile coloration and finishing / Warren S. Perkins
        p.   cm.
    Includes bibliographical references and index.
    ISBN 0-89089-885-5 (casebound : alk. paper)
    1. Dyes and dyeing—Chemistry.   2. Color in the textile industries.
3. Textile finishing.
I. Title
TP893.P47 1996   677'.02825—dc20   96-2516

Contents

Textile Coloration
and
Finishing

Chapter 1

Textile Chemicals

The Textile Chemist and Colorist Buyer's Guide lists over one hundred categories of chemical specialties containing thousands of individual products. These chemical specialties are manufactured and distributed by hundreds of companies ranging in size from small companies serving limited markets to large multinational corporations serving many and diverse markets. Textile specialty chemicals are classified according to general chemical types such as acids, alkalies, starches, oxidizing agents, reducing agents and according to function of the chemical product such as adhesive, softener, flame retardant, surfactant, thickener, and many others. Categories according to function of chemicals overlap a lot because a particular chemical substance may perform more than one function in textile manufacturing. For example, a particular substance may be a lubricant, softener, dispersing agent, dyeing assistant and may have other functions. Therefore, the same chemical substance could be used in several different ways depending on the function required of the substance for a particular application. Similarly, several different classes of chemicals may be used to perform a particular function. For example, softness may be imparted to textile products by several different types of chemical substances.

Many textile chemical specialties are blends or mixtures of substances formulated by the manufacturer or distributor for a specific application. For example, two or more agents may be mixed to produce a fabric softener which will impart different fabric properties than either of the agents by itself. The exact composition of formulated products is often proprietary to the manufacturer or distributor. Usually, a general description of the composition of a formulated product is divulged by the supplier.

The following sections discuss the chemistry and function of some common classes of substances found in textile specialty chemicals.

Specific applications of many of these chemicals are discussed in other chapters.

Water

Water is the chemical most used in dyeing and finishing of textiles. Treatment of water for use in textile manufacturing and treatment and disposal of wastewater effluent from textile manufacturing plants is a complex and important subject. The subjects of water and wastewater treatment are not covered in this chapter.

Acids, Bases, and Salts

Almost all textile wet processes require control of pH, acidity, alkalinity, or salt concentration. Furthermore, many textile functional chemicals fall into one of these classes. Selection of acids, bases, and salts for use in textile manufacturing is based mainly on the usefulness of the chemical for the intended application and cost of the chemical. Following is a discussion of some of the important acids, bases, and salts used in textile manufacturing.

Acids

For most practical purposes it is sufficient to say that an acid is a substance that makes the hydrogen ion content of a solution higher than that of pure water, which has hydrogen ion concentration of 1×10^{-7}M. Since pH = -log [H$^+$], this means that acids make solutions having pH of less than 7. Some acids commonly used in textile process are shown in Table 1-1 along with their typical pH values.

The strongest acids, such as hydrochloric, ionize completely in water while the weaker acids, such as acetic, ionize only partially in water.

Acids are used for pH adjustment, pH control, and neutralization of fabrics after alkaline treatment in various preparation, dyeing, and finishing steps. In many cases a buffered acid system is preferable to a single component pH control system.

Bases

For most practical purposes it is sufficient to say that a base is a substance which makes the hydrogen ion concentration of a solution

Table 1-1.   pH Values[1] of Some Acids Commonly Used in Textiles

Acid	Concentration	pH
Hydrochloric	0.1 N	1.1
Sulfuric	0.1 N	1.2
Citric	0.1 N	2.2
Formic	0.1 N	2.3
Acetic	0.1 N	2.9
Carbonic	saturated	3.8
Monosodium phosphate[2]	1%	4.4
Boric	0.1 N	5.2

1. *CRC Handbook of Chemistry and Physics*
2. *The Condensed Chemical Dictionary*

lower than that of pure water, or conversely, makes the hydroxyl ion concentration higher than that of pure water. Therefore, bases make solutions having pH greater than 7. Some common bases are shown in Table 1-2 along with their pH values.

Bases are used for pH adjustment, pH control, and neutralization of fabrics after acidic treatment in various preparation, dyeing, and finishing steps.

Salts

A salt is any substance which forms ions other than hydrogen or hydroxyl ions. A salt is formed by the reaction of an acid with a base. Neutral salts do not change the pH when dissolved in water. The two most common neutral salts used in textile manufacturing

Table 1-2.   pH Values[1] of Some Bases Commonly Used in Textiles

Base	Concentration	pH
Sodium hydroxide	0.1 N	13.0
Potassium hydroxide	0.1 N	13.0
Sodium metasilicate	0.1 N	12.6
Trisodium phosphate	0.1 N	12.0
Sodium carbonate	0.1 N	11.6
Ammonia	0.1 N	11.1
Disodium phosphate[2]	1%	8.8
Sodium bicarbonate	0.1 N	8.4

1. *CRC Handbook of Chemistry and Physics*
2. *The Condensed Chemical Dictionary*

are sodium chloride (common salt) and sodium sulfate (Glauber's salt). Neutral salts are those formed by the reaction of strong acids with strong bases.

Many salts behave as acids or bases because they hydrolyze in water. Some of the acids and bases in the above tables fit the definition of salt. Acidic and basic salts are those which were derived from acids and/or bases which do not completely ionize in water.

Salts are frequently used as dyeing assistants and catalysts in textile chemical formulations.

Oxidizing and Reducing Agents

The term "oxidation" implies the addition of oxygen to a substance. "Reduction" is the opposite of oxidation. Usage of these terms has been broadened to include any chemical reaction in which electrons are transferred between atoms. Oxidation and reduction occur simultaneously, so the reactions are called oxidation-reduction (or "redox") reactions. Oxidation numbers are used to keep track of electrons in redox reactions. An atom which increases in oxidation number has been oxidized. An atom which decreases in oxidation number has been reduced.

The reducing agent is the substance which does the reducing and becomes oxidized as a result of the reaction. The oxidizing agent is the substance which does the oxidizing and becomes reduced as a result of the reaction. In the first reaction shown below, the carbon atom is oxidized so the aldehyde is the reducing agent. In the second reaction the carbon atom is reduced so the aldehyde is the oxidizing agent.

$$R-\overset{\overset{\textstyle O}{\|}}{C}-H \ + \ \text{oxidizing agent} \ \longrightarrow \ R-\overset{\overset{\textstyle O}{\|}}{C}-O-H$$

$$R-\overset{\overset{\textstyle O}{\|}}{C}-H \ + \ \text{reducing agent} \ \longrightarrow \ R-\overset{\overset{\textstyle OH}{|}}{\underset{\underset{\textstyle H}{|}}{C}}-H$$

As shown above in the reactions of aldehydes, a particular substance can be either an oxidizing or a reducing agent depending on the reaction. However, following is a list of some chemicals which are used as oxidizing agents in reactions in textile chemical processes and chemical tests.

> hydrogen peroxide
> dichromates (sodium or potassium)
> potassium permanganate
> sodium hypochlorite
> sodium chlorite
> sodium perborate
> potassium iodate
> sodium persulfate
> other peroxygen compounds

Following is a list of some chemicals which are used as reducing agents in reactions in textile chemical processes and chemical tests.

> sodium hydrosulfite ("hydro")
> sodium bisulfite
> sulfur dioxide
> glucose
> sodium formaldehyde sulfoxylate
> sodium polysulfide
> others

Redox reactions involving both organic compounds and inorganic compounds are important in several textile manufacturing processes, especially bleaching and dyeing. Oxidation-reduction reactions are also common in analytical tests on textile materials and textile chemicals.

Surface Active Agents

A surface active chemical is one which tends to accumulate at a surface or interface. Surface active chemicals have remarkable effects on chemical processes many of which are observed in our everyday lives.

An interface is the area of contact between two substances. The following five types of interfaces are possible.

1. Liquid/gas—surface of a lake
2. Solid/liquid—textile fabric in water
3. Solid/solid—stack of bricks
4. Solid/gas—smoke polluted air

5. Liquid/liquid—oil on water

Where the interface is between two substances not in the same phase, the interface is usually called a surface. The type of interfaces that are of greatest interest in textiles are surfaces, for example, the area of contact between fibers and a chemical treatment formulation. Solid/liquid surfaces are important in many textile wet processes such as washing, dyeing, and chemical finishing.

Natural phenomena often occur at interfaces or surfaces. Following are examples of events that usually happen at interfaces. Each of these has direct importance in textile chemical processes.

dissolution
wetting
dispersion
emulsification
chemical adsorption
chemical absorption
adhesion
vaporization
sublimation
melting
heat transfer
catalysis
foaming
defoaming

These phenomena are observed or utilized to advantage in many ways in the textile chemical industries and in textile manufacturing. Some specific examples where these phenomena are important are as follows:

Removing soil (scouring)
Wetting
Rewetting
Softening
Retarding dyeing rate
Fixing dyes
Making emulsions
Stabilizing dispersions
Coagulating suspended solids
Making foams

Table 1-3.   Surface Tension of Some Liquids

Substance	Surface Tension (dynes/cm)
water	73
mercury	480
benzene	28
ethanol	22

Preventing foam formation
Defoaming liquids

Surface phenomena depend on the interaction of substances with one another at their surfaces. The surface tension of a liquid is an internal pressure caused by the attraction of molecules below the surface for those at the surface of a liquid. This molecular attraction creates an inward pull, or internal pressure, which tends to restrict the tendency of the liquid to flow and form a large interface with another substance. Surface tension is responsible for the meniscus on a liquid in a narrow tube.

The surface tension (or interfacial tension if the interface is not a surface) determines the tendency for surfaces to establish contact with one another. Therefore, surface tension is responsible for the shape of a droplet of a liquid. If the surface tension is high, the molecules in the liquid are greatly attracted to one another and not so much to the surrounding air. The droplet minimizes its contact with air by forming an almost spherical shape. The shape will not be exactly spherical because of the gravitational effect. If the droplet of water is in contact with a solid such as a fabric, its shape will also be affected by the interfacial tension at the solid/liquid interface. If the surface tension in the liquid is lower, the droplet forms a more ellipsoidal shape. Force must be applied and work must be done in order to distort the shape of the droplet; that is, to increase the area of the interface. By definition the interfacial tension is the amount of work required to create a unit area of interface or to increase the area of interface by one unit.

Polar substances have high surface tension while nonpolar substances have low surface tension. Table 1-3 shows the surface tensions for some liquid substances.

Because of its lower surface tension, ethanol will flow and form a larger area of contact (surface) with a solid than will water. Mer-

Figure 1-1. Schematic of surfactant molecule

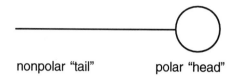

nonpolar "tail"   polar "head"

cury with its very high surface tension does not flow but breaks into droplets if given the opportunity.

The term surfactant is derived from the words surface active agent. A surface active agent, surfactant, is a substance which tends to concentrate at a surface. Surface active agents interfere with the ability of the molecules of a substance to interact with one another and, thereby, lower the surface tension of the substance. Surfactants used in industrial applications usually cause a dramatic decrease in surface tension when used at low concentration.

Chemically, surfactants are amphipathic molecules. That is, they have two distinctly different characteristics, polar and nonpolar, in different parts of the same molecule. Therefore, a surfactant molecule has both lyophilic (solvent-loving) and lyophobic (solvent-hating) characteristics. If the solvent is water, the surfactant has both hydrophilic (water-loving) and hydrophobic (water-hating) characteristics. Symbolically, a surfactant molecule can be represented as having a polar "head" and a nonpolar "tail" as shown in Figure 1-1.

While surface chemistry is important in almost all natural and man-made processes, most textile applications of surfactants concern the interaction of water with fibers and fabrics. Therefore, this discussion of surfactants will concentrate mainly on the behavior of surfactants in water.

The hydrophobic group in a surfactant for use in aqueous medium is usually a hydrocarbon chain but may be a fluorocarbon or siloxane chain of appropriate length. The hydrophilic group is polar and may be either ionic or nonionic.

Since surfactant molecules have both hydrophilic and hydrophobic parts, the most attractive place for them in water is at the surface where the forces of both attraction and repulsion to water can be satisfied. One other way that surfactants interact to satisfy natural forces of attraction and repulsion between molecules is by formation of micelles as shown in Figure 1-2. Surfactant molecules

Figure 1-2.   Schematic representation of surfactant molecules at surface and surfactant micelle in bulk liquid

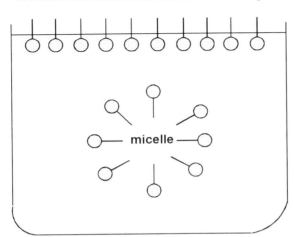

aggregate in water forming micelles. Micelles consist of hydrophobic interior regions, where hydrophobic tails interact with one another. These hydrophobic regions are surrounded by the hydrophilic regions where the heads of the surfactant molecules interact with water.

The number of surfactant molecules in a micelle is called the aggregation number. The aggregation number varies from only a few molecules to several thousand molecules depending on the chemical structure of the surfactant and other factors such as temperature and the presence of impurities in the mixture.

At very low concentration in water surfactant molecules are dissociated. At higher concentration of surfactant in water, micelles form. The concentration at which micelles form is called the critical micelle concentration (CMC). The concept of critical micelle concentration is very important because dramatic changes in the properties of the water/surfactant mixture occur at the CMC. As shown in Figure 1-3, the surface tension of water undergoes a precipitous decrease, and the detergency (ability to remove soil) of the mixture increases dramatically at the CMC. Surfactant concentration increases beyond the CMC have little additional effect on these properties of the surfactant/water mixture. Obviously, it is advantageous for the user to know and minimize the concentration of surfactant required to perform a particular function for both economical and environmental reasons.

Figure 1-3.   Surface tension and detergency of surfactant solution

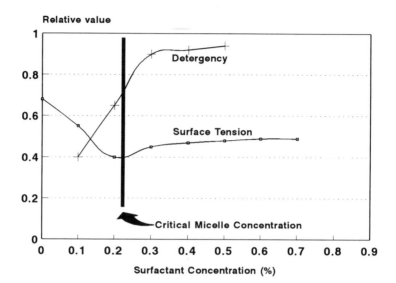

When the concentration of surfactant is near the CMC, surfactant micelles are believed to be spherical in shape. The radius of the micelle is approximately the length of the extended hydrophobic tail of the surfactant molecule. At greater surfactant concentrations or with the addition of other agents, the shape of micelles may be complex. Some micellar shapes which have been identified include extended parallel sheets (lamellar), rod-like structures, and long cylinders packed together.

Types (classes) of Surfactants

Surfactants fall in the following classifications according to the nature of the hydrophilic group:

anionic—hydrophilic head is *negatively* charged
cationic—hydrophilic head is *positively* charged
nonionic—hydrophilic head is polar but not fully charged
amphoteric—molecule has both potential positive and negative groups; charge depends on pH of the medium

Anionic Surfactants

Anionic surfactants are the most widely used of the four classes. Soaps are anionic surfactants which are made from fats. Some other important types of anionic surfactants are linear alkylbenzenesulfonates (LAS), lignin sulfonates, sulfosuccinate esters, and sulfated alcohols.

Soap

Soaps are alkali metal salts of fatty acids.

$$C_XH_YCOO^-M^+ \quad \text{X usually 15–17}$$
$$\text{H usually 31–35}$$
$$\text{M usually Na, K, or NH}_4$$

Fatty acids are carboxylic acids derived from or contained in animal or vegetable fats or oils. They contain linear hydrocarbon groups and may be either saturated or unsaturated. The most important fatty acids used for manufacture of surfactants are as follows:

stearic acid $C_{17}H_{35}COOH$ (saturated); solid at room temperature
palmitic acid $C_{16}H_{33}COOH$ (saturated); solid at room temperature
lauric acid $C_{11}H_{23}COOH$ (saturated); solid at room temperature
oleic acid $C_{17}H_{33}COOH$ (unsaturated at C_9-C_{10}); liquid at room temperature

Stearic, palmitic, and oleic acids are derived from tallow (animal fat). Lauric acid is usually derived from coconut oil. As a general rule, any carboxylic acid salt with a hydrocarbon group from C_{10} to C_{20} will make a soap. Those with less than 10 carbons are too soluble in water to have good surface activity. Those with more than 20 carbons in a linear configuration are too insoluble in water to use in aqueous medium. Economics and availability determine which particular fatty acids are used.

The most common cation in soap is sodium although potassium and ammonium are also common. Soaps are effective as cleaning agents in aqueous medium. Since soaps are relatively weak acids, the free acid is liberated in acidic medium. The free acids are insoluble in water. Therefore, soaps are only effective in alkaline medium. Another disadvantage of some soaps, especially those derived from tallow, is that they are precipitated by divalent cations. Therefore, the calcium and magnesium ions present in hard water can precipitate soap from water making it ineffective and leaving an undesirable deposit on surfaces. Soap deposited by hard water often forms a deposit on the sides of a bathtub.

Soaps can be made by neutralization of free fatty acids by alkali metal hydroxides.

$$C_{17}H_{35}COOH \quad + \quad NaOH \quad \longrightarrow \quad C_{17}H_{35}COO^-Na^+ + HOH$$

stearic acid   caustic soda   sodium stearate (soap)

Soaps can also be made by alkaline hydrolysis (saponification) of fats and oils. Fats and oils belong to the lipid family. The chemistry of oils as used in making soaps is identical to that of fats. Fats are solid. Oils are liquid. Generally, lipids with more saturated hydrocarbon content are more firm and have higher melting temperatures than those with unsaturated hydrocarbon groups. Fats are esters of the trihydric alcohol, glycerol. Fatty acids are produced by alkaline hydrolysis (saponification) of fats.

$$
\begin{array}{l}
C_{17}H_{35}COO\,CH_2 \\
\;\;\;\;\;\;\;\;\;\;\;\;\;| \\
C_{17}H_{35}COO\,CH \;\; + \;\; 3\,NaOH \;\; \longrightarrow \;\; 3\,C_{17}H_{35}COO^-Na^+ \;\; + \\
\;\;\;\;\;\;\;\;\;\;\;\;\;| \\
C_{17}H_{35}COO\,CH_2
\end{array}
\quad
\begin{array}{l}
CH_2OH \\
| \\
CH-OH \\
| \\
CH_2OH
\end{array}
$$

glycerol tristearate   fatty acid salt   glycerol
   (a fat)   (soap)

The soap (fatty acid salt) thus formed is separated from the glycerol byproduct by neutralization of the alkali or addition of salt to precipitate the soap. Commercial soaps produced from fats and fatty acids are generally mixtures of fatty acid salts.

Linear alkylbenzenesulfonates

These are called LAS detergents. They consist of a hydrocarbon chain usually 12 carbon atoms long with random distribution of benzene rings along the hydrocarbon chain. Acid-resistant equipment is required for the sulfonation reaction to produce the LAS. The general structure is as follows:

$$C_xH_y \!-\!\!\bigcirc\!\!-\! SO_3H$$

LAS as the sodium salt is the most common surfactant in industrial and household detergents. Since the sulfonate group is a strong acid, the LAS detergents are soluble and effective in acidic as well as in alkaline medium. The calcium and magnesium salts are soluble in water so LAS detergents are not affected by hard water. The sodium salt LAS detergents are soluble and effective even in the presence of electrolytes such as sodium chloride and sodium sulfate. Since the LAS detergents are resistant to hydrolysis by both hot acid and alkali, they are very useful for textile scouring formulations. LAS detergents resist degradation under anaerobic conditions but are degradable under aerobic conditions.

Ligninsulfonates

Lignin is a byproduct of paper manufacture. Sulfonated lignin is a very good dispersing agent for solids in water and finds textile applications mainly as a dispersing agent in specialty chemicals and dyes. Lignin sulfonates are among the least expensive surfactants and are readily available. They are unsuitable for many applications because of their dark color and because they do not produce much lowering of the surface tension of water.

Sulfosuccinate esters

Esters of sulfosuccinic acid, such as dioctyl (2-ethylhexyl) sulfosuccinate (DOSS), are excellent fast-wetting surfactants.

$$C_8H_{17}OOCCH_2CH{-}COOC_8H_{17}$$
$$|$$
$$SO_3^-Na^+$$

DOSS (as sodium salt)

Sulfosuccinate ester surfactants are very soluble in water. They do not emulsify oils so are not good scouring agents. They are soluble in organic solvents making them useful in dry cleaning. They are not acceptable for some aqueous applications since they are hydrolyzed by hot acid or alkali.

Sulfated alcohols

Various fatty alcohols, obtained by reduction of the corresponding fatty acid, can be reacted with chlorosulfonic acid or sulfur trioxide to produce their sulfuric acid esters.

$$C_{12}H_{23}{-}OH \;+\; ClSO_3H \;\longrightarrow\; C_{12}H_{23}{-}OSO_3H$$

lauryl alcohol   chlorosulfonic   lauryl sulfate
                 acid

These surfactants are *sulfates* rather than *sulfonates* like those described above. The sodium salt is most common although salts with diethanolamine, triethanolamine, or ammonia are used in cosmetics and shampoos. Sodium lauryl sulfate (free acid form shown above) is an excellent foaming agent. Foaming properties are enhanced when some unsulfated fatty alcohol is retained in the product.

Nonionic surfactants

Although less widely used than anionic surfactants, nonionic surfactants have diverse uses in textiles and the volume used is large. Of the several types of nonionic surfactants, the polyoxyethylenated alkylphenols and the polyoxyethylenated linear alcohols are the most common.

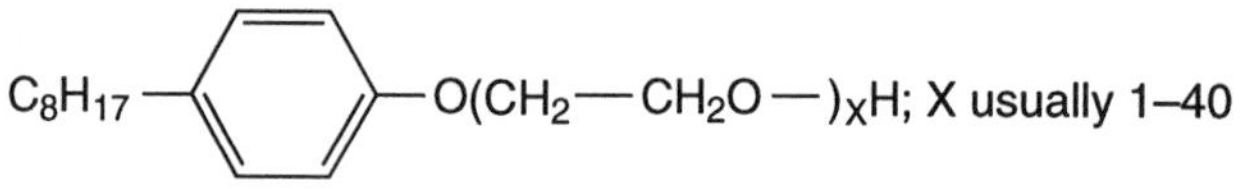

$$C_8H_{17} - \langle\!\!\bigcirc\!\!\rangle - O(CH_2 - CH_2O -)_xH; \; X \; usually \; 1\text{--}40$$

ethyloxylated p-octylphenol

The reaction of ethylene oxide with lauryl alcohol to produce a nonionic surfactant is shown below.

$$C_{12}H_{23} - OH + X \; \overset{H_2C - CH_2}{\underset{O}{\diagdown\;\diagup}} \longrightarrow C_{12}H_{23} - O(CH_2 - CH_2O -)_xH$$

The hydrocarbon group is the hydrophobic part of the surfactant while the chain of ethylene oxide groups is the hydrophilic part of the molecule. The length of the ethylene oxide chain is controlled by the relative amounts of reactants used and determines how hydrophilic the surfactant is.

When the reactant is a linear alcohol such as lauryl alcohol, the product usually contains some unreacted alcohol. This can be a disadvantage. Fortunately, the reaction with the phenolic hydroxyl group is usually complete since the phenolic hydroxyl is more reactive than the alcoholic hydroxyl. Therefore, there are no toxicity or dermatology problems due to free phenol in these products.

Nonionic surfactants are compatible with other types of surfactants. They are generally poor foamers which can be an advantage or disadvantage depending on requirements. They are good dispersing agents in many cases. They are more effective than LAS detergents in removing soil from hydrophobic fibers but are inferior to anionic surfactants for soil removal from cotton. Nonionic surfactants, like most ethylene oxide derivatives, exhibit inverse solubility characteristics and may precipitate with increase in temperature of their solutions. This sometimes precludes their use in high temperature applications but can be an advantage in that elevation of the temperature can be used to destroy activity of the surfactant if desired. The temperature at which precipitation occurs is called the "cloud point" of the surfactant.

The properties of a nonionic surfactant can be tailored somewhat for a particular use by controlling the relative amounts of hydrophilic and hydrophobic character. The relative amounts of hydrophilic and hydrophobic character may be expressed as the hydrophile-lipophile balance (HLB) of the surfactant. HLB values are sometimes assigned by observation of and experience concerning the emulsification behavior of surfactants. Likewise, HLB values can be assigned to substances that must be emulsified. Matching the HLB values of substance to be emulsified and the surfactant is a good starting point for selection of an appropriate surfactant.

HLB values for nonionic surfactants are often calculated using the formula

$$20 \times \frac{M_H}{M_H + M_L},$$

where M_H is the molecular weight of the hydrophilic portion of the molecule (the ethylene oxide chain) and M_L is the molecular weight of the hydrophobic portion of the molecule. HLB values calculated using this formula will range from 0 to 20.

HLB values may be used as an indicator of the emulsification behavior of surfactants. As a general rule, surfactants with good oil solubility produce water-in-oil (w/o) emulsions while more water soluble surfactants produce oil-in-water (o/w) emulsions. HLB values are a good indicator of behavior of surfactants in water as is shown below.

HLB Values	Behavior in Water
1–4	Not dispersible
3–10	Form milky dispersions
10–13	Form translucent dispersions
>13	Form clear solutions

Therefore, emulsification behavior should be predictable from HLB values. In practice, HLB values can only be used as a rough guide to surfactant selection because variables such as temperature and nature of the substances to be emulsified are important. In many cases, a mixed surfactant system will produce better emulsification than a single surfactant.

Cationic Surfactants

Most of the uses of cationic surfactants result from their ability to adhere to and modify solid surfaces. Cationic surfactants are important as corrosion inhibitors, fuel and lubricating oil additives, germicides, and hair conditioners. Important applications of cationic surfactants in textiles include their use as fabric softeners, fixatives for anionic dyes, and dyeing rate retarders for cationic dyes. Cationic and anionic surfactants are usually incompatible. Cationic surfactants are compatible with nonionics and zwitterionics. Usage of cationic surfactants is small compared to anionics and nonionics.

Two common types of cationic surfactants are long chain amines and quaternary amine salts. The long chain amine types are made from natural fats and oils or from synthetic amines. A typical example is

$$C_{18}H_{37}NH_3^+Cl^-.$$

The amine N may be primary, secondary, or tertiary. They are soluble in strongly acidic medium but become uncharged and insoluble in water at pH greater than 7.

Quaternary amine type cationic surfactants are very important as fabric softeners. They absorb on the surface of fibers with their hydrophobic groups oriented away from the fibers. This reduces the friction between fibers and imparts a soft, fluffy feel to the fabric. This same mechanism accounts for the behavior and use of cationic surfactants as hair conditioners.

A typical quaternary cationic surfactant is

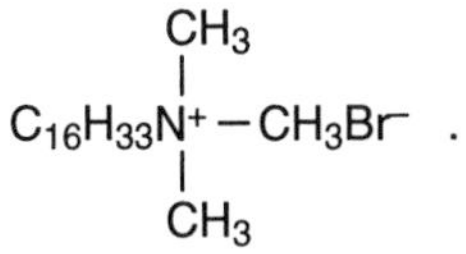

$$
\begin{array}{c}
CH_3 \\
| \\
C_{16}H_{33}N^+ - CH_3Br^- \\
| \\
CH_3
\end{array}
$$

cetyl trimethylammonium bromide

Unlike long chain amine cationic surfactants, quaternary ammonium salts are useful and effective in neutral and alkaline as well as acidic medium.

Zwitterionic Surfactants

Like cationic surfactants, zwitterionic surfactants impart a feel of softness to textile materials. An example is

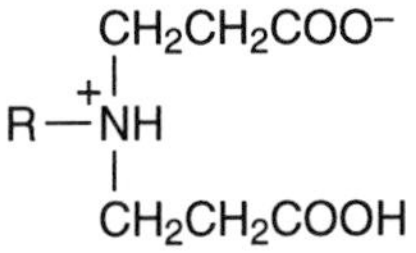

$$
\begin{array}{c}
CH_2CH_2COO^- \\
+| \\
R-NH \\
| \\
CH_2CH_2COOH
\end{array}
$$

N-Alkyl-β-iminodipropionic acid; R= long chain hydrocarbon

Zwitterionic surfactants are compatible with all other classes of surfactants and are soluble and effective in the presence of high concentrations of electrolytes, acids, and alkalies. They exhibit cationic behavior near or below their isoelectric points and anionic behavior at higher pH. The isoelectric point depends on the structure of the surfactant.

Polymers

Both natural and synthetic polymers have a multitude of uses in a wide range of products including the following:

adhesives
agricultural chemicals
ceramics
construction products
cosmetics

foods
leather
paints
paint removers
paper products
pharmaceuticals
printing inks
rubber
tobacco products
textile chemical products
textile products

The use of polymers in textile auxiliary products and textile chemical processes is broad and extensive. Polymers are used to modify or add desirable properties to a chemical formulation or product. Binders, coatings, thickeners, sizes, and finishes usually use polymers as their major ingredient.

Latex paint is a good example of the use of polymers to improve properties of a product. Polymers for use in paints are usually pseudoplastic meaning that the viscosity of the liquid decreases when it undergoes shearing. Thus, the paint flows readily during spreading with the applicator but becomes resistant to flowing when not under shear. This prevents the paint from running after it is applied. The flow requirements of a print formulation for textiles are much like those for paints. The print paste must flow readily through a screen with small holes during application but must keep the color from spreading after application until the printed design can be dried. Polymers provide these required flow characteristics in the textile print paste.

Polymers provide essential adhesion between particles and parts in products like pharmaceutical, construction products, paper and textile products. The addition of polymeric agents to textile fabrics can improve fabric properties such as appearance, durability, strength, abrasion resistance, hand, drape, flexibility, and stiffness. The following sections describe some of the common polymers used as auxiliary chemicals in textile manufacturing.

Starch

Starch is one of several polysaccharides commonly used in textile manufacturing. Starch is a carbohydrate polymer of molecular formula $(C_6H_{10}O_5)_X$. The repeat unit in the starch molecule is α-anhydroglucopyranose.

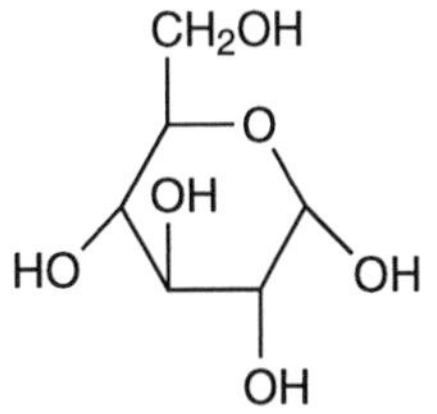

α-glucopyranose

Plants store starches in their roots, stems, and seeds as their energy reserve. Examples of starches of these three types are potato, sago, and corn, respectively. While the molecular formula for all starches is the same, starches do differ chemically from one another. Most starches are mixtures of two main components, amylose and amylopectin. The ratio of amylose to amylopectin in corn starch is about 28/72, but the ratio varies in starches from different sources. Amylose is usually the minor of these two components but varies from as little as 2% in waxy maize to as much as 80% in amylomaize. Amylose is mostly a linear polymer having the following structure:

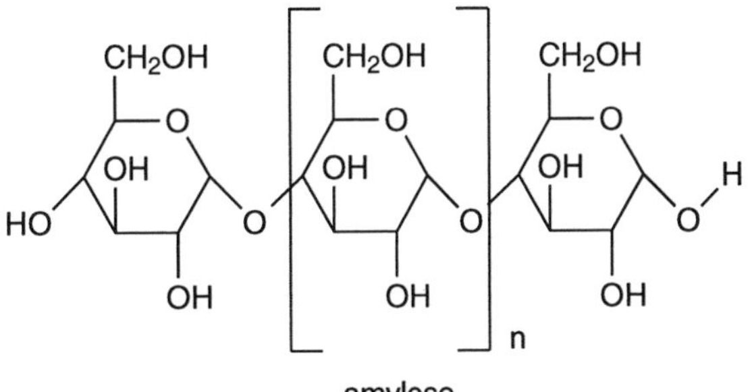

amylose

Note that all anhydroglucopyranose units are linked to one another by an oxygen atom bridging the number 1 and number 4 carbon atoms on adjacent units. The atoms around the number 1 carbon atom are in the α configuration in starch. (Cellulose is also a carbohydrate consisting of a chain of 1,4-linked anhydroglucose units. However, in cellulose the atoms around the number 1 carbon atom are in the ß configuration.) Amylose is believed to contain a few

Table 1-4.   Properties of Amylose and Amylopectin

Property	Amylose	Amylopectin
General structure	mostly linear	branched
Typical DP	1000–3000	10^4–10^5
Molecular weight	160000–500000	10^7–10^9
Color of iodine complex	deep blue	purple
Behavior in paste	retrogrades	stable
Structure	partially crystalline	amorphous
Solubility in water	variable	soluble

(Table derived from references 4 and 7)

short branches resulting from 1,6 anhydroglucose linkages. The number of repeat units in amylose molecules in starch in nature is around 1000–3000 although samples outside this range can be found. The molecular weight of amylose is usually in the range of 160,000–500,000.

Amylopectin also contains 1,4-linked α-anhydroglucose units. However, amylopectin also contains some 1,6 α-anhydroglucose linkages. These 1,6 linkages occur about every 20 units and make amylopectin a branched chain polymer. Branching of the structure results in very high molecular weights of 10^7–10^9. Amylopectin is similar to glycogen (animal sugar), a branched chain carbohydrate which the human body stores in the liver until it is needed for energy. Properties of amylose and amylopectin are different as indicated in Table 1-4.

Since the properties of amylose and amylopectin are different, and starches from various sources contain different ratios of the two components, the starches themselves differ in properties. Differences in molecular weight and amounts and types of impurities also cause starches from different sources to differ in properties.

Corn is the most common source of starch in the United States. Corn is refined to separate it from other components in the corn kernel. Other components in the corn such as oil and gluten also have value. Dry starch for industrial use is a white powdery substance.

Although starch is not completely soluble in water, it swells in water forming a viscous, cloudy dispersion which is referred to as the starch paste. Heat and agitation are required to produce swelling and dispersion of starch in water. The process of swelling and dis-

Figure 1-4. Hypothetical cooking curve of starch

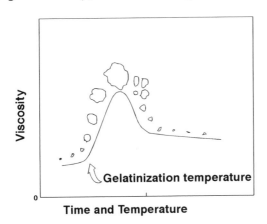

persing starch in water is called "cooking." Figure 1-4 shows the general shape of a cooking curve for starch. The actual shape of the curve depends on the type of starch and whether or not it has been chemically modified.

In cold water, the starch granules make a thin slurry. As the temperature rises and the mixture is stirred, the starch granules begin to swell. The temperature at which swelling of starch begins is characteristic of a particular starch and is called the gelatinization temperature. As the starch granules swell, they begin to interfere with one another and restrict the movement of water in the vessel, i.e. the viscosity of the mixture rises. The granules continue to swell, and the viscosity continues to rise to a peak. The peak viscosity is the point at which some of the granules begin to rupture. As the granules continue to rupture, the viscosity continues to fall until the starch is "cooked out" to a smooth paste. The cooked starch paste is usually cloudy indicating that the starch is not fully dissolved. However, a fully cooked starch will contain little or no granular material when viewed under a microscope. The length of the cooking cycle for many starches is about 1.5 hours. Vigorous agitation and high temperature in special cooking vessels is often used to lower the time required to cook starch.

The cooked starch paste is temperature sensitive and may gel if its temperature decreases much. The gelling characteristic of starch may be a desirable property for use such as food thickening, but it is a nuisance for most industrial applications of starches. The gel formation is called retrogradation. Retrogradation is often irreversible even with vigorous stirring and reheating.

Modified starches

Starch can be modified to produce a variety of products for many applications. Some of the modifications resulting in important textile chemicals are as follows:

> Depolymerization
> Crosslinking
> Derivatization

Depolymerization reduces the viscosity of the starch while crosslinking can either increase or decrease the viscosity depending on the extent of crosslinking. Chemical derivatization can dramatically alter the properties of starch.

Depolymerization

Depolymerized starches for textile applications are mainly of two types, acid modified and oxidized. Amylopectin is attacked preferentially in the early stages of degradation followed later by degradation of the amylose fraction. Therefore, slightly depolymerized starch tends to retain the character of amylose more so than the character of amylopectin. While acid modified and oxidized starches are both lower viscosity products than unmodified starch, they differ from each other in other properties such as ease of solubility, strength, and gelling tendency.

Acid modified starch, often called thin-boiling starch, is made by treating a starch with a mineral acid such as sulfuric or hydrochloric or sometimes with an organic acid. Thin-boiling starches are often designated by fluidity numbers. Since fluidity and viscosity are inversely related, a starch having a higher fluidity number forms a lower viscosity solution at a given solids concentration than does a starch having a lower fluidity number. The treatment with acid is done using an aqueous suspension (milk form) of starch granules in water at temperatures below the gelatinization temperature. The acid hydrolyses some glucosidic linkages decreasing the molecular weight of the starch. The acid is neutralized to stop the reaction after the desired extent of degradation has been achieved. Finally, the converted starch is collected and dried.

Depolymerization of Starch

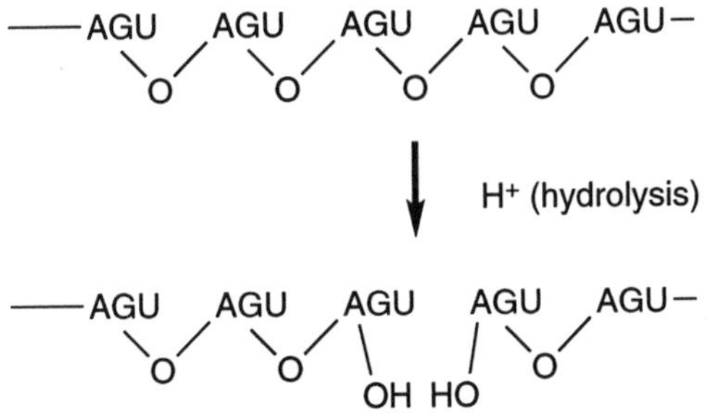

——AGU AGU AGU AGU AGU—
        \ / \ / \ / \ /
         O   O   O   O

↓ H⁺ (hydrolysis)

——AGU AGU AGU AGU AGU—
        \ / \ / \   / \ /
         O   O   OH HO   O

AGU= anhydroglucose unit ($C_6H_{10}O_5$)

Because of their lower viscosity, more concentrated solutions can be prepared from thin-boiling starches than is possible with unmodified starch. This can be an advantage when a high concentration level of starch is required for some application. Acid modified starches tend to retrograde easily. They are used mostly where firm gel characteristics are desirable. Since the strength of a polymer depends on molecular weight of the polymer, converted starches produced by degradation of the starch are weaker than unmodified starches.

The manufacture of oxidized starch is similar to that of acid modified starch except that an oxidizing agent is substituted for acid in the depolymerization process. Oxidized starches are sometimes referred to as bleached starch. Sodium hypochlorite is the classic oxidizing agent used to make oxidized starches, but other oxidizing agents are sometimes used. In addition to lowering the molecular weight of the starch by scission of the glucosidic linkages, oxidizing agents oxidize some alcohol groups in the starch to aldehyde and carboxyl groups.

$$\text{Starch—CH}_2\text{OH} \xrightarrow{[O]} \text{Starch—}\overset{\text{H}}{\underset{}{\text{C}}}\!\!=\!\!\text{O} \xrightarrow{[O]} \text{Starch—COOH}$$

Although the primary hydroxyl group is used in the example shown, the secondary hydroxyl groups can also participate in oxidation reactions. The incorporation of aldehyde and carboxyl groups improves solubility and stability of the starch in water. Oxidized starches have good film forming characteristics and are commonly found in coating and sizing formulations in paper and textile manufacturing.

Starch gums and dextrins are also produced by acid hydrolysis of starch or by roasting of dry starch. They are depolymerized to a greater extent than thin boiling starches and are used mostly as thickeners and adhesives.

Crosslinking

Starch may also be crosslinked using bifunctional or polyfunctional reactants. The resulting products are more resistant to swelling than are unmodified starches. They can be made in a wide range of viscosities and types of products depending on the degree of crosslinking imparted.

Derivitization

Chemical derivatives of starch are common and useful products in textile manufacturing. Ethers and esters are two common types of chemical derivatives of starch.

Starch—O—R   R = alkyl or alkyl derivative
                  O is from primary or secondary hydroxyl
(starch ether)

$$\text{Starch}-\text{O}-\overset{\overset{\displaystyle O}{\|}}{\text{C}}-\text{R}\qquad R = alkyl$$

(starch ester)

The properties of the starch derivative depend on the chemistry of the particular derivative and on the degree of substitution. The degree of substitution in products for textile applications in aqueous medium is generally low, just enough to interfere with the normal orientation and interaction of the molecular chains in the starch. The incorporation of new chemical groups usually makes the starch more water soluble and easier to dissolve. The gelatinization temperature is usually lowered, and the product is usually more resistant to gelling and retrogradation than is unmodified starch. Derivatized starches sometimes produce virtually clear solutions or dispersions in water. Toughness and flexibility of the derivatized starch is usually much greater than that of unmodified starch.

Starch ethers

Hydroxyethyl, hydroxypropyl, and carboxymethyl starches are in common use in textiles. Hydroxyethyl starches are made by reacting starch with ethylene oxide. The reaction is called ethoxylation.

$$\text{Starch-CH}_2\text{OH} + \; X \; \underset{\substack{\diagdown \diagup \\ O \\ \text{ethylene oxide}}}{\overset{H_2C-CH_2}{}} \longrightarrow \text{Starch-CH}_2\text{O} - (\text{CH}_2-\text{CH}_2\text{O}-)_x\text{H}$$

ethylene oxide   hydroxyethyl starch

Since ethylene oxide polymerizes, a chain of hydroxyethyl groups can form from the hydroxyl group on starch where the reaction began. Therefore, degree of substitution is not completely descriptive of the extent of the derivatization. The total amount of ethylene oxide reacted with the starch must be specified to indicate the extent of the reaction. The term *mole substitution* is used to express the extent of the reaction between ethylene oxide and starch. In addition to disrupting the ability of the starch molecules to interact with each other, ethoxylation also increases the hydrophilic character of the starch polymer.

Hydroxypropyl starch is similar to hydroxyethyl starch. It is produced by reacting starch with propylene oxide. Some hydroxyethylated starches and hydroxypropylated starches lose water of hydration when their solutions are heated and either separate from solution or gel. This is similar to the cloud point observed with some nonionic surfactants.

The reaction of starch with monochloroacetic acid produces carboxymethyl starch. The carboxyl group on carboxymethyl starch is acidic and easily forms a sodium salt. Carboxymethylation can dramatically enhance the water solubility of starch.

$$\text{Starch}-\text{CH}_2\text{OH} + \text{ClCH}_2\text{COOH} \xrightarrow{\text{NaOH}} \text{Starch}-\text{CH}_2\text{OCH}_2\text{COOH}$$

(carboxymethyl starch)

Starch esters

Starch acetate is produced by reacting starch with acetic anhydride.

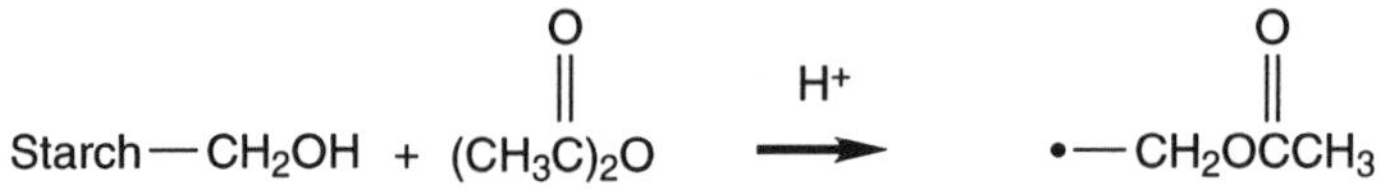

$$\text{Starch—CH}_2\text{OH + (CH}_3\text{C})_2\text{O} \xrightarrow{\text{H}^+} \bullet\text{—CH}_2\text{O}\overset{\displaystyle O}{\overset{\|}{\text{C}}}\text{CH}_3$$

A low degree of substitution of acetate groups for hydroxyl groups disrupts the molecular chain interaction. This disruption of molecular chain interaction increases accessibility of the polymer to water. Therefore, even though the ester group formed in the reaction is less polar than the hydroxyl group it replaced, the starch acetate is more water soluble than unmodified starch if the degree of substitution is low. Other esters of starch include phosphates, succinates, and xanthates.

Other polysaccharides

Several other polysaccharides that have textile uses are shown in Table 1-5. These natural polysaccharides may be separated from impurities that they contain and used without further modification. Alternatively, they may be chemically modified, as was described earlier for starch, to give them special properties.

Carboxymethyl cellulose

Carboxymethyl cellulose (CMC) is a water soluble derivative of cellulose. CMC is usually supplied as a white or brownish granular

Table 1-5.   Polysaccharides Used in Textile Manufacturing

Polysaccharide	Origin	Major Uses
Guar gum	Cyanopsis tetra-gonoloba (plant)	print paste thickener; etc.
Carrageenan	seaweed	dispersant; viscosity control
Locust bean gum	carob seed	print paste thickener
Gum tragacanth	plant	dispersant; thickener
Gum Arabic	acacia (plant)	adhesive; thickener; dispersant
Xanthan gum	fermentation of carbohydrates	dispersant; thickener; etc.
Alginates	seaweed (usually used as sodium salt)	thickener; antimigrant

solid. Molecular weight of the cellulose and degree of substitution of the carboxymethyl groups is controlled during manufacture to make a family of grades for a multitude of uses. Historically, the largest textile use of CMC was as a warp size. However, CMC fell out of favor as a warp size in recent years except as an ingredient in preblended size products. Certain grades of CMC produce solutions having very high viscosity. This accounts for its use as a thickener in chemical formulations. Synthesis of CMC is similar to synthesis of carboxymethyl starch. CMC for textile uses is usually supplied as the sodium salt form.

$$\text{Cellulose}-CH_2OH + ClCH_2COOH \xrightarrow{\text{NaOH}} \text{Cellulose}-CH_2OCH_2COOH$$

Polyvinyl acetate and polyvinyl alcohol

Polyvinyl acetate and other vinyl polymers are used as firming finishes, hand modifiers, hand builders, coatings, and binders for textile fabrics. Other uses include flock binding, print binding, and warp sizing.

Polyvinyl acetate (PVA) is a linear polymer made by polymerization of vinyl acetate.

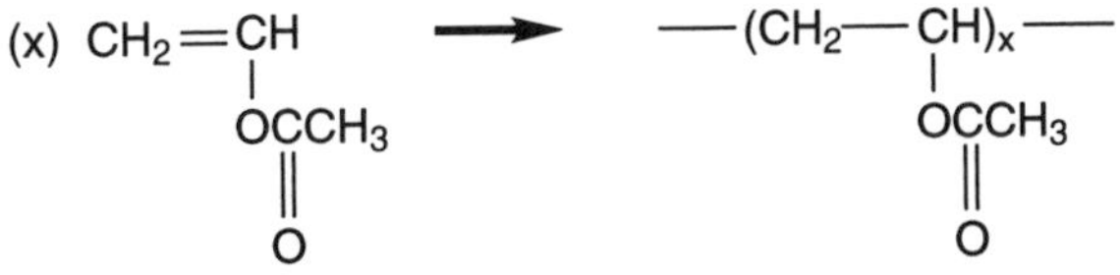

$$(x)\ CH_2{=}CH \longrightarrow {-}(CH_2{-}CH)_x{-}$$

vinyl acetate   polyvinyl acetate

PVA is insoluble in water and soluble in some organic solvents. Since PVA is insoluble in water, it is supplied to the textile finisher as an emulsion in water. PVA emulsions contain about 25 or 30% active solids. Surfactants are used to stabilize the emulsion. The emulsion is easy to use since the finisher needs only to dilute it to the concentration required for his application.

Table 1-6.   Hydrolysis levels of PVOH

Hydrolysis type	% of acetate groups hydrolyzed
Super hydrolyzed	almost 100
Fully hydrolyzed	about 99
Intermediate hydrolyzed	95–98
Partially hydrolyzed	about 87

Polyvinyl alcohol (PVOH) is made by hydrolysis of polyvinyl acetate.

$$—(CH_2—CH)_x— \quad \xrightarrow{\quad NaOCH_3 \quad} \quad —(CH_2—CH)_x—$$
$$\underset{\underset{O}{\|}}{OCCH_3} \quad CH_3OH \qquad OH$$

The extent of hydrolysis has a major influence on properties of PVOH and can be controlled to produce a family of products having a range of properties. Table 1-6 shows the various hydrolysis levels of PVOH that are available.

Because of internal hydrogen bonding, the partially hydrolyzed types of PVOH are more soluble in water even though they contain fewer hydrophilic groups. The residual acetate groups on the lower hydrolysis types of PVOH interfere with the internal hydrogen bonding capability of the polymer and make it more accessible to water. The partially hydrolyzed types adhere better to hydrophobic materials because of the presence of the residual acetate groups.

Polyvinyl alcohol is produced in a range of molecular weight grades as shown in Table 1-7. Molecular weight determines the viscosity type of the PVOH product.

Since both the extent of hydrolysis and the degree of polymerization of the product can be controlled during manufacture of PVOH,

Table 1-7.   Molecular weight and viscosity types of PVOH.

Viscosity type	Molecular weight (viscosity average)
Low	11000–31000
Medium	77000–79000
High	106000–110000

products having a broad range of properties can be produced. Higher molecular weight has the following effects on the product:

- higher viscosity aqueous solutions
- less tacky polymer
- higher tensile strength
- higher adhesive strength
- higher water resistance
- higher solvent resistance.

Lower molecular weight has the following effects:

- higher solubility
- greater flexibility
- increased water sensitivity
- increased ease of solvation.

Higher extent of hydrolysis has the following effects:

- increased water resistance
- higher tensile strength
- higher solvent resistance
- greater adhesion to hydrophilic surfaces.

Lower extent of hydrolysis has the following effects:

- greater solubility in water
- greater flexibility
- increased water sensitivity
- greater adhesion to hydrophobic surfaces.

As is true of most water soluble polymers, the viscosity of a solution of polyvinyl alcohol depends on the concentration and temperature of the solution as well as the molecular weight of the polymer. Figure 1-5 shows these effects for a commercial PVOH product.

One important commercial PVOH product is a copolymer. The comonomer used with vinyl acetate in making the product is methyl methacrylate. Properties of this product differ somewhat from other grades of PVOH.

Other vinyl polymers and copolymers

Another important group of polymers and copolymers used in textiles is based on acrylic acid, substituted acrylic acid, and esters of

**Figure 1-5.   Effect of concentration and temperature on
viscosity of aqueous polyvinyl alcohol solution**
(courtesy of Air Products and Chemicals, Inc.)

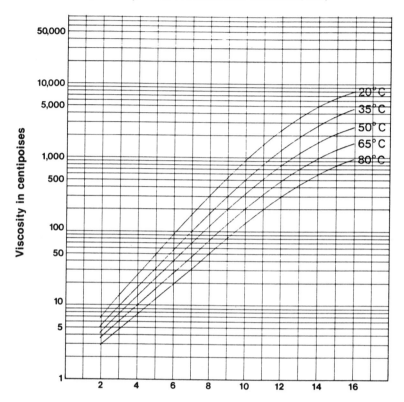

these compounds. Following are the chemical structures of these
monomers.

$$CH_2{=}CH \qquad CH_2{=}CH \qquad CH_2{=}CR'$$
$$| \qquad\qquad | \qquad\qquad |$$
$$COOH \qquad COOR \qquad COOR$$

R, R' = alkyl group

Acrylic acid   Alkyl acrylate   Ester of substituted
                    (ester)   acrylic acid

Polymers, copolymers, and terpolymers made from these and other monomers vary in properties depending on what monomers are used in what proportions. Properties such as hardness/softness, tackiness, water solubility, elasticity, elongation, and tensile strength can be tailored for a particular application by judicious selection of the monomers and their ratio in the copolymer or terpolymer. Polyacrylic acid homopolymer is very water soluble, and incorporation of acrylic acid promotes solubility of acrylic copolymers in water and alkali.

Hardness of a polymer is partially determined by the structures of the monomers from which it is made. A series of acrylates giving polymers from hardest to softest is as follows:

methyl methacrylate
methyl acrylate
ethyl acrylate
butyl acrylate
2-ethyl-hexyl acrylate

Copolymers from monomers whose homopolymers differ in hardness usually have glass transition temperatures (T_g) between those of the two homopolymers.

Other vinyl monomers like vinyl acetate, acrylic acid, ethylene, vinyl chloride, butadiene, acrylonitrile, styrene and maleic anhydride are used to make polymers and copolymers useful for textile finishing.

Silicones

Silicones comprise an important group of polymers in textile manufacturing. They are used mostly as fabric softeners, water repellents, lubricants, and defoamers. Silicone polymers are so important as defoamers that defoamers are usually classified as either silicone type or nonsilicone type.

Silicon has the capability to form covalent compounds. However, since the Si-Si bond is thermally unstable, there are no polymers having a silicon backbone. Siloxane bonds (Si-O) are stable, and polymers containing this group are used commercially.

Silicone chemicals for textile use are usually emulsified silicone oils. The silicone emulsions must be used carefully to prevent separation of the emulsion and deposition of silicone oil spots on fabrics. Dimethyl polysiloxane is used as a defoamer.

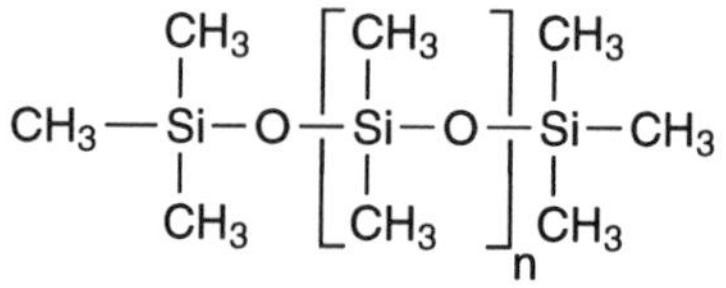

$$CH_3 - \underset{\underset{CH_3}{|}}{\overset{\overset{CH_3}{|}}{Si}} - O - \left[\underset{\underset{CH_3}{|}}{\overset{\overset{CH_3}{|}}{Si}} - O \right]_n \underset{\underset{CH_3}{|}}{\overset{\overset{CH_3}{|}}{Si}} - CH_3$$

dimethyl polysiloxane

Silicone rubbers are high molecular weight versions of dimethyl poly-siloxane.

Methyl hydrogen silicone polymers are usually present in silicones used for fabric treatments.

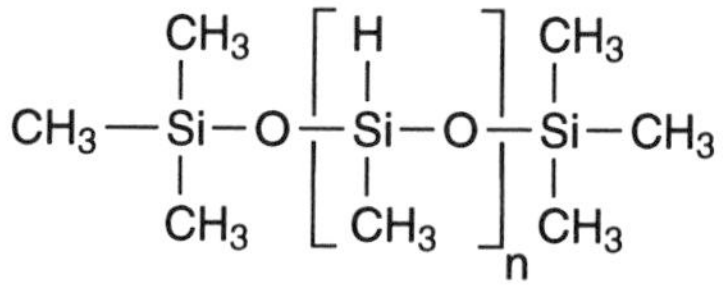

$$CH_3 - \underset{\underset{CH_3}{|}}{\overset{\overset{CH_3}{|}}{Si}} - O - \left[\underset{\underset{CH_3}{|}}{\overset{\overset{H}{|}}{Si}} - O \right]_n \underset{\underset{CH_3}{|}}{\overset{\overset{CH_3}{|}}{Si}} - CH_3$$

methyl hydrogen polysiloxane

In practice, mixtures of fully methylated and methyl hydrogen poly-siloxanes usually give the preferred combination of hand and other properties. Organometallic compounds act as hardening agents or catalysts in application of silicone polymers to textile materials.

Fluorocarbon polymers

Fluorocarbon polymers provide both water repellency and oil repellency to textile materials. The polyacrylate made from perfluorobutyl acrylate is an example of such a polymer.

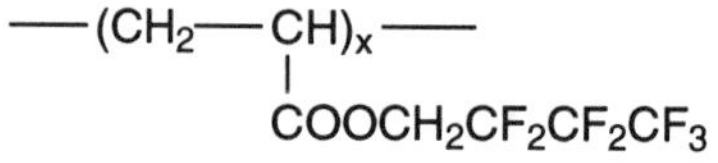

$$-(CH_2 - \underset{\underset{COOCH_2CF_2CF_2CF_3}{|}}{CH})_x -$$

polyperfluorobutylacrylate

These polymers are elastomeric and form a protective coating on the textile material.

Aminoplast resins

The aminoplast resins are used to impart easy care characteristics, durable press behavior, and dimensional stability to fabrics containing cellulosic fibers. They also improve the fastness properties of some dyes when applied to dyed fabrics.

The term "resin" is so broadly used that it is almost meaningless. It can refer to water insoluble vegetable-derived substances like oils and terpenes exuded on the bark of certain trees and shrubs. Synthetic "resins" are usually defined as high polymers resulting from a chemical reaction between two or more substances. This definition includes almost all synthetic polymers but excludes natural polymers. Even these natural polymers are sometimes referred to with the term "resin." The most common use of the term "resin" in textile chemistry is in connection with the aminoplast compounds. Aminoplast resins are thermosetting substances made by the reaction of an amine with an aldehyde. The most important aldehyde used in commercial aminoplast resins is formaldehyde. The most important amine used in commercial aminoplast resins for textile applications is urea. Urea and formaldehyde react with one another under alkaline conditions to first form monomethylol urea.

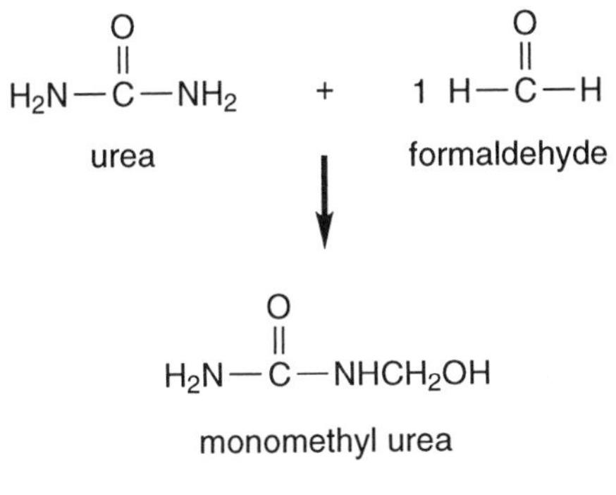

$$H_2N-\underset{\underset{O}{\|}}{C}-NH_2 \quad + \quad 1 \ H-\underset{\underset{O}{\|}}{C}-H$$

urea   formaldehyde

$$H_2N-\underset{\underset{O}{\|}}{C}-NHCH_2OH$$

monomethyl urea

Further reaction produces dimethylol urea. These methylolated urea compounds are called resin precondensates.

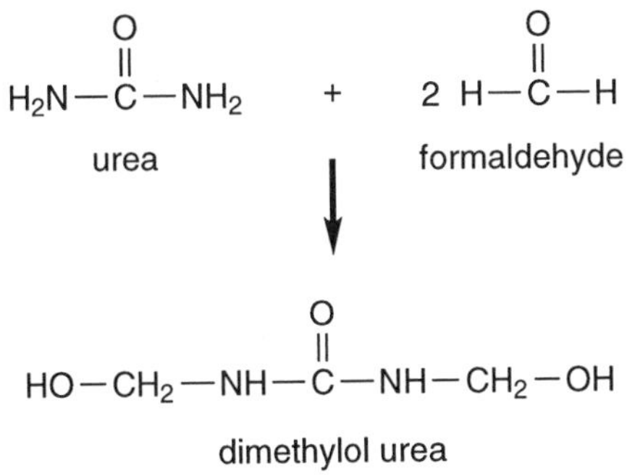

$$H_2N-\underset{\underset{O}{\|}}{C}-NH_2 \quad + \quad 2 \ H-\underset{\underset{O}{\|}}{C}-H$$

urea   formaldehyde

$$HO-CH_2-NH-\underset{\underset{O}{\|}}{C}-NH-CH_2-OH$$

dimethylol urea

Trimethylol urea and tetramethylol urea also exist but the amounts are negligible under controlled reaction conditions.

Methylolated urea compounds participate in condensation reactions. Therefore, they can polymerize or they can react with the hydroxyl groups of cellulose. Since the methylolated ureas are bifunctional, the reaction with cellulose can produce crosslinking between molecular chains in the amorphous regions of the fiber.

$$
\text{Cell}-\text{O}-\text{H} \quad \text{HO}-\text{CH}_2-\text{NH}-\overset{\overset{\textstyle O}{\|}}{\text{C}}-\text{NH}-\text{CH}_2-\text{OH} \quad \text{H}-\text{O}-\text{Cell}
$$

$$
\downarrow
$$

$$
\text{Cell}-\text{O}-\text{CH}_2-\text{NH}-\overset{\overset{\textstyle O}{\|}}{\text{C}}-\text{NH}-\text{CH}_2-\text{O}-\text{Cell} \quad +\,2\,\text{H}-\text{O}-\text{H}
$$

The aminoplast resin can be made in or on the fiber by applying a formulation containing the urea and formaldehyde. However, the preferred method is to use precondensates of these reactants. The precondensate can be made on site, but usual practice is for the finisher to obtain the precondensate from a chemical vendor.

The methylolated urea resins have limitations. These limitations include chlorine retention and high degree of formaldehyde release.

Chlorine retention refers to the reaction of the aminoplast compound with chlorine bleaches to form chloramines.

$$
-\overset{\overset{\textstyle O}{\|}}{\text{C}}-\underset{\underset{\textstyle H}{|}}{\text{N}}-\text{R} + \text{NaOCl} \;\underset{\longleftarrow}{\overset{\longrightarrow}{}}\; -\overset{\overset{\textstyle O}{\|}}{\text{C}}-\underset{\underset{\textstyle Cl}{|}}{\text{N}}-\text{R} + \text{NaOH} \quad (1)
$$

$$
-\overset{\overset{\textstyle O}{\|}}{\text{C}}-\underset{\underset{\textstyle Cl}{|}}{\text{N}}-\text{R} + \text{HOH} \;\longrightarrow\; -\overset{\overset{\textstyle O}{\|}}{\text{C}}-\underset{\underset{\textstyle H}{|}}{\text{N}}-\text{R} + \text{HCl} + 1/2\,\text{O}_2 \quad (2)
$$

Theoretically, any resin with a -N-H bond remaining on the structure can form chloramines. Chloramines are yellow. The chloramines may also degrade under hot wet conditions forming acids which can weaken cellulosic fibers.

Formaldehyde release refers to loss of formaldehyde from the resin finished fabric. The chlorine retention and formaldehyde release characteristics of methylolated urea resins makes them unacceptable for many applications.

Methylation of the methylolated ureas improves the stability of the resin.

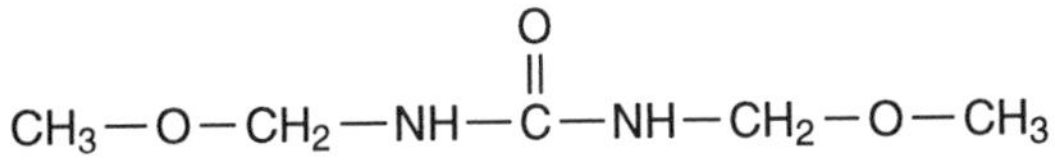

$$CH_3-O-CH_2-NH-\overset{\overset{\displaystyle O}{\|}}{C}-NH-CH_2-O-CH_3$$

Since aminoplast resins are of major importance in chemical finishing of textiles, much research has been done to develop and improve this technology. Later generation aminoplast resins are often referred to as "reactants" rather than as "resins" because they tend to react with and crosslink cellulose rather than polymerizing.

Dimethylol ethylene urea (DMEU) is an example of an improved aminoplast resin. DMEU is made by reacting ethylene diamine with carbon dioxide to form 2-imidazolidone which is then methylolated by reaction with formaldehyde.

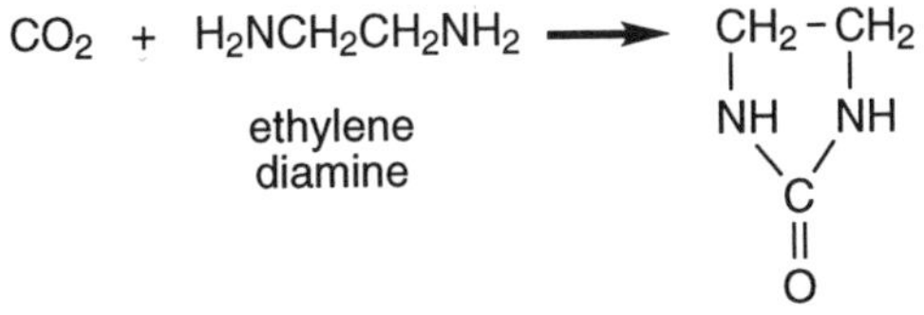

$$CO_2 \;+\; H_2NCH_2CH_2NH_2 \longrightarrow$$

ethylene
diamine

2-imidazolidone

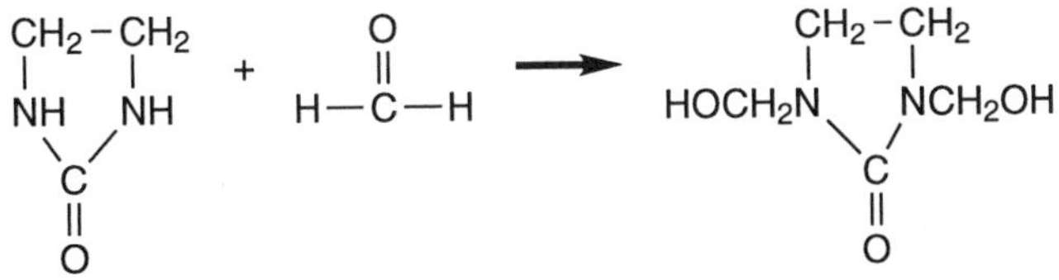

DMEU

Theoretically, DMEU should not be chlorine retentive since it contains no -N-H groups. In practice, it is chlorine retentive because of the presence of other substances in the product or because hydrolysis during application or storage produces -N-H groups.

Dimethylol dihydroxy ethylene urea is a popular aminoplast resin. It is made by reacting urea with glyoxal to produce dihydroxy ethylene urea which is then methylolated by reaction with formaldehyde.

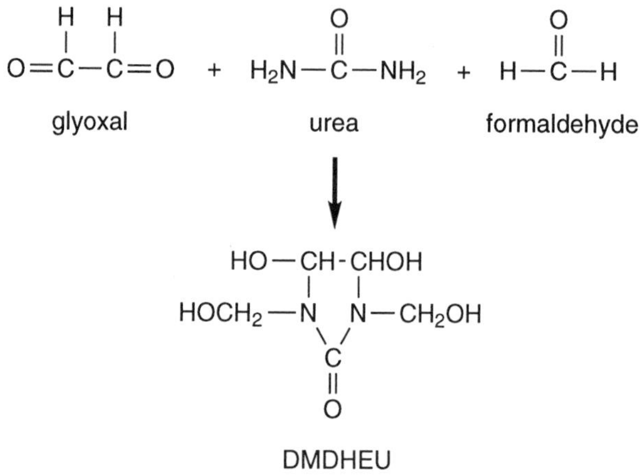

$$O{=}C{-}C{=}O \quad + \quad H_2N{-}C{-}NH_2 \quad + \quad H{-}C{-}H$$

glyoxal   urea   formaldehyde

$$HO{-}CH{-}CHOH$$
$$HOCH_2{-}N \quad N{-}CH_2OH$$
$$C$$
$$\|$$
$$O$$

DMDHEU

Like DMEU, DMDHEU is not immune to chlorine retention even though it has no -N-H groups in the pure compound.

Other aminoplast resins which are or which have been used in textile finishing include carbamates (urethanes), triazones, and triazines (melamines).

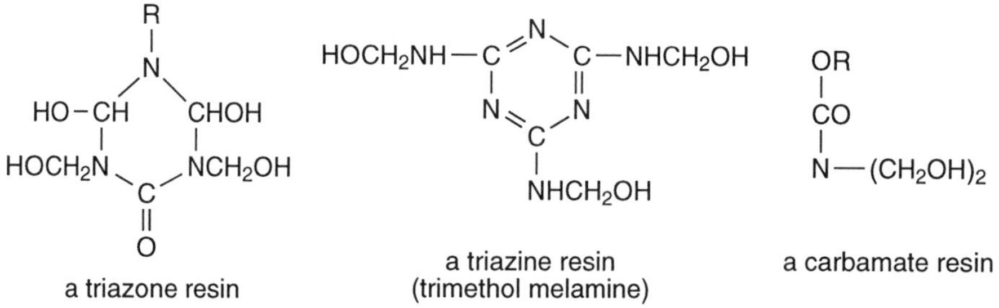

a triazone resin

a triazine resin
(trimethol melamine)

a carbamate resin

Development of low formaldehyde or formaldehyde-free finishes which impart durable press and dimensional stability to textiles has been a goal of textile researchers for a long time. New crosslinking technology for cellulose has been developed as a result of these efforts. Since these products are not aminoplast resins, they are discussed elsewhere in this text.

The aminoplast resins are used to overcome two of the most important limitations of cellulosic fibers, the tendency to shrink when washed and the tendency to wrinkle during use. Both of these limitations are related to hydrogen bonding between cellulose molecules in the amorphous regions of the fiber. When cellulose fibers are severely deformed, by creasing a fabric for example, some of the hydrogen bonds are broken allowing chain slippage in the amorphous regions. New hydrogen bonds form and tend to hold the fabric in the creased configuration when the deforming force is released. Therefore, the crease or wrinkle tends to remain in the fabric.

Shrinkage of fabrics made from cellulosic fibers is complex and involves mechanical phenomena in structure of the fiber, yarn, and the fabric itself. However, the behavior of the fiber in water is the primary causative factor in fabric shrinkage. When cellulosic fibers are wetted, water penetrates the amorphous regions breaking internal hydrogen bonds. The absorption of water into the fiber structure results in swelling of the fiber. Swelling is mostly in the transverse direction rather than the longitudinal direction. Since the fiber diameter increases, the fiber requires more space. The greater space requirement of the swollen fiber is partially satisfied by increased crimping of yarn in the fabric. This increased yarn crimping results in shrinkage of the fabric.

Swelling has other effects. Since swelling decreases interaction between the fiber molecules, the modulus is lowered. This results in reduced tensile strength in rayon and acetate. However, cotton is stronger when wet because the increased mobility of the amorphous regions allows greater load sharing by the chains and crystalline regions of the fiber. Swelling allows relaxation of strains which have been induced in the fibers so that axially aligned molecules retract to more random configurations. As the fibers become more relaxed and flexible, strains induced in the yarn and fabric during processing are also relaxed, and the entire structure shrinks.

The mechanism by which aminoplast resins improve durable press and shrinkage is mainly crosslinking. Crosslinking decreases the ability of fibers to swell. This minimizes mobility of the amorphous regions decreasing chain slippage and preventing relaxation of stresses in the polymer structure. Although crosslinking of cellulose improves its wrinkle resistance dimensional stability, other fiber properties are also affected. Some of the effects of crosslinking on fiber properties are as follows:

Stiffness—usually increased
Tear strength—decreased
Tensile strength—decreased
Abrasion resistance—decreased
Water absorbency—decreased
Dyeability—decreased dramatically

Bibliography

1. Billmeyer, Fred W. Jr., Textbook of Polymer Science, John Wiley and Sons, Inc., New York, NY, 1962.
2. CRC Handbook of Chemistry and Physics, 65th ed., Robert C. Weast, Ed., CRC Press, Inc., Boca Raton, Florida, 1984.
3. Farrow, J.C., D.M. Hall, and Warren S. Perkins, Textile Slashing Theory and Practice, Auburn University and Alabama Textile Operating Executives, Auburn, AL, 1973.
4. Galliard, T. Ed., Starch: Properties and Potential, Critical Reports on Applied Chemistry Volume 13, John Wiley and Sons, Inc., New York, NY, 1987.
5. Mark, H., N.S. Woodling, and S.M. Atlas, Chemical Aftertreatment of Textiles, John Wiley and Sons, Inc., New York, NY, 1971.
6. Nettles, J. E., Handbook of Chemical Specialties, John Wiley and Sons, Inc., New York, NY, 1983.
7. Radley, J. A., Starch and Its Derivatives, 4th Edition, Chapman and Hall Ltd., London, England, 1968.
8. Rosen, Milton J., Surfactants and Interfacial Phenomena, John Wiley and Sons, Inc., New York, NY, 1978.
9. Seydel, Paul V. and James R. Hunt, Textile Warp Sizing, Phoenix Printing, Inc., Atlanta, Georgia, 1981.
10. Sienko, Michael J. and Robert A. Plane, Chemistry, 2nd Edition, McGraw-Hill Book Company, Inc. New York, NY, 1961.
11. Smith, J. B., The Technology of Warp Sizing, Columbine Press Ltd., Manchester, Great Britain, 1964.
12. Textile Chemist and Colorist-Buyer's Guide, American Association of Textile Chemists and Colorists, Research Triangle Park, NC, published annually.
13. The Condensed Chemical Dictionary, 9th ed., Gessner G. Hawley, Ed., Van Nostrand Reinhold Company, New York, NY, 1977.
14. Trotman, E.R., Dyeing and Chemical Technology of Textile Fibres, Sixth Edition, John Wiley and Sons, Inc., New York, NY, 1984.

15. Vaidya, A.A. and S.S. Trivedi, Textile Auxiliaries and Finishing Chemicals, Ahmedabad Textile Industry's Research Association, Ahmedabad, India, 1975.

16. Van Beynum, G.M.A. and J.A. Roels, Ed., Starch Conversion Technology, Marcel Dekker, Inc., New York, NY, 1985.

Chapter 2

Preparation for Dyeing and Finishing

Most textile materials and fabrics require pretreatments before they can be dyed and finished. The preparatory treatments needed depend on the type of fiber in the material and particular dyeing and finishing treatments that are to be done. Preparatory treatments can be done on material in almost any stage of assembly into textile products from fiber to yarn, fabric, or garments. Generally, fibers containing the most types and the greatest amount of impurities require the greatest amount of preparation for dyeing and finishing.

Most often the preparatory treatments are done on the material in fabric form. Fabrics which have been prepared for dyeing and finishing must have sufficient absorbency and whiteness. Fabrics which will be dyed or finished using padding techniques must be very absorbent because they must be completely wetted and saturated with chemical formulations which they may be in contact with for only a few seconds or less. Fabrics being dyed using batch processes will be in contact with the chemical formulations for a greater length of time, and absorbency may not be as critical as in continuous processes. Fabrics which will go into white products require a very high degree of whiteness. Fabrics which will be dyed pastel or very bright shades also require a good level of whiteness since the base color of the fabric will contribute to the final shade after the fabric is dyed. Fabrics which will be dyed dark or dull shades require less whiteness than fabrics for white products or pastel shades.

Most preparatory processes for dyeing and finishing involve heating the fabric or treating it with chemicals. Therefore, the potential is present for thermal and chemical damage to the fibrous polymer comprising the fabric. Fabrics can also be damaged mechanically in most preparatory processes.

Often preparatory processes for dyeing and finishing are specific to the type of fibers in the material. For example, the treatments needed to prepare wool-containing fabric are much different from those required for cotton or synthetic fibers. Furthermore, the preparation requirements for cotton-containing fabrics are somewhat different from those for polyester, nylon, acrylics, and other synthetics. Preparation of woven fabrics must include treatment to remove size materials. This is not required for knit fabrics and carpets since no size is present in these materials. Knit fabrics may contain large amounts of lubricants which were added to make the fabric manufacturing process run efficiently. These lubricants must usually be removed in order to dye the fabric satisfactorily. High temperature thermal treatments are often beneficial to fabrics containing thermoplastic fibers while these treatments are not beneficial or desirable on fabrics containing only non-thermoplastic fibers.

The following discussion of preparation for dyeing and finishing is general and reference is made to many types of fibers and textile materials. The continuous preparation of polyester-cotton woven fabrics is discussed later in the text.

Preparatory Processes

Typical processes for preparation of materials for dyeing and finishing are as follows:

Heat setting
Singeing
Desizing
Scouring
Mercerizing
Bleaching

The sequence shown is common but many variations may be used. Virtually all materials go through some of these processes prior to dyeing and some materials in fabric form are subjected to all of them. Each of these processes is discussed in the following sections.

Heat Setting

The dimensional stability, dyeability, and other properties of thermoplastic fibers are affected by repeated heating and cooling, or the "heat history," of the material. The main purposes of heat setting are as follows:

1. to stabilize the material to shrinkage, distortion, and creasing,
2. to crease, pleat, or emboss fabrics, and
3. to improve the dyeability of fabrics.

Heat relieves stresses in the amorphous regions of thermoplastic fibers. When the fiber is heated above its glass transition temperature, the molecules in the amorphous regions can move, and the material can be formed into a new shape. When the temperature is decreased, the material stays in its new shape. Thus, creases that have developed in the fabric can be pulled out, and the width of the fabric can be changed somewhat in the heat setting process. Creases can be permanently set in the fabric by heat setting if desired. Heat setting is used to permanently set twist in yarns.

Heat setting may be done before any wet treatments, after scouring and mercerizing, or after dyeing of the fabric. Fabric heat set before dyeing resists undesirable creasing and wrinkling in the dyeing process and accepts dye more uniformly if the heat setting process is controlled well. On the other hand, heat setting can cause nonuniform dyeing if the setting temperature varies along the length or across the width of the fabric. Heat setting of greige goods can make size materials and stains in the fabric more difficult to remove. Heat setting after dyeing helps to remove carrier from carrier-dyed polyester. However, undesirable discoloration (usually yellowing) of the fabric may occur in fabric heat set after dyeing. Dye migration or loss of dye by sublimation may also occur in fabrics heat set after dyeing.

Heat history affects the rate at which fibers absorb dye and the amount of dye the fibers will absorb. Figure 2-1 shows rate of dyeing isotherms for a disperse dye on polyester which was heat set at 230°C compared to a control sample which was not heat set. Differences in rate of dye absorption due to differences in heat history may cause nonuniform dyeing of fabrics. The heat setting process subjects the fibers to higher temperatures than they have previously experienced. This tends to minimize the effect of previous heat history and improves the chances for uniform dyeing of the material. Certainly, the material must be heated uniformly during the heat setting process if uniform dyeing is to be expected.

Heat setting can be done with either dry heat or steam. Polyester is usually heat set dry while nylon may be heat set either dry or with steam. Continuous heat setting of flat fabrics is usually done with

Figure 2-1.   Effect of heat setting of polyester at 230°C on dyeing rate (9)

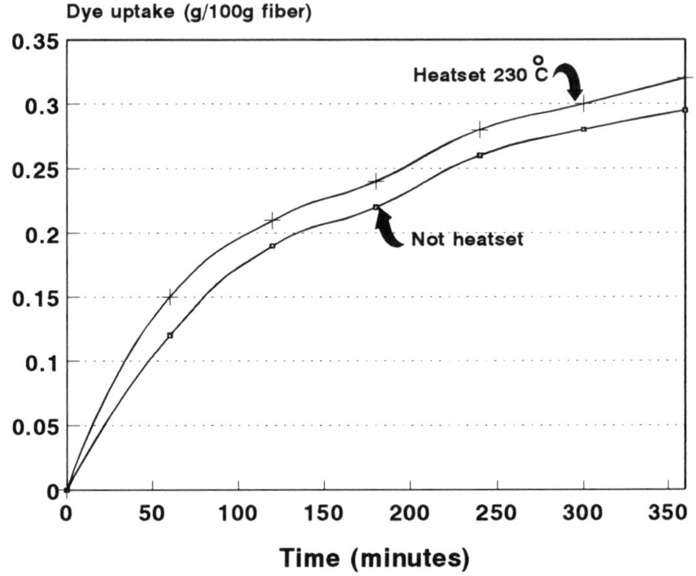

Dye uptake (g/100g fiber)

Time (minutes)

dry heat by contacting the fabric with heated rolls, impinging hot air on the fabric in a tenter frame, a combination of these two methods, or by heating with infrared radiation. Steam heat setting is often done in an autoclave or may be done using continuous steaming equipment. Nylon carpet yarns are often steam set.

The temperature used for dry heat setting of polyester is usually 180–200°C although temperatures in the range of 175–220°C can be used. Higher setting temperature generally gives better dimensional stability and resistance to pilling. However, the fabric increases in stiffness and loses crease recovery characteristics when set at higher temperatures.

The temperature selected for heat setting is often that temperature at which dyeability of the fabric can be best controlled. As shown in Figure 2-2, the temperature used to heat set polyester affects the dye uptake of the fiber. The saturation value of various disperse dyes is affected to different degrees by heat setting, but the general effect shown in Figure 2-2 occurs with most dyes.

The saturation value of the dye on the fabric is more critical in batch dyeing than continuous dyeing. Heat setting temperature affects rate of dye uptake as well as saturation value and can affect continuous as well as batch dyeing. Heat setting of polyester at tem-

Figure 2-2.   Effect of heat setting temperature on saturation value of disperse dye on polyester (derived from reference 9)

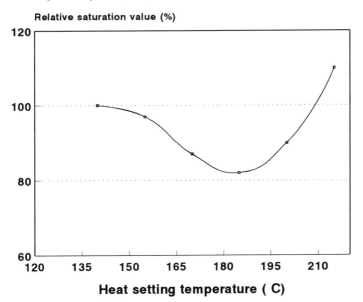

peratures higher than 200°C is difficult because small changes in setting temperature greatly affect dyeability of the fiber.

The effect of dry heat setting on dyeability of nylon is similar to its effect on dyeability of polyester. Dyeing rate of the fiber decreases with higher heat setting temperature up to a point and then increases at even higher setting temperatures as is shown in Figure 2-3. Dry heat setting temperatures of 190–200°C are typical for nylon.

Steam setting increases the dyeing rate of nylon with both acid and disperse dyes. The presence of water apparently promotes molecular chain rearrangements which increase the size of openings through which dyes can diffuse.

Lower temperatures are used for heat setting fabrics containing texturized yarn because the crimp may be lost if the yarn is heated to higher temperatures. Typical dry heat setting temperatures are 150–175°C for texturized nylon and 160–180°C for texturized polyester.

Problems or defects that may be caused by heat setting or improper control of the heat setting process include the following:

1. permanent set wrinkles
2. strength loss
3. improper hand or feel in the fabric

Figure 2-3.   Effect of dry heat setting on dyeing of nylon 6,6 with C.I. Acid Black 52 at pH 9.0. (Derived from reference 4)

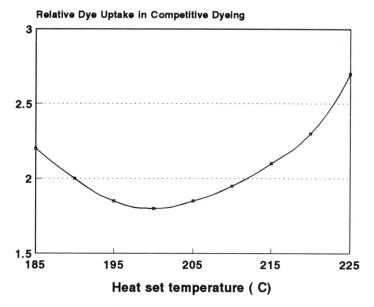

Relative Dye Uptake in Competitive Dyeing

Heat set temperature (C)

4. permanent set stains
5. nonuniform dyeing
6. improper fabric width or weight

Singeing

In singeing, the fibers which protrude from the fabric are burned away to give the fabric a smoother surface. Singeing is usually done by passing the fabric through a burning gas flame at high speed followed by quenching in water or the desizing bath to extinguish the smoldering fibers. Alternatively, the fabric may be passed close to a very hot plate to ignite the protruding fibers. Singeing is sometimes done after scouring since heating of the fabric in the singer can increase the difficulty of removing size and soil from the fabric.

Extreme care must be taken when singeing fabrics containing thermoplastic fibers in order to avoid dyeing problems. Thermoplastic fibers such as polyester melt when singed, and the fiber ends form beads on the fabric surface. These beads have greater dye affinity than the polyester fibers so the dyeability of singed fabrics by batch processes is usually not satisfactory. Therefore, fabrics that will be dyed by exhaust methods are usually heat set after dyeing. Singed fabric can usually be dyed satisfactorily by pad-thermosol methods.

Yarns, sewing threads, felts, and carpet backing can also be singed. Yarn singeing is usually called "gassing." Singeing of carpet backing has been reported to reduce latex binder requirements by as much as 10%.

Desizing

Desizing is the process of removing the size material from the warp yarns in woven fabrics. Most of the size must be removed before the fabric can be dyed satisfactorily. Residual size prevents the yarns and fibers from wetting quickly and can affect dye absorption in either batch or continuous dyeing. Most synthetic sizes are water soluble by design so that they can be easily washed from the fabric. Typical synthetic sizes are polyvinyl alcohol, acrylic copolymers, and carboxymethyl cellulose. Starch is also common in size formulations. Starch is not very soluble in water and must be chemically degraded in order to remove it from the fabric. Starch used in sizing is often modified to improve its properties and removability in desizing. Lubricants added to size formulations to enhance the fabric manufacturing process may be more difficult to remove than the size itself. Virtually all size formulations contain lubricants derived from natural fats and waxes. Virtually complete removal of these lubricants is required before the fabric can be dyed. The desizing step removes mostly size and not much lubricant. Most of the lubricant is removed in the scouring process.

Fabrics containing only water soluble sizes can be desized using hot water perhaps containing wetting agents and a mild alkali. Fabrics that contain starch are usually desized with enzymes. Enzymes are complex organic substances that catalyze chemical reactions in biological processes. They are formed in the living cells of plants and animals. A particular enzyme catalyzes a very specific reaction. An enzyme is usually named by the kind of substance degraded in the reaction it catalyzes. Thus, enzymes which hydrolyze and reduce the molecular weight of starch are called amylases because they hydrolyze the amylose and amylopectin molecules in starch. The hydrolysis of starch catalyzed by amylase enzymes produces starch fragments which are soluble enough to be washed from the fabric.

Figure 2-4.   Schematic diagram of a size reclamation process

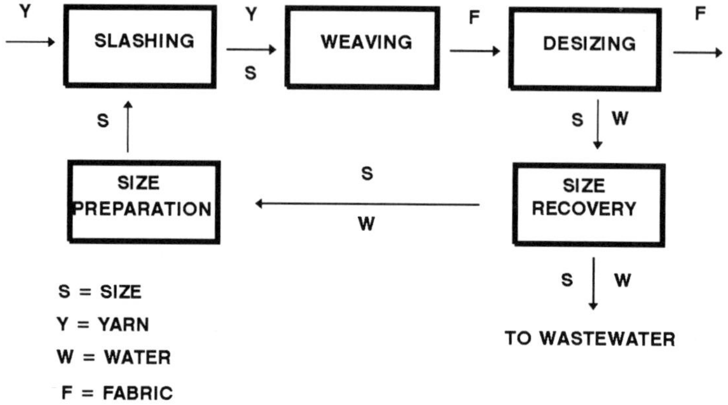

Desizing may be done using either batch or continuous methods. Continuous desizing consists of application of the enzyme solution followed by a digestion period to allow the hydrolysis to take place. Finally, the fabric is washed to remove the water soluble digestion products. The digestion period may consist of holding the fabric saturated with enzyme solution at room temperature for several hours. Alternatively, some high temperature stable enzymes can be steamed for a few minutes to heat the fabric and accelerate hydrolysis of the starch. Mineral acids and oxidizing agents can also be used to degrade starch in desizing.

Size Reclamation

The high value of the polymers used for sizing makes reclamation and reuse of size materials economical. Therefore, size materials are sometimes recovered and recycled. The size material in wash water from the desizing process is usually 0.5 to 3.0% which is too dilute for direct reuse in slashing. The concentration required in size formulations for slashing is usually 8% or higher. In order to concentrate a size solution from 1.0% in desize wash water to 8.0% for reuse in slashing, approximately 88% of the water in the dilute solution must be removed. As shown in Figure 2-4, a size reclamation process consists of a desize washer and a system to concentrate the size in the wash water to a level that can be used in the slashing process.

Several methods to reclaim size have been developed, but only ultrafiltration has achieved commercial acceptance. Ultrafiltration is

Figure 2-5. Schematic diagram of ultrafiltration principle

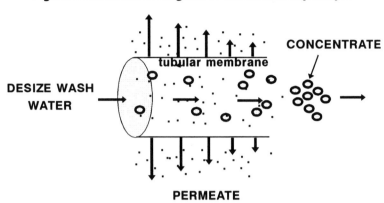

a separation process which can increase the concentration of size in dilute desize wash water to a level required for reuse in slashing. In ultrafiltration, some of the water and other small molecules in the dilute size solution are induced to diffuse through a polymer membrane by reverse osmosis. The polymer molecules in the size which are too large too diffuse through the pores of the membrane are left behind forming a more concentrated solution of size. As indicated in Figure 2-5, the material which diffuses through the membrane is called the permeate, and the size solution which is left is called the concentrate.

Pressure must be applied to the desize wash water in contact with the membrane to force the diffusion to take place. Ultrafiltration requires relatively low pressure and can use relatively coarse membranes because the polymer molecules to be excluded from diffusion are relatively large. Greater pressure and smaller pore sizes in the membranes are required to remove very small species such as salt ions using membrane separation technology. For this reason, a distinction is usually made between ultrafiltration technology such as is used for concentrating polymer solutions in size recovery and higher pressure hyperfiltration which is used for removal of very small molecular species from water.

Theoretically, any polymer which is not depolymerized or otherwise altered chemically in the sizing and desizing process should be recoverable using ultrafiltration. However, polyvinyl alcohol is the size most often recycled using ultrafiltration.

One manufacturer of ultrafiltration equipment for reclamation of warp size uses tubular membranes in the process shown schemati-

Figure 2-6.   Schematic diagram of ultrafiltration process

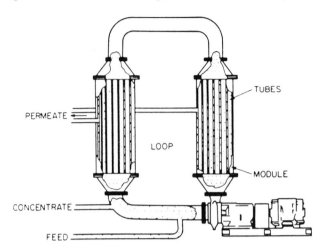

cally in Figure 2-6. The membrane is coated on the inside of 6 mm inside diameter ⅓ meter long porous carbon support tubes. Approximately 1000 of these tubular membranes are assembled into a module. Two of these modules make up a loop. As the desize wash water is circulated through the tubes parallel to the membrane surface, water diffuses through the membranes and the concentrate becomes progressively more concentrated.

Ultrafiltration processes can be run in either batch or continuous mode. In batch mode, the concentrate is returned to a feed tank and passed through the loop repeatedly until the desired concentration is obtained. In continuous mode, multiple loops are used so that the concentrate from one loop becomes the feed for a subsequent loop. The number of loops is sufficient so that only concentrate of the desired concentration comes from the final loop.

The capacity of the reclamation system depends on the total surface area of membrane, the flux rate, the concentration of the desize wash water, and the concentration required in the concentrate. Flux rate is volume of permeate that flows through a unit of surface area of membrane per unit of time.

Scouring

Scouring of textile materials refers to removal of impurities by wet treatments so that the impurities do not interfere with dyeing and finish applications. The amounts and types of impurities present depend on the type of fiber in the material. Materials containing only synthetic fibers usually contain only the lubricants which have been added to aid in manufacturing of the material and soil deposited on the material in manufacturing processes and handling.

Cotton contains natural impurities which must be removed in scouring and bleaching. The exact composition of cotton fibers depends on its source, maturity, and other factors. Typical composition of dry cotton fiber is as follows: (15)

Composition of Cotton (%)	
Cellulose	94.0
Protein	1.3
Pectic matter	0.9
Ash	1.2
Wax	0.6
organic acids	0.8
sugars	0.3
other materials	0.9

The waxy substances on cotton are esters of fatty alcohols or glycerol and have relatively high melting point of 80–85°C. Therefore, high temperature treatments assist greatly in removal of natural waxes from cotton. The exact nature of the protein material in cotton fibers is unknown, but these materials are removed by hot alkaline treatments. The pectins are high molecular weight carbohydrates and appear to exist as calcium and magnesium salts of pectic acid or its derivatives. Pectic acid is a polymer containing galactouronic acid as the repeat unit.

galactouronic acid
(repeat unit in pectic acid)

Because of the acidic carboxyl groups, alkaline treatments are effective in removing pectic substances. The ash content of cotton is mainly potassium, calcium, and magnesium carbonates, phosphates, sulfates, and chlorides. Cotton also contains various extraneous matter such as leaves, stems, and seed coat fragments (generally called motes). This vegetable matter is swollen by the hot alkaline treatments so that it can be removed or decolorized by the bleaching processes subsequent to scouring. Most of these impurities are soluble or removable by hot alkaline scouring.

Up to ⅔ of raw wool is impurities such as suint (dried perspiration), dirt, and fat or grease. Most of these impurities must be removed so preparation of wool is quite different from and more extensive than preparation of cotton and synthetic fibers. Details concerning the scouring of wool are not covered in this text.

Scouring of Cotton and Blends

Cotton can be scoured in either batch or continuous processes. The chemical formulation usually contains caustic soda (sodium hydroxide) and surfactants. Other ingredients such as organic solvents and builders may also be added. The caustic soda solubilizes many of the impurities in cotton making them removable in aqueous medium. The process is done at elevated temperature for an extended period of time. The chemical concentrations, temperature, and time required vary with the particular process being used. Since polyester is subject to alkaline degradation, the treatment conditions are sometimes milder when processing blends of cotton with polyester. Lower temperatures may be used and soda ash (sodium carbonate) may be substituted for caustic soda.

Mechanisms of Cleaning of Textile Substrates

The mechanisms of cleaning and removal of impurities from fibrous structures are complex, and much has been written on the subject. Cleaning of textiles involves surface and interfacial phenomena so surfactants play a vital role in the process. Much of the surface chemistry involved in cleaning of textiles is directly applicable to other areas of textile manufacturing. Water repellant finishing, stain repellant finishing, wetting, emulsifying, dispersing, aggregating, foaming and defoaming all involve generally the same principles as detergency and cleaning.

The three elements of a scouring process are

1. the fibrous substrate to be cleaned,
2. the impurities to be removed, and
3. the bath or scouring formulation.

Since the first two elements in the list are very diverse, several different mechanisms are involved in scouring. Chemically, substrates can be classified as hydrophobic or hydrophilic depending on polarity of the polymer comprising the fiber. Textile substrates also differ greatly in construction, and this can affect scouring. Soils and impurities that must be removed can be solid or liquid (or a mixture of both), polar or nonpolar, finely divided or coarse. Adhesion of soil to textiles is mostly by van der Waals forces so nonpolar soils are generally more difficult to remove using aqueous medium than are polar soils. Nonpolar soils are also more difficult to remove from hydrophobic substrates such as polyester and polypropylene than from hydrophilic substrates such as cotton and wool. Conversely, hydrophilic soils are more difficult to remove from hydrophilic substrates than from hydrophobic substrates.

Cleaning of textile materials requires both removal of the soil and suspension of the soil in the bath. Suspension of soil in the bath to prevent its redeposition on the substrate is just as important as removal of the soil in most cases.

The two general types of soil, solid and liquid, are removed by entirely different mechanisms. Removal of each of these two types of soils is discussed below.

Removal of Solid Soil

Removal of solid soils in an aqueous bath involves two mechanisms:
1. wetting of the substrate and the soil particles by the bath and
2. adsorption of surfactant at the liquid/substrate and the liquid/particle interfaces

Wetting of substrate

Wetting means that the scouring formulation spreads on the surface to be cleaned. Soil on a textile material is mostly on the surface of the material and not inside of the fibers. Wetting of the solid soil particles results in formation of electrical double layers at the soil/liquid and substrate/liquid interfaces causing repulsion between

Figure 2-7. Liquid/solid interfaces having various contact angles

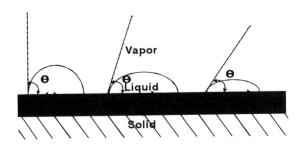

the soil and substrate. Water may also cause differential swelling of the fibrous material and the soil. Both of these mechanisms represent forces which counteract the van der Waals forces between the soil and substrate and facilitate removal of the soil.

Wetting of solid surfaces (textile substrate and soil) requires that a liquid (scouring formulation) spread out on the solid. Spreading of a liquid on a solid surface is defined by the area of contact between the liquid and solid. The concept of "contact angle" is used to express the degree of contact between the liquid and solid. As shown in Figure 2-7, the greater the contact angle, θ, the lower is the degree of wetting of the solid by the liquid.

If the contact angle is less than 90°, the liquid has spread spontaneously on the solid. If the contact angle is greater than 90°, the liquid has not spread spontaneously on the surface. A liquid having a contact angle of 0° with a solid wets the solid surface completely, liquids having contact angles between 0 and 90° wet the surface partially, and liquids having contact angles greater than 90° do not wet the surface. The contact angle is determined by the surface forces acting at the boundary of the three phases: air, liquid, and solid. These forces are represented by the vectors in Figure 2-8.

The Young-Dupré equation relates the contact angle to the surface and interfacial tensions.

$$\cos \theta = \frac{\gamma_{SA} - \gamma_{LS}}{\gamma_{LA}}$$

Since larger value of cos θ (smaller contact angle) means greater wetting, the Young-Dupré equation indicates that wetting is improved

Figure 2-8.   Forces acting at boundaries of liquid, solid, and vapor

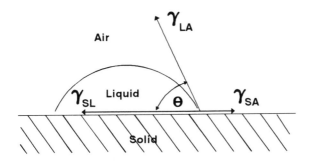

by higher solid/air surface tension (γ_{SA}) and lower liquid/air surface tension (γ_{LA}) or liquid/solid interfacial tension (γ_{LS}).

Of the three surface tensions in the Young-Dupré equation, only the liquid/air surface tension can be measured. However, the contact angle can be observed and is used as a measure of the wetting of a solid by a liquid.

The wettability of polymer surfaces can be expressed in terms of the so-called "critical surface tension." The critical surface tension is determined by observing the contact angle with the polymer of liquids having various surface tensions. The critical surface tension is the highest surface tension which gives a contact angle of 0°, or complete wetting. Critical surface tensions of some fiber-forming polymers are shown in Table 2-1. Based solely on critical surface tension values, none of these polymers are wettable with pure water which has surface tension of 72 dynes/cm. The surface of most textile materials is rough rather than smooth, and both the surface and the treating liquid are usually contaminated rather than pure. Therefore, the

Table 2-1.   Critical Surface Tensions of Common Polymers at 20°C (from reference 5)

Polymer	Critical surface tension (dynes/cm)
Polytetrafluoroethylene	18.5
Polypropylene	28
Polyethylene	31
Polyacrylonitrile	37
Polyvinyl alcohol	37
Polyvinyl chloride	39
Polyethylene terephthalate	43
Polyhexamethylene adipamide	46

wetting behavior in practice may be much different than is predicted by these values measured using pure chemicals and polymers.

Textile materials like fabrics usually have a rough surface and porous structure. Fabrics (or other textile structures) can be viewed as a system of capillaries the walls of which are the fibers comprising the fabric. Wetting requires penetration of liquid and displacement of the air occupying these capillaries. The movement of liquid into capillaries is determined by the parameters in the LaPlace equation:

$$\Delta P = \frac{2\gamma_{LA}\cos\theta}{r} = \frac{2(\gamma_{SA}-\gamma_{SL})}{r}$$

γ_{LA}, γ_{SA}, and γ_{SL} = surface tensions
r = radius of capillary
ΔP = capillary pressure

The capillary pressure, ΔP, is the difference in hydrostatic pressure of the liquid in the capillaries and the hydrostatic pressure of the liquid surrounding the capillaries. If ΔP is positive (P greater surrounding capillary than inside capillary), liquid spontaneously enters the capillary. This occurs when the contact angle is less than 90°. If ΔP is negative (P greater inside than surrounding capillary), liquid is ejected from or does not spontaneously enter the capillary in the absence of some external force. This is the case when the contact angle is greater than 90°.

Adsorption of surfactant

There is always an unequal distribution of electrical charge at the interface of two phases. One side of the interface assumes a net charge of one sign, and the other side assumes a net charge of the opposite sign to preserve electrical neutrality. This electrical double layer produces an electrical potential which decreases with distance from the charged surface. The Stern model of the electrical double layer is shown in Figure 2-9.

The absorption of surfactant molecules by the substrate and the soil is believed to increase the electrical potential. This increases electrical repulsion and reduces the amount of work required to separate the soil from the substrate. This mechanism is consistent with the observation that anionic surfactants are effective in removing solid soils from textile substrates while nonionic surfactants are not par-

Figure 2-9.   Stern model of the electrical double layer

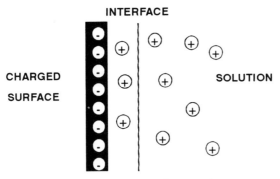

ticularly effective. Soils having a small particle size are more difficult to remove from textiles than are soils having larger particles. Small particles have greater area of contact with the substrate. Furthermore, the velocity of liquid movement caused by agitation of the cleaning liquid becomes very low near the substrate surface, and smaller particles encounter only liquid moving at low velocity.

Removal of Liquid Soils

The same forces that determine wetting of a substrate by a liquid also control removal of liquid soils. For example, complete removal of an oil droplet from the substrate requires that the contact angle of the droplet with the substrate be greater than 90°. Figure 2-10 shows the surface and interfacial tensions operating on an oil droplet on a surface. The Young-Dupré equation in this case is

$$\cos \theta = \frac{\gamma_{SB} - \gamma_{SO}}{\gamma_{BO}}$$

Figure 2-10.   Forces acting on an oil droplet on a textile substrate

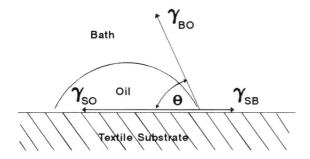

Figure 2-11.   Rollback mechanism for oily soil removal from substrate

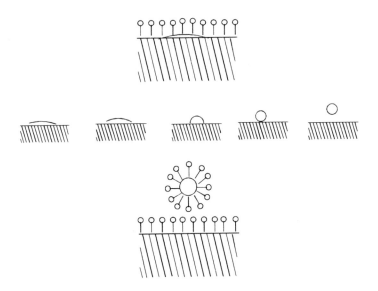

where γ_{SB}, γ_{SO}, and γ_{BO} are surface or interfacial tensions at the substrate/bath, substrate/oil, and bath/oil boundaries, respectively.

The adsorption of surfactant at the interface of the substrate and bath decreases γ_{SB} which increases the value of θ and aids in the removal of the oil. If the surfactant adsorbs at the interface of the bath and oil to decrease γ_{BO} or if it dissolves in the oil to decrease γ_{SO}, then it will decrease the value of θ and impede the removal of oil by this mechanism. The practical implication of this is that surfactants with different degrees of attraction to the various phases will differ from one another in their ability to remove soil from textile substrates.

An oily (liquid) soil is generally present as a thin layer on the surface of fibers. This oily soil is removed from the textile substrate by a mechanism called "rollback." Preferential wetting of the substrate by the bath liquid causes the oil to roll up into droplets which are then removed from the substrate by hydraulic action as is illustrated in Figure 2-11.

If the contact angle is less than 90°, part of the oil droplet may break away and be removed but part will stay attached to the substrate. If the contact angle is greater than 90° but less than 180°, the droplet can be completely removed if assisted by mechanical

Figure 2-12. Schematic diagram of an oil in water emulsion

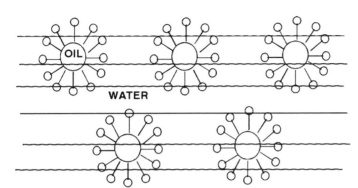

action. If the contact angle is 180°, the droplet releases from the substrate without application of mechanical action.

Suspending Soil in the Bath

Suspension of soil in the bath to prevent its redeposition on the substrate may occur by several different mechanisms.

1. Electrical and steric barriers may be formed.

Adsorption of surfactant molecules on solid soil particles which have been detached from the fabric increases the electrical potential near the surface of the particles causing mutual repulsion and preventing particles from agglomerating. Adsorption of surfactant molecules on the soil particles may also produce steric barriers that prevent the particles from approaching one another closely enough to agglomerate. Polymeric agents such as carboxymethyl cellulose which aid in keeping soil suspended in the bath are believed to function by forming steric barriers to agglomeration of soil particles.

2. Small amounts of oily soil may be dissolved into the hydrophobic portions of surfactant micelles.

The observation that many surfactants are effective in removing oily soil only if the concentration of surfactant in the bath is much above the critical micelle concentration is supportive of this mechanism.

3. Emulsification of oily soil in the bath may also contribute to keeping the soil suspended.

An emulsion consists of finely divided droplets of a discontinuous phase suspended in a continuous phase. Figure 2-12 is a schematic of an oil in water (o/w) emulsion. Water in oil emulsions (w/o) can be made by judicious selection of surfactants.

Emulsification requires that the interfacial tension between the oil and the bath be very low. Adsorption of surfactant molecules at the oil/water interface makes the interfacial tension low enough for the emulsion to form.

Bleaching

Cellulose and most other fiber-forming polymers are white in their natural state. However, impurities in fibers may absorb light causing the fibers to have a creamy, yellowish, or dull appearance. Cotton fibers usually require bleaching unless the material will be dyed very dark or dull shades. Synthetic fibers are often very white as supplied by the fiber producer but may require bleaching in some cases. The goal of bleaching is to decolorize the impurities which mask the natural whiteness of fibers. Oxidizing agents are used to bleach fibers. Bleaching processes must be closely controlled so that the color in the fibers is destroyed while damage due to oxidation of the fibrous material is minimized.

The exact nature of coloring matter in fibers is not known and, presumably, varies for different fiber types and origins. Color in organic substances is usually due to the presence of mobile electrons. These mobile electrons in organic compounds are usually in systems of conjugated double bonds involving carbon, nitrogen, and oxygen atoms. A simple alkene can be used to illustrate the effect of oxidation on color of an organic molecule. Oxidation of an alkene can produce carbonyl compounds. The resulting break in conjugation in the molecule decreases the delocalization of electrons and produces colorless oxidation products.

$$\text{—C=C—} \quad \xrightarrow{\text{oxidation}} \quad \text{—C=O} + \text{O=C—}$$

Cellulose may be damaged by oxidation during bleaching. Oxidation of cellulose produces carbonyl and carboxyl groups which can affect the ability of the fiber to interact with dyes. Oxidized cellulose is also subject to depolymerization under alkaline conditions so oxidative damage can decrease strength and change other physical properties of the fibers.

Bleaching with Hydrogen Peroxide

Industrial bleaching of cotton is most commonly done using hydrogen peroxide (peroxide). Commercially available peroxide is usually either a 35 or 50% solution in water. Hydrogen peroxide is stable under acidic conditions and unstable in alkaline medium. The activity of peroxide in bleach baths is regulated by controlling pH and alkalinity of the bath. Both ionic and free radical mechanisms have been proposed to account for bleaching of fibers with peroxide. The ionic mechanism proposes that the active species in peroxide bleaching is the perhydroxyl ion.

$$H_2O_2 \rightleftharpoons HO_2^- + H^+$$

The fact that bleaching rate increases with higher alkalinity in the bath is explained by this ionic mechanism since higher alkalinity would increase the concentration of perhydroxyl ions formed. As the perhydroxyl ions are consumed in reactions with coloring matter and cellulose, they are replenished by ionization of peroxide in the bath.

The free radical mechanism (11, 12) proposes that a donor substance, D, transfers one electron to peroxide which then forms a radical.

$$H_2O_2 + D \longrightarrow D^+ + HO^- + HO^\bullet$$

A chain reaction ensues to form new radicals which propagate the process as the free radicals react with coloring matter and cellulose. The free radical mechanism accounts for the effect of pH by proposing that perhydroxyl ions can be an electron donor substance to initiate formation of free radicals.

$$H_2O_2 + HO_2^- \longrightarrow HO^\bullet + HO^- + HO_2^\bullet$$

The free radical mechanism is consistent with the observation that certain ions (Ca^{2+}, Mg^{2+}) inhibit the decomposition of peroxide while other ions (Cu, Fe, etc.) catalyze the decomposition of peroxide.

Regardless of the mechanism of decomposition of peroxide by which bleaching occurs, the decomposition of peroxide to release the active bleaching species must be carefully controlled to achieve optimum bleaching action. Formation of molecular oxygen in the bleach bath is undesirable since this oxygen is lost to the atmosphere. Molecular oxygen has also been associated with depolymerization of cellulose under alkaline conditions. Peroxide bleaching is usually activated by addition of alkali such as caustic soda or soda ash to the bath. The bath is stabilized by addition of sodium silicate or other agents. Wetting agents and chelating agents may also be added. A stabilizer is vital in peroxide bleaching because the rate of peroxide decomposition is difficult to control with caustic soda alone. Sodium silicate has been the preferred stabilizer in peroxide bleaching for many years. Various organic hydroxy compounds, phosphates, hardness ions such as calcium and magnesium, and certain proteins tend to stabilize peroxide bleach baths. Proprietary bleach bath stabilizers are provided by many chemical suppliers. These proprietary formulations are sometimes used in combination with sodium silicate as peroxide bleach bath stabilizers.

The time, temperature, and concentration of peroxide used vary depending on the process used in peroxide bleaching. Continuous, batch, and pad/batch processes can all be used in peroxide bleaching. High temperature greatly accelerates peroxide bleaching.

Bleaching with Sodium Hypochlorite

Sodium hypochlorite, NaOCl, is made in the chlor/alkali process by electrolysis of brine. It is also formed by dissolving chlorine gas in a solution of caustic soda. Sodium hypochlorite is available commercially as a 5.25% solution in water. Lowering the pH of a solution of sodium hypochlorite causes the formation of hypochlorous acid which is believed to be the active species in hypochlorite bleaching.

$$NaOCl + H^+ \rightleftharpoons HOCl + Na^+$$

Figure 2-13 shows the position of this equilibrium as a function of pH of the bath. At pH values higher than 10, the hypochlorite exists mainly as the hypochlorite ion, and little bleaching occurs. At pH between 9 and 10, the above equilibrium moves slightly to the right producing some hypochlorous acid, and bleaching begins. The frac-

Figure 2-13.   Effect of pH on fraction of hypochlorite existing as hypochlorous acid

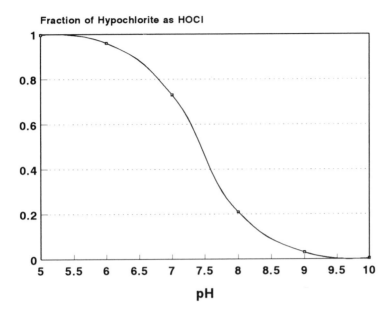

tion of hypochlorite existing in the hypochlorous acid form increases steadily as pH is lowered from about 9.0 to about 5.0.

At pH below about 5.0 hypochlorous acid is in equilibrium with free chlorine in aqueous medium. Since chlorine gas is not very soluble in water, hypochlorite bleach baths must be kept alkaline.

$$HOCl + Cl^- + H^+ \rightleftharpoons Cl_2 + H_2O$$

The pH chosen for hypochlorite bleaching is usually 9.5 to 10.0, but the bleaching action is greatly accelerated by lowering the pH slightly. Hypochlorite bleaching is most often done at room temperature, but slight heating greatly accelerates the bleaching rate and reduces the concentration of hypochlorite required. Very short bleaching times can be obtained using a pad/steam process, but the process is more difficult to control than low temperature hypochlorite bleaching.

After hypochlorite bleaching, residual chlorine must be removed to prevent damage to the fibers. This treatment is called the antichlor and is done with a mild reducing agent such as sodium bisulfite.

Hypochlorite bleaching may be followed by a peroxide bleaching stage using less peroxide and other chemicals than would be used in a regular peroxide bleaching cycle. In this process, the peroxide also serves as an antichlor for the hypochlorite.

Bleaching with Sodium Chlorite

Sodium chlorite is an effective bleach for both natural and synthetic fibers. Sodium chlorite is a white powder which when mixed with an alkali such as sodium carbonate can be stored indefinitely. A solution of sodium chlorite in water decomposes when acidified and heated forming chlorine dioxide, the active bleaching species.

$$5\,NaClO_2 + 2\,H^+ \longrightarrow 4\,ClO_2 + Cl^- + 5\,Na^+ + 2\,OH^-$$

sodium chlorite   chlorine dioxide

Cotton may be bleached with sodium chlorite at pH of 4.0 to 4.5. Synthetic fibers usually require lower pH of 2.0 to 4.0 and higher concentration of sodium chlorite than does cotton. Temperature near the boiling point of water is generally used in chlorite bleaching. The pH must be carefully controlled to prevent release of gaseous chlorine and chlorine dioxide from the bath. These substances, if released, cause odor problems and may be hazardous to workers. Auxiliary chemicals that scavenge chlorine are used as additives to help prevent odor problems. Since chlorine dioxide is very corrosive to metals (including stainless steel), fiber glass equipment is preferred for bleaching with sodium chlorite.

Sodium chlorite is used mostly on synthetic fibers such as acrylic, polyester, and nylon which are difficult or impossible to bleach with hydrogen peroxide. Acrylic fibers may yellow if heat set after bleaching with sodium chlorite.

Other Bleaching Agents

Various peroxygen compounds can be used as bleaches. Peracetic acid may be used to bleach polyamides. Accelerated and combination desize/scour/bleach processes based on persulfate and perphosphate chemistry have been devised for cotton and polyester/cotton blends. (2)

Figure 2-14. Spectrophotometric curves of greige, bleached, and bleached/optically whitened fabric

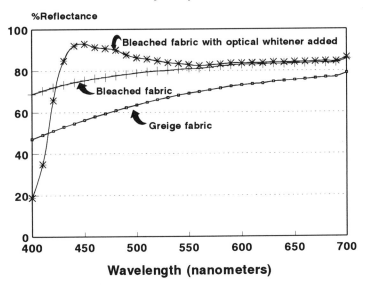

Use of Fluorescent Whitening Agents

The creamy, yellowish color of textile materials can be only partially destroyed by bleaching. Fluorescent whitening agents can be used to further improve the whiteness of textile materials. Fluorescent whitening agents, which are sometimes called optical brighteners, absorb ultraviolet (UV) light. Some of the absorbed energy is emitted at longer wavelengths. If the wavelengths at which the energy is emitted are in the visible region, the brightness of the textile substrate is increased. If the emitted energy is in the blue region, its addition to the light reflected by the yellowish substrate makes the substrate appear whiter. Figure 2-14 shows spectrophotometric curves of samples of a 100% cotton fabric in the greige state, after bleaching with hydrogen peroxide, and after addition of a fluorescent whitening agent to the bleached fabric.

Fluorescent whitening agents are like dyes in that they have affinity for the fibers to which they are applied. Therefore, the chemical nature of the fiber must be considered in selection of a fluorescent whitening agent.

Fluorescent whitening agents may be added to the bleach bath or applied in a separate step. Fluorescent whitening agents are often added during the manufacture of synthetic fibers and are a common ingredient in laundry detergents.

Tests for Scoured and Bleached Fabrics

Many different analytical methods may be useful in evaluating quality of preparation, controlling preparation processes, and detecting damage caused by preparatory treatments. (17) Following are some tests commonly done for quality control and detection of problems in preparation processes.

Whiteness

Reflectance of visible light from the fabric is compared to that from a white standard such as magnesium oxide. Standard methods for measurement and reporting of whiteness are available (17).

pH

Fabric is extracted with water, and the pH of the extract is measured. A standard method for pH measurement is published by AATCC.

Absorbency

Absorbency is affected by many variables and its unambiguous measurement is difficult. A standard method of AATCC uses the length of time required for the fabric to absorb a droplet of water carefully placed on the surface of the fabric as a measure of absorbency.

Fluidity

Fluidity is inversely related to viscosity. The viscosity of a polymer solution is a function of the molecular weight (and degree of polymerization) of the polymer. Viscosity of a solution of cellulose in cuprammonium hydroxide (CUAM) or cupriethylene diamine (CUEN) can be used to detect depolymerization of cellulose. The results are usually expressed as fluidity values where higher fluidity means that the molecular weight of the polymer is lower indicating that damage has occurred. Fluidity measurement is difficult and time consuming and is not done routinely in most plants.

Presence of aldehyde groups

Chemical damage from over oxidation or hydrolysis of cellulose produces aldehyde groups. Fehling's test may be used to detect aldehyde groups in cellulose. Aldehyde groups in oxidized cellulose reduce copper ions to copper which is deposited on the fibers as a reddish

Figure 2-15.   Schematic diagram of continuous preparation range

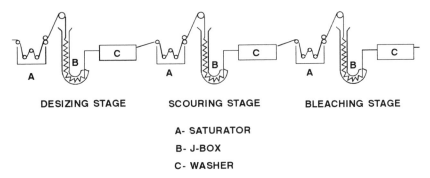

DESIZING STAGE   SCOURING STAGE   BLEACHING STAGE

A- SATURATOR

B- J-BOX

C- WASHER

brown solid. The test can be used as a qualitative spot test or can be done quantitatively. When done quantitatively, the result is called the "copper number."

Presence of carboxyl groups

Severe over oxidation of cellulose produces carboxyl groups. Several methods have been devised to detect carboxyl groups in cellulose. In one of these methods, the fibers are dyed with methylene blue, a basic dye. Since the carboxyl groups are dye sites for methylene blue, cellulose containing carboxyl groups is dyed. The depth to which it dyes with methylene blue is a measure of the carboxyl group content of a cellulose sample.

Continuous Preparation Range

The preparatory processes described in the preceding sections may be done in a continuous manner by placing the appropriate stages in tandem so that the material proceeds from one stage to the next without interruption. Figure 2-15 shows a schematic of the process. The wet steps of the process are usually done in three separate stages—desizing, scouring, and bleaching. Knit fabrics which normally do not contain sized yarn would require only the scouring and bleaching stages.

Fabric is usually dry upon entering the desize saturator. Therefore, the concentration of desizing formulation in the fabric is the same as the concentration of chemicals in the saturator. However, since the fabric entering the caustic saturator and peroxide saturator is wet, the formulations in these stages are diluted by exchange of a portion of the water in the fabric for formulation in the saturator. These dilutions must be taken into account in preparing and replenishing the formulation in the saturators as the process runs.

The concentration of alkali in the saturators is measured by titration with a standard acid reagent. The concentration of peroxide in the saturator is usually measured by titration with a standard solution of potassium permanganate. Measurement of these concentrations provides the basis for either manual or automatic control of the concentrations of chemicals in the saturators.

Continuous preparation processes provide the time required for diffusion of chemicals and chemical reactions by using J-boxes or bins to accumulate and hold fabric for extended periods of time in a stage. J-boxes are often heated to accelerate chemical reactions and lower the dwell time required. Open width steamers may also be used to heat and hold fabrics for the time required for chemicals to accomplish their function.

Washing of the fabric between stages is important so that carry over of decomposition products and chemicals from one stage to the next is minimized.

Sometimes two, or even all three, stages in a preparation range are combined to save energy and processing time. Combination of stages usually results in a compromise between better quality of preparation with the three stage process and savings of time and energy that may be achieved in a combined stage process.

Mercerization

The process of treating cotton with a concentrated solution of sodium hydroxide is called mercerization because it was discovered by John Mercer around 1850. Treatment of cotton with alkali has many beneficial effects including:

increased tensile strength
increased softness
increased luster (if done under tension)
improved affinity for dyes
improved dyeability of immature fibers
higher water sorption.

The chemical effect of concentrated caustic soda solutions is unusual because the crystalline as well as the amorphous regions of the fiber are affected while most beneficial treatments of cotton affect only the amorphous regions of the fiber. Treatment of cellulose with caustic soda forms soda cellulose.

$$Cell—OH \ + \ NaOH \ \longrightarrow \ Cell—O^-Na^+ \ + \ H_2O$$

Subsequent neutralization of the soda cellulose regenerates cellulose forming a hydrated cellulose which when dried has a slightly different arrangement of the glucose units in the crystal structure than does unmercerized cellulose. This change in the crystal structure is responsible for the difference in properties of mercerized and unmercerized cotton.

The changes that occur in cotton upon mercerization depend on the concentration of caustic soda used, temperature of treatment, and whether or not the material is under tension during treatment. Caustic soda solution of concentration up to about 9% causes some untwisting of the fibers. Above 9% (and especially at about 15%) caustic concentration, untwisting is accompanied by swelling of the fibers. At concentrations of about 17.7 to 26% caustic soda solutions cause rapid and simultaneous untwisting and swelling of cotton. Full mercerization of cotton is usually done with 20–25% caustic soda solution. Some of the benefits of mercerization, especially improvement in dyeability of immature fibers, are obtained with lower concentrations of caustic soda.

Swelling in caustic soda solution is accompanied by shrinkage in length of the fibers. If the fabric or yarn being mercerized is slack, fiber shrinkage results in lengthwise shrinkage of the yarn or shrinkage in area of fabric. If tension is applied during mercerization, shrinkage is minimized. Application of tension during mercerization is also required in order to develop luster in the material. Mercerization under tension produces smoother fiber surfaces. The high luster of mercerized cotton results from increased specular reflectance of light from the smooth fiber surfaces.

The temperature of the caustic soda solution used affects mercerization of cotton. Mercerization at room temperature or lower allows the use of lower concentration of caustic soda than is required at higher temperature. However, higher temperature produces better wetting of the fabric by the caustic soda solution and may improve uniformity of mercerization if the fabric is difficult to wet.

Mercerization may be done either before or after the fabric is scoured and bleached. If done on greige goods, the concentration of the caustic soda formulation is relatively easy to control. When mercerization is done on wet fabric, dilution of the caustic soda formulation by water in the entering fabric can make control of concentration difficult. The water content of wet fabric entering the mercerization process must be uniform to prevent nonuniform pickup of the caustic soda solution by the fabric.

Mercerization of fabrics is usually done in a continuous process. The fabric is saturated with caustic soda solution. The machine may be equipped with a series of cylinders called "timing cans" to provide the caustic time to penetrate and swell the fibers. A second padding may be done after the fabric leaves the timing cans. Alternatively, the mercerizing range may be equipped with two padders without intermediate timing cans. After leaving the padding and timing section the fabric passes through a tenter frame where the fabric is placed under tension in both the warp and filling directions. While still in the tenter frame, the fabric passes under cascades which wash away part of the caustic soda. The caustic soda concentration in the fabric is lower than mercerizing strength when the fabric exits the cascade washers in the tenter frame. Further washing is done on the fabric, which is no longer under tension, with either hot or cold water. Finally, the fabric is neutralized with acetic acid or sodium bicarbonate to remove the last traces of caustic soda.

The washers in mercerizing ranges are designed for counter-flow of wash water to minimize the use of water. Fresh water enters the washers nearest to the end of the range. The overflow passes through the various washers counter to the direction of movement of fabric through the range. Counterflow washing produces an effluent containing a high concentration of caustic soda. The effluent from the first cascade washer is returned to a recovery unit where it is further concentrated by evaporation so that the caustic soda can be recycled.

Since mercerization affects dyeability of cotton fibers, tests for measuring the degree to which a fabric is mercerized are useful. The following tests can be used:

1. Dye samples with direct dyes such as C.I. Direct Blue 1 or C.I. Direct Red 2. Lighter dyeings indicate lower degrees of mercerization. Comparison of the test dyeings to permanent standards is helpful in determining degree of mercerization.

2. Stain samples of the fabric with a solution of iodine/potassium iodide. Mercerized fibers are stained blue or black while unmercerized fibers are not stained by this reagent.

3. Spot the fabric with 30% sodium hydroxide solution and then dye it with C.I. Direct Red 2. If the fabric was not completely mercerized, darker dyed spots will be present where the fabric was spotted with sodium hydroxide.

4. Examine the mercerized fabric under a microscope and estimate the number of twisted and untwisted fibers present. Completely mercerized material will contain few twisted fibers.

Liquid Ammonia Treatment

Treatment with liquid ammonia produces changes in cotton similar to those produced by mercerization. However, the magnitude of the changes in cotton is not as great with liquid ammonia as with caustic soda mercerization.

Bibliography

1. AATCC, Technical Manual, American Association of Textile Chemists and Colorists, Research Triangle Park, NC, published annually.
2. AATCC Southeastern Section, Textile Chemist and Colorist, vol. 14, no. 1, 1982.
3. Datye, K.V. and A.A. Vaidya, Chemical Processing of Synthetic Fibers and Blends, John Wiley and Sons, New York, NY, 1984.
4. Gibson, M.E. et. al., Textile Chemist and Colorist, vol. 18, no. 9, p55, 1986.
5. International Dyer and Printer, November, 1988, p23.
6. Mark, H., Norman S. Woodling, and Sheldon M. Atlas, eds., Chemical Aftertreatment of Textiles, Wiley-Interscience, New York, NY, 1971.
7. Merian, E. et. al., Journal of the Society of Dyers and Colourists, vol. 79, p505, 1963.
8. Nettles, J.E., Handbook of Chemical Specialties, John Wiley and Sons, New York, NY, 1983.
9. Olson, E.S., Textile Wet Processes, Vol. 1, Noyes Publications, Park Ridge, NJ, 1983.
10. Rosen, M.J., Surfactants and Interfacial Phenomena, John Wiley and Sons, New York, NY, 1978.
11. Steinmiller, W.G. and D.M. Cates, Textile Chemist and Colorist, Vol. 8, no. 1, p30, 1976.

12. Taher, A.M.M. and D.M. Cates, Textile Chemist and Colorist, Vol. 7, no. 12, p30, 1975.
13. Trotman, E.R., Dyeing and Chemical Technology of Textile Fibres, 6th Ed., John Wiley and Sons, New York, NY, 1984.
14. Trotman, E.R., Textile Scouring and Bleaching, Charles Griffin and Company Ltd., London, England, 1968.
15. Ward, Kyle, Jr., Chemistry and Technology of Cotton, Interscience Publishers, New York, NY, 1955.
16. Warwicker, J.O., Journal of the Society of Dyers and Colourists, vol 88, p142, 1972.
17. Weaver, J.W., Ed., Analytical Methods for a Textile Laboratory, 3rd ed., American Association of Textile Chemists and Colorists, Research Triangle Park, NC, 1984.

Color

Colors are sensory perceptions produced when light waves reflected from an object strike the eye. Color is the phenomenon which allows one to differentiate otherwise visually identical objects. Everything has color if we include white and black as colors. The color of textile products has a profound effect on the appeal of the products to the consumer.

The existence of color requires a source of light, an object, and an observer to see the light. All three of these conditions are variables in the perception of color. Each of these conditions for color is discussed in the following sections.

Light

Visible light consists of the narrow band of the electromagnetic spectrum having wavelengths in the range of about 380–780 nanometers (nm). While visible light is most often specified by its wavelength, it can be denoted as well by its frequency or wavenumber. Frequency is the number of wave cycles occurring per unit of time. Frequency is most often specified as cycles per second, or Hertz (Hz), and is inversely proportional to wavelength.

$$\text{frequency (Hz)} = \frac{\text{speed of light (length/time)}}{\text{wavelength (length)}}$$

Wavenumber is the number of wave cycles occurring per unit of length and is the reciprocal of wavelength.

$$\text{wavenumber} = \frac{1}{\text{wavelength}}$$

Table 3-1. Colors of the Visible Spectrum

Color Perceived	Wavelengths (nm)
Red	700–610
Orange	610–590
Yellow	590–570
Green	570–480
Blue	480–430
Violet	430–390

The approximate wavelengths of visible light that produce various color perceptions are shown in Table 3-1.

Since an object can only reflect light waves which shine on the object, the color of the object depends on the intensity of the various wavelengths which are present in the light source. A light source is defined by its spectral energy distribution. Blackbody temperature is a concept based on the fact that the relative spectral energy distribution emitted by an object depends on the temperature of the object. For example, when a metal is heated it glows, first becoming reddish and then progressively whiter and brighter as its temperature rises. A blackbody is a real or theoretical object that emits a certain energy distribution depending on its temperature. Light sources are sometimes described by their "color temperature", the blackbody temperature in °K which produces the spectral energy distribution approximating the light source.

The Commission Internationale de l'Éclairage (CIE) defines several standard light sources. Having standard light sources is important so that standard conditions can be established for viewing, comparison, acceptance, and rejection of colors in commerce. The spectral energy distributions of some of these standard sources are shown in Figure 3-1.

CIE sources A,B, and C are all incandescent. Source A is a tungsten-filament lamp operating at a color temperature of 2854°K. Source A is more intense in the long wavelengths making it appear reddish. Sources B and C are filtered tungsten-filament sources operating at color temperatures of 4800°K and 6500°K, respectively. Source B is intended to simulate noon sunlight while source C is intended to simulate overcast-sky daylight.

The tungsten-filament sources described above approximate the appearance of daylight but contain less ultraviolet waves than natural daylight. Because many textile products and colors are fluores-

Figure 3-1. Spectral energy distributions of illuminants A and C

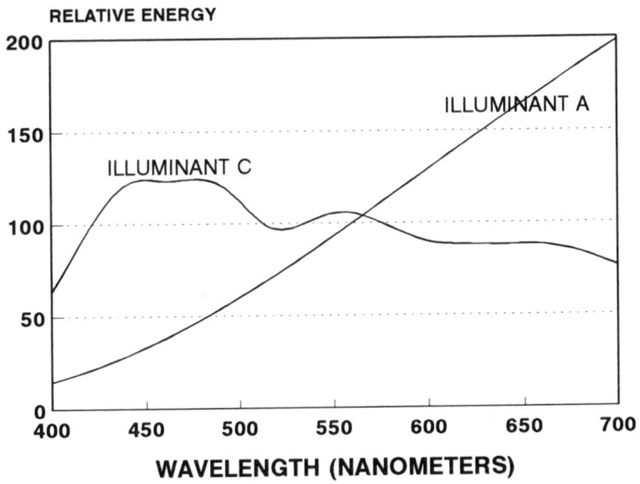

RELATIVE ENERGY

WAVELENGTH (NANOMETERS)

cent, their appearance changes depending on the ultraviolet wave content of the light source. The CIE specified a series of illuminants to supplement A,B, and C. Illuminant D_{65} (color temperature of 6500°K) is now widely used in colorimetry. D_{55} and D_{75} (colors temperatures of 5500° and 7500°K) were also specified by the CIE. Note that the term *illuminant* is used instead of *source* when referring to the D illuminants. A source is a real light that can be physically turned on and off. An illuminant is an imaginary spectral power distribution. It may or may not be possible to make a physical source identical to a defined illuminant.

Some light sources are continuous meaning that they contain all wavelengths of the visible spectrum. Other light sources are discontinuous having all of their energy concentrated in a few narrow bands. These are called line sources. Mercury arc lamps and fluorescent lamps are examples of line sources. "Prime color" fluorescent lamps have high relative energy output in the wavelength regions which stimulate most strongly the color receptors in the human eye. These sources make colors appear especially intense and bright.

Object

The modification of incident light by an object affects the color perceived by the observer. Following are some ways that an object can modify light.

Transmit

Light passes through without a change in direction. The object is said to be transparent. If some wavelengths are transmitted to a greater degree than others, the object is colored as opposed to white or colorless.

Reflect

Light waves bounce off at an angle equal to the angle of incidence in "specular reflection." If certain wavelengths of light are reflected to a greater degree than other wavelengths, the object has color as opposed to being white. If no light is reflected by the object, the object is black.

Scatter

Light waves bounce off at various angles. This is called scattering or "diffuse reflection." If all of the incident light is reflected, scattered, or absorbed, and no light is transmitted; the object is opaque. If part of the light is transmitted, the object is said to be translucent. Light scattering is an important phenomenon which is responsible for the blue color of the sky and colors of smoke and clouds. Light scattering greatly influences the color of textile materials.

Absorb

Light is transformed to some other form of energy, typically heat. Much of the light not transmitted, reflected, or scattered is absorbed.

Refract

Speed of light is changed as light passes through an object resulting is bending of the waves. Refraction is responsible for the appearance of a dividing line between two immiscible liquids in contact with one another and for the apparent bending of a stick at the point that it is submerged in water.

Fluoresce

Light of some wavelengths is absorbed by an object and quickly emitted at longer wavelengths. Fluorescence is responsible for the brightening effect of optical whiteners in textiles and for the brightness of certain dyes when viewed under a source containing ultraviolet waves.

Phosphoresce

As in fluorescence, light of some wavelengths is absorbed and emitted at longer wavelengths. However, a phosphorescent object may store the energy for an extended period of time before emitting it while a fluorescent object emits the absorbed light almost instantaneously.

Observer

We usually think of the observer as a person, but an electronic instrument also satisfies this requirement for color. The human observer sees color when light enters the eye and strikes the retina. The term "color blind" is often used to refer to an individual having a color vision deficiency. Although defective color vision is common, the term "color blind" is an overstatement in most cases since total inability to see color is very rare. The most common color vision deficiency is difficulty in distinguishing between red and green, but other types of deficiencies also exist. About 8% of all men and ½% of women suffer color vision deficiencies ranging from very mild to severe.

People having normal color vision see wavelengths of light in the range from about 380–780 nanometers (nm). The sensitivity of the eye is low near both ends of this range, so the "visible region" is often said to be from 400–700 nm. Nerves in the retina send signals to the brain so that the observer perceives an image. The retina contains two types of cells, rods and cones. The rods are very sensitive but only to wavelengths near 505 nm. Rods make it possible for humans to see in low light conditions, but they do not play a role in color perception. The cones are much less sensitive to light than the rods and vary in sensitivity to different wavelengths of light. The cones are responsible for the perception of color.

The maximum sensitivity of the eye to wavelengths of about 450, 540, and 575 nm is the basis for the tristimulus theory of color vision. This theory is often referred to as the Young-Helmholtz theory after its early proposers. The theory contends that the eye contains pigments which absorb light at or near the above wavelengths and undergo chemical reactions. The details of how messages are transmitted from the cones in the eye to the brain are not completely understood and are not within the scope of this text.

The opponent theory of color vision contends that the eye perceives one of each of three opponent pairs (red/green, blue/yellow, and black/white) but not both of a particular pair simultaneously. For example, a greater perception of red would be accompanied by a corresponding lesser stimulus of green. According to the opponent theory, the stimulus produced by each opponent pair contributes to the color perceived by the observer.

The spectral energy distribution of a light source can be defined and controlled very accurately. The modification of light by an object is inherent in the object and can be accurately measured. These elements in the perception of color can be handled very objectively. On the other hand, acuity of color vision varies greatly among individuals. Even individuals considered to have normal color vision probably see colors slightly differently, and the psychological response to color is certainly very different from one individual to another. Therefore, the perception of color by an individual is a subjective matter, a fact which can have significant influence in acceptance or rejection of colors in commerce.

Color Measurement

The reflectance of light by an opaque object or transmittance of light through a transparent object as a function of wavelength describes the color of the object. The practice of color measurement with instruments is called spectrophotometry. Although the instruments used may be very different, the basic principles of visible spectrophotometry are the same as those applicable to infrared, near infrared, ultraviolet, microwave and other types of spectroscopy. Spectrophotometers have three essential parts: a light source, a monochromator, and a detector. An output device such as a chart recorder, CRT, or printer is often present. A spectrophotometer may be relatively simple and inexpensive having a simple meter as the output device and manual controls. However, typical spectrophotometers for color measurement for industrial and research purposes are more sophisticated having electronic controls, automated operations, and extensive computer programs to assist in analysis of data.

As shown in diagrams of scanning spectrophotometers in Figure 3-2, the geometry of the optics is designed to measure the transmittance of light through transparent objects or the reflectance of light from opaque objects.

Figure 3-2.   Schematic diagram of spectrophotometers for measuring transmittance (top) and reflectance (bottom)

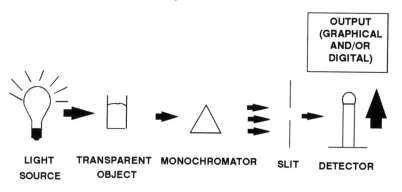

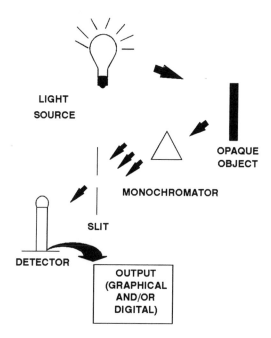

A white source such as a tungsten lamp usually provides the light for the spectrophotometer. The monochrometer is a prism, spectrum filter, or diffraction grating which spreads the light from the source into a spectrum. Although the word "monochromatic" means one color or one wavelength, the monochrometer and slit select a narrow band of light rather than a single wavelength to be measured. The slit scans across the spectrum selecting the band of light to be measured. The monochromator and slit may be placed either before the sample position giving monochromatic illumination or after the sample position giving polychromatic illumination. However, only polychromatic illumination followed by separation of the reflected light by a monochromator gives an accurate spectrophotometric curve if the sample is fluorescent. The detector is a photoelectric device which converts the transmitted or reflected light to an electrical signal which a chart or computer records.

An abridged spectrophotometer measures a few narrow bands across the spectrum rather than scanning wavelength by wavelength. Typically about 16 bands each about 20 nm wide are measured. These instruments use a series of filters to select the bands to be measured or may use a series of detectors to measure the reflectance at all of the wavelengths simultaneously. Abridged spectrophotometers are simpler and less expensive than scanning spectrophotometers, but provide less information.

Abridged spectrophotometers containing only 3 or 4 colored filters are sometimes called "colorimeters" to distinguish them from instruments measuring 16 or more bands. Colorimeters can be used to measure color but give less information than spectrophotometers.

Color Mixing

When colors are mixed, new colors result. The color perceived by an observer results from the stimulus produced by the mixture of wavelengths of light that enter the eye. A color mixture which results in an increase in the number of wavelengths or intensity of light entering the eye is an "additive color mixture." Mixing of lights is an example of additive color mixing. Figure 3-3 shows the colors produced by additive mixing of red, blue, and green primary lights.

The circles in Figure 3-3 can be viewed as spots from colored lamps on a white screen. Where the spots overlap, the amount of light reflected by the screen is greater and a brighter secondary color is formed. Where the light from all three primary colors overlap, the reflected light mixture is white. Additive color mixing is used to produce colors in color television picture tubes.

A color mixture which results in a decrease in the number of wavelengths or intensity of light entering the eye is a "subtractive color mixture." Subtractive color mixing results from mixing of dyes, pigments, or inks that absorb light. Figure 3-4 shows the effect of sub-

Figure 3-3.   Additive color mixing

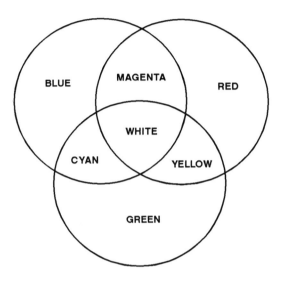

tractive mixing the primary colors yellow, cyan, and magenta. The secondary colors produced are duller because the total light reflectance is lower than that of either of the primary colors. Where all three of the primaries are mixed the color is black. Subtractive color mix-

Figure 3-4.   Subtractive color mixing

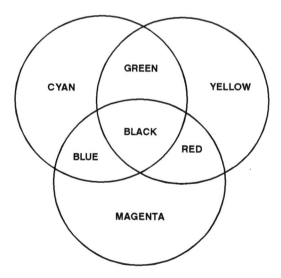

Figure 3-5.   Reflectance curve of an orange color

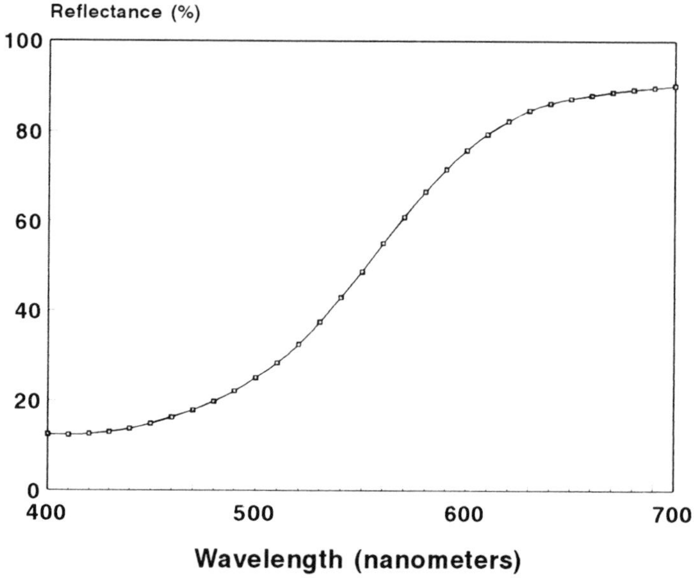

Reflectance (%)

Wavelength (nanometers)

ing is used in dyeing of textile materials, formulation of paints, and for coloration of most objects.

Spectrophotometric reflectance curves are best interpreted by thinking in terms of additive mixtures. For example, a dyer starts out with white cloth. If an orange color is needed, the dyer uses an orange dye or a mixture of a red and a yellow dye. As is indicated in Figure 3-5, the resulting fabric absorbs most of the violet, blue, and green wavelengths and reflects mostly red, orange, and yellow. The observer sees the reflected light and the stimulus produced is the additive mixture of the reflected colors.

Laws of Absorption of Light by Transparent Objects

The Beer-Lambert Law relates light absorption in a transparent material to concentration of colorant in the material and the thickness of the material. The Law is usually written in the form

$$A = \varepsilon \, c \, l \, , \quad (1)$$

where "c" is the concentration of colorant and "l" is the path length or thickness of the sample. "A" is the absorbance and is sometimes called the "optical density." "ε" is the extinction coefficient and is

Figure 3-6.   Absorbance vs. concentration of color

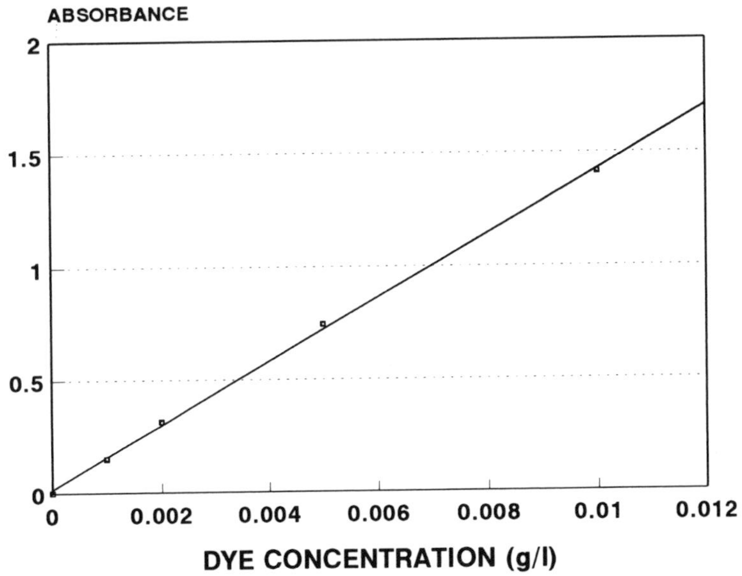

ABSORBANCE

DYE CONCENTRATION (g/l)

sometimes called the "molar extinction coefficient" when the concentration, c, is expressed in molarity. The Law applies to either solid or liquid materials, but it is used most often in textiles for measuring the color of solutions of dye in water or other solvents.

The Beer-Lambert Law is actually a combination of two separate laws. Beer's Law relates absorbance of light by a colored solution to the concentration of absorbing substance. Lambert's Law relates absorbance of light by a colored solution to the thickness of the absorbing solution. The Beer-Lambert Law is usually valid only when monochromatic light is used. Furthermore, Beer's Law may not be valid in dye solutions of high concentration or when the dye is in an aggregated state in the solvent. The validity of Beer's Law must be established experimentally before it can be used with confidence to analyze a particular dye in solution.

Absorbance and transmittance are related by the equation

$$A = \log_{10}(100/\%T), \quad (2)$$

where %T is the percentage of incident light that passes through the solution.

The path length (sample thickness), l, is often fixed or predetermined so that it can be treated as a constant. Figure 3-6 shows that the amount of light absorbed is directly proportional to the concentration of colorant in the sample.

The extinction coefficient, ε, is the slope of the line and is constant for a particular colorant. Therefore, the extinction coefficient is a measure of the tinctorial strength of the dye. If the extinction coefficient of a colorant (dye) is known, the concentration of dye can be determined simply by measuring the light absorption using a spectrophotometer.

The fact that most dyes in solution absorb light independently of one another is very useful in analyzing dye mixtures. The absorbance of a mixture of dyes is equal to the sum of the absorbance of each of the components in the mixture at a particular wavelength. In mathematical terms,

$$A_{mixture} = A_{dye\ 1} + A_{dye\ 2} + \cdots\cdots + A_{dye\ x}\ ,\ at\ \lambda_x. \quad (3)$$

Combining equations 1 and 3 yields equation 4.

$$A_{mixture} = \varepsilon_1 c_1 l + \varepsilon_2 c_2 l + \cdots\cdots + \varepsilon_x c_x l\ ,\ at\ \lambda_x, \quad (4)$$

where the subscripts refer to the individual dyes in the mixture. A series of simultaneous equations can be used to determine the concentrations of the individual dye components in a mixture, since all of the terms in equation 4 except the concentrations of dyes are constant or measurable. The number of simultaneous equations required is the same as the number of dyes in the mixture.

Laws of Absorption of Light by Opaque Objects

The mathematical relationships relating light reflectance from opaque objects to concentration of colorant in the object are analogous to those discussed above for transparent objects. However, reflectance measurements of dyed materials usually include the influence of the textile substrate as well as the influence of the dye. Reflectance is usually measured relative to a very white standards such as barium sulfate or magnesium oxide. Since these standards are difficult to handle and tend to discolor quickly, glass tiles which are more stable in color are usually used as secondary standards for routine measurements. On the other hand, transmittance measurements are usually made in a solvent where the light absorbing characteristics of the solvent are eliminated by measuring the transmittance relative to a blank containing only the solvent.

Light scattering and light absorption of visible light determine the color of an opaque object. Scattering changes the direction of light while absorption converts some of the rays to heat, or to longer wavelengths in the case of fluorescent materials. Complete mathematical treatments of absorption and scattering are very complex. However, Kubelka and Munk in 1939 developed a relatively simple treatment that is the basis for color measurement and computer-assisted prediction of color matches on textile materials. The Kubelka-Munk equation provides for calculation of a ratio , K/S ("K over S value"), from measured reflectance values as is shown in equation 5.

$$K/S = \frac{(1 - R)^2}{2R} \quad (5)$$

K is called the coefficient of absorption and S is called the coefficient of scatter. R is the fractional reflectance at a specific wavelength. The ratio K/S is analogous to absorbance, A, as measured in transparent substrates and used in Beer's Law.

Assuming that the fabric and the dyes contained in the fabric absorb and scatter light independently of one another, the K/S for a fabric containing a mixture of dyes is

$$K/S = \frac{K_1 C_1 + K_2 C_2 + \cdots\cdots + K_F}{S_1 C_1 + S_2 C_2 + \cdots\cdots + S_F}, \quad (6)$$

where C is concentration of dye; and the subscripts 1, 2, and F refer to the individual dyes and the fabric, respectively. Since reflectance measurements include the influence of the substrate, the mathematical equations include terms, K_F and S_F, for this effect. If scattering of light by the dyes is small compared to scattering of light by the fabric, equation 6 can be further simplified to

$$K/S = (K_1/S_F)C_1 + (K_2/S_F)C_2 + \cdots\cdots + (K/S)_F . \quad (7)$$

The K_x/S_F factors in equation 7 are constants for a particular dye at a particular wavelength and are analogous to the extinction coefficient, E, as used in Beer's Law. Therefore, a series of simultaneous equations can be used to determine what concentrations of dye are contained in a fabric if the constants for the particular dyes in the fabric are known and the K/S of the fabric is measured.

When a fabric contains only one dye, equation 7 simplifies to

Figure 3-7.   K/S vs. concentration

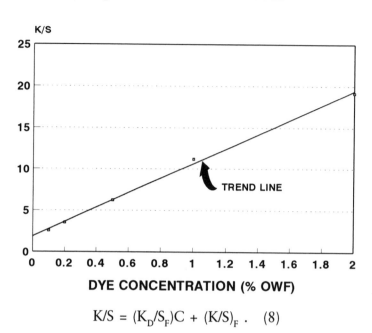

$$K/S = (K_D/S_F)C + (K/S)_F \ . \quad (8)$$

As shown in Figure 3-7, a plot of K/S of a dyed fabric as a function of concentration of dye yields a straight line if equation 8 is valid. The slope of the line is K_D/S_F, and the intercept on the ordinate is K/S for the fabric when it contains no dye.

Equation 7 is the basic equation for computer-assisted prediction of color matches. If the dyes or pigments in the sample to be matched are identical to those that will be used to match the color, color matching is trivial. A simple set of simultaneous equations equal in number to the number of dyes in the mixture is used to solve for the concentrations of dyes present. However, the textile colorist is usually asked to match an almost unlimited variety and number of colors on textile materials using a relatively small number of available dyes and pigments. Since the spectral reflectance characteristics of the dyes or pigments available to the textile colorist are usually not identical to those of the colorants in the sample to be matched, an exact match can not usually be made. However, an acceptable match usually can be made by determining the concentrations that produce an approximate solution to a large number of simultaneous equations. Typically, 16 simultaneous equations in the form of equation 7, each representing a different wavelength, are used. A com-

Figure 3-8.   Diagram of Munsell color space

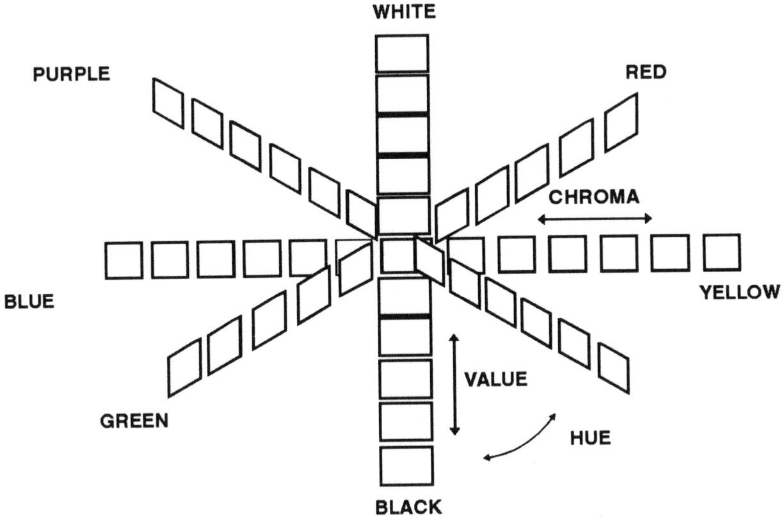

puter is necessary to do the many calculations required to solve the equations.

Often the relationship between K/S and concentration of dye in the fabric is not linear, indicating that equation 8 is not valid. These deviations from linearity are incorporated into the mathematics and software used in computer color matching programs.

The Munsell Color Order System

A color order system is a logical arrangement of a large number of colors. Such a system may be either a set of physical samples or purely numerical. Any logical arrangement of a large number of widely different colors requires three dimensions so the term "color space" is commonly used when describing a color order system.

The Munsell System is a widely-used color order system consisting of a set of painted color samples arranged in three dimensions. The three "dimensions", or color attributes, in the Munsell System are hue, value, and chroma. Figure 3-8 shows a diagram of the arrangement of colors in the Munsell System. Samples in the Munsell set differ from adjacent samples in approximately equal visual steps.

Munsell hue is that quality of color described by the traditional words used to describe color such as red, blue, green, etc. The ten (10) principal hues in the Munsell System are as follows:

yellow
yellow-red
red
red-purple
purple
purple-blue
blue
blue-green
green
green-yellow

Each hue has ten subdivisions with the principal hue being designated "5".

Value is the lightness or darkness of a color along a white to black scale. The value scale is from 1 to 10 with 1 being black and 10 being white.

Chroma (sometimes called saturation) is used to describe the intensity of a color. Chroma is that attribute which makes two colors different even though they have the same hue and value. Chroma has no theoretical upper limit. This allows the system to accommodate additional samples when pigments having greater saturation than existing colors are found.

The Munsell Color system can be viewed as a book having its pages fanned out to make a cylinder with the binding at the center of the cylinder. The pages of the book would represent the various hues. The binding would represent the value scale, and the distance from the binding out toward the edge of the pages would represent the chroma of a color.

Each sample in the Munsell System has a designation, 5Y 2/12 for example, which indicates hue of 5 yellow, value of 2 and chroma of 12. The fact that the Munsell System is a set of physical samples has advantages and disadvantages. The greatest advantages are that the colors can be viewed and measured and parties involved in trade can both have a set of Munsell Color samples. Disadvantages are lack of permanency of the color, discoloration of colors due to handling of samples, and the fact that construction of the color space is subjective.

The CIE Color Order System

The CIE color order system is numerical. The CIE System integrates the three conditions for existence of color: light source, object,

Figure 3-9.   Standard observer experiment

LAMPS

(RED, GREEN, BLUE)

OBSERVER

WHITE SCREEN

BLACK PARTITION

TEST (SPECTRUM) LAMP

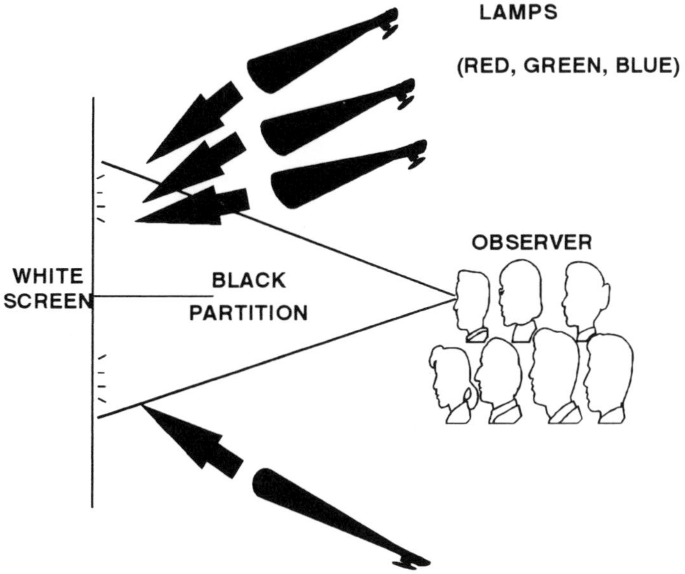

and observer. Two of these, the spectral energy distribution of light sources and reflectance curves of objects, were discussed previously. Curves representing these two variables comprise two of the elements of the CIE System.

The third element in the CIE System is the Standard Observer. The concept of Standard Observer is best explained by describing the experiment that was used to establish the Standard Observer. The experiment is shown schematically in Figure 3-9.

Participants in the experiment were individuals having "normal" color vision. Each individual viewed the color from a spectrum lamp on one side of a split white screen. The individual then matched the spectrum color by adjusting the intensity of light from three colored lamps (primaries) being mixed on the other side of the split screen. The experiment was repeated by each observer for spectrum lamps for each wavelength across the visible spectrum. The results produced values of r, g, and b which represented the relative amounts of the three primaries used by the observers to match the spectrum colors.

One complication of the Standard Observer experiment was that not all of the spectrum lamps could be matched by mixing different

**Figure 3-10.   Tristimulus values for the equal energy spectrum obtained
from the standard observer experiment**

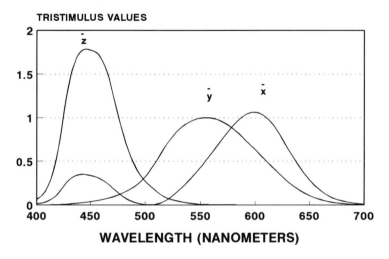

intensities of the primary lamps. In some cases, the colors on the two sides of the screen could only be made to match by adding energy from a primary lamp to that of the spectrum color. Adding energy from a primary lamp to the spectrum color is equivalent to using a negative amount of light from the primary lamp, so the results contained some negative numbers. In order to eliminate the need for negative numbers, the CIE subjected the results to a mathematical transformation based on a set of imaginary primary lamps which cannot be produced by any real source lamps.

The results of the Standard Observer experiment and transformation of the data are shown in Figure 3-10. The values $\bar{x}, \bar{y}$, and $\bar{z}$ are called the "color matching functions" and represent the amount of the three imaginary primaries that would be required by a person with normal color vision to match the spectrum colors. The results are the average of responses of a relatively small number of observers. The original CIE experiment was done in 1931 using a 2° field of view which produced a colored spot about the size of a 25 cents coin. The experiment was repeated in 1964 using a 10° field of view which produced colored circles many times larger than those viewed in the original experiment. The results of the 1931 and 1964 experiments produced slightly different results. The results of the 1964 experiment are often referred to as the 1964 Supplementary Standard Observer, or sometimes simply the 10° observer.

The three dimensions in CIE color space are the tristimulus values. The tristimulus values X, Y, and Z are given by the following integrals:

$$X = \int_{400}^{700} E\,\bar{x}\,R\,d\lambda$$

$$Y = \int_{400}^{700} E\,\bar{y}\,R\,d\lambda$$

$$Z = \int_{400}^{700} E\,\bar{z}\,R\,d\lambda$$

The tristimulus values are the areas under the curves produced by multiplying wavelength by wavelength the power of the light source, the reflectance of the object, and the color matching function $\bar{x}$, $\bar{y}$, or $\bar{z}$.

Since the variables R and E cannot be expressed in terms of wavelength, the integration must be done by a summation technique. The equations for the summations are as follows:

$$X = \sum_{400}^{700} E\,\bar{x}\,R\,\Delta\lambda$$

$$Y = \sum_{400}^{700} E\,\bar{y}\,R\,\Delta\lambda$$

$$Z = \sum_{400}^{700} E\,\bar{z}\,R\,\Delta\lambda$$

The manual integrations required to determine tristimulus values are tedious and time consuming to perform. The advent of high speed digital computers made routine calculation of tristimulus values practical.

The Chromaticity Diagrams

The chromaticity diagram provides a convenient way to view a plane in CIE color space. Chromaticity coordinates x, y, and z are calculated using the following equations:

$$x = \frac{X}{X + Y + Z}$$

Figure 3-11. CIE chromaticity diagram

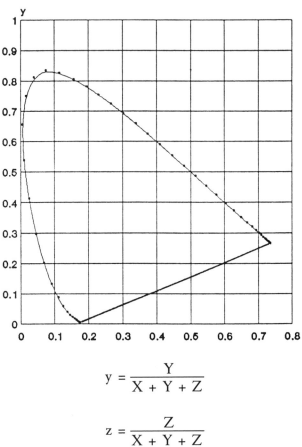

$$y = \frac{Y}{X + Y + Z}$$

$$z = \frac{Z}{X + Y + Z}$$

Lower case letters represent chromaticity coordinates while upper case letters represent tristimulus values. The chromaticity coordinates relate to the hue and chroma of colors. Plotting chromaticity coordinates x versus y yields the horseshoe-shaped chromaticity diagram shown in Figure 3-11.

Since x+y+z=1, the chromaticity coordinates x and y provide only two of the coordinates necessary to describe the color. One of the tristimulus values must also be specified. The tristimulus value Y is ordinarily specified along with chromaticity coordinates x and y.

An alternative set of coordinates is sometimes used to locate a color on the CIE chromaticity diagram. These coordinates, dominant wavelength and purity, are illustrated in Figure 3-12. Dominant wavelength and purity are similar to the visual aspects of color, hue and

Figure 3-12.   Chromaticity diagram showing purity and dominant wavelength

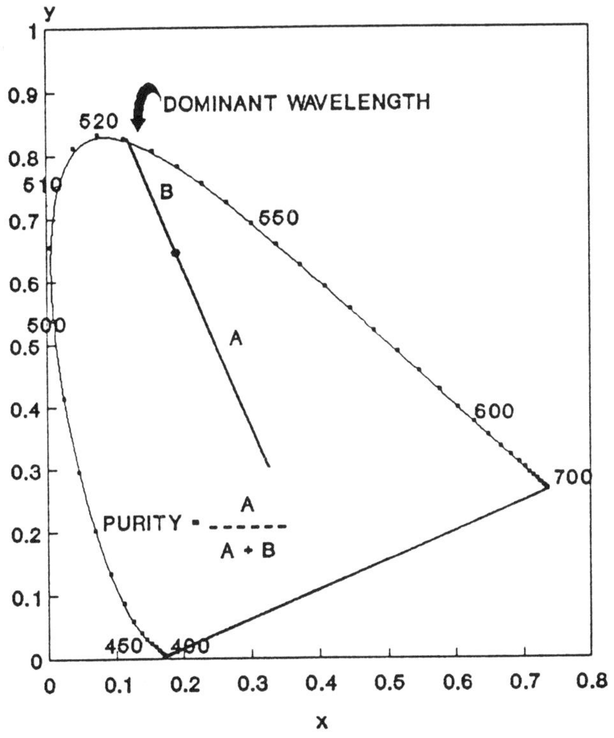

chroma. The dominant wavelength is found by drawing a straight line from the coordinates of the illuminant to the spectrum locus. The wavelength at which the line intersects the spectrum locus is the "dominant wavelength" of the color. The color of the dominant wavelength is similar to hue as in the Munsell System. Purple colors do not have a dominant wavelength. If the line from the coordinates of the illuminant through the coordinates of the color does not intersect the spectrum locus, the line is drawn in the opposite direction and the point of intersection is then referred to as the "dominant wavelength (complimentary)." The purity is the distance of the coordinates of the color from the coordinates of the illuminant divided by the distance from the coordinates of the illuminant to the spectrum locus. Purity is an indication of intensity of the color and is similar to chroma as in the Munsell System.

The greatest limitation of the CIE Chromaticity Diagram is that distances between various points on the diagram do not correlate to visual perceptions of the magnitude of color differences between sam-

Figure 3-13.   MacAdam ellipses in CIE color space

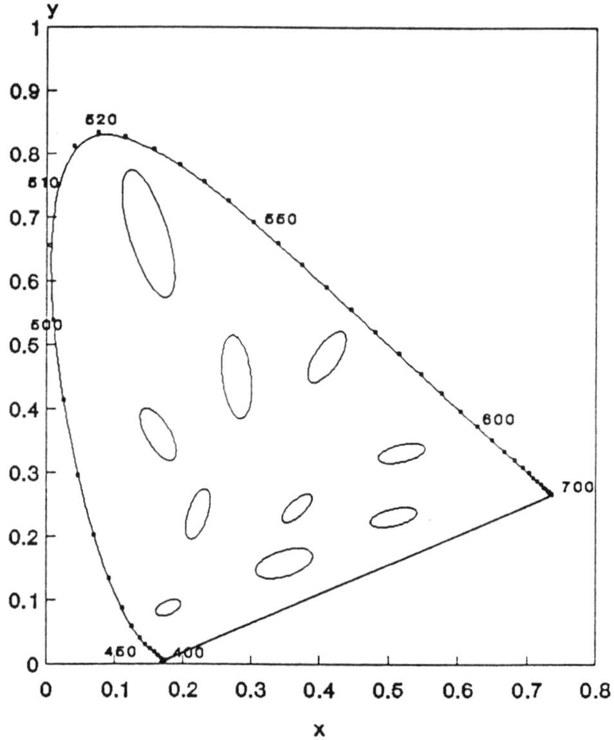

ples. This is illustrated by the well-known MacAdam Ellipses in Figure 3-13 which show areas (enlarged by a factor of ten) of equal visual perception in the CIE Chromaticity Diagram. The ellipses which vary in size for different regions of the diagram represent the areas within which colors are not visually distinguishable from reference colors having coordinates at the centers of the ellipses.

LAB Color Space

LAB color space (illustrated in Figure 3-14) is based on the theory of "opponent colors" which contends that a color cannot be red and green at the same time, or blue and yellow at the same time. According to the opponent theory of color vision, the human color vision system encodes signals from cone receptors in the eye into light-dark, red-green, and yellow-blue signals. Thus in LAB color space, redness-greenness and blueness-yellowness of a color are

Figure 3-14.   LAB color space

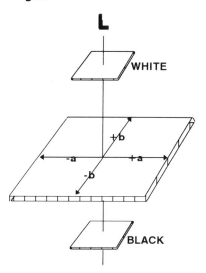

expressed as single numbers, usually "a" and "b," respectively. The third coordinate, lightness, is usually designated "L." Coordinate "a" is positive for red colors and negative for green colors. In 1976, the CIE recommended use of the CIE L*, a*, b* (officially abbreviated CIELAB) color space which is the system now most widely used in textiles, the CIELAB system. Equations for CIELAB color space are as follows:

$$L^* = 116 \ (Y/Y_o)^{1/3} - 16$$
$$a^* = 500 \ [(X/X_o)^{1/3} - (Y/Y_o)^{1/3}]$$
$$b^* = 200 \ [(Y/Y_o)^{1/3} - (Z/Z_o)^{1/3}]$$

Although CIELAB is not a perfectly visually uniform color space, the magnitude of distances between points in the CIELAB space correlates better with visual perceptions of color differences than is the case in the CIE Chromaticity Diagram.

Expression of Color Differences

Assessment of color is vital in manufacturing and marketing of textile products. Color can be assessed either visually or by the use of instruments. Assessment consists of determining whether a color difference exists, describing the difference, and determining whether or not color differences are tolerable. Assessment of color differences is fraught with difficulties, and literally dozens of systems have been devised to express color differences. Some of these systems are based on some theory of color vision while others are purely empirical. The difference in location of samples in CIELAB color space is used widely in textiles to assess color differences between samples.

The difference in coordinates in the CIELAB space can be resolved into the three components to give an indication of the magnitude and direction of the color difference between two colors, 1 and 2.

$$\Delta a^* = a^*_1 - a^*_2$$
$$\Delta b^* = b^*_1 - b^*_2$$
$$\Delta L^* = L^*_1 - L^*_2$$

The sign of the difference indicates the direction of difference in color while the magnitude of the difference indicates the size of the color differences. Total color difference, ΔE, is the actual distance in CIELAB color space between samples.

$$\Delta E = [(\Delta a^*)^2 + (\Delta b^*)^2 + (\Delta L^*)^2]^{1/2}$$

The location of a color in CIELAB color space can also be specified in terms of coordinates L^*, C^*, and H^*, where C^* represents chroma and H^* is the "hue angle." C^* is the distance between the sample and the L axis and H is the angle made by the chroma line and the a^* axis. The total color difference between two samples expressed in terms of chromaticity and hue angle is

$$\Delta E = [(\Delta C^*)^2 + (\Delta H^*)^2 + (\Delta L^*)^2]^{1/2}.$$

A color difference between two samples is often expressed by the differences in hue angle, ΔH, and chroma, ΔC, of the two samples.

Metamerism

When two objects, fabrics for example, match in color under one set of lighting conditions but fail to match under other lighting conditions, the objects are said to be a metameric pair. This means that the two objects have different spectrophotometric curves. A pair of objects can have identical coordinates in color space and still be metameric since the light source affects how the color is seen by the observer. A given set of coordinates in color space can correspond to many different spectrophotometric curves. Metameric pairs have different spectophotometric curves but identical color space coordinates for one set of conditions. Conversely, nonmetameric pairs have identical spectrophotometric curves. Metamerism is a common problem in textiles because the dyes used to formulate colors usually have different light absorbing characteristics from the colorants in the object being matched. Therefore, formulating an exact, nonmetameric match of the desired color on a textile material may not always be possible.

"Observer metamerism" refers to the case where two objects appear to some observers to be the same color, but seem to other observers to be different in color. This occurs when the observers have slight differences in their respective spectral response curves even though all have "normal" color vision. The "observers" in observer metamerism need not be humans. Color measuring instruments can also have variations in their response curves.

Bibliography

1. Billmeyer, F.W. Jr. and M. Saltzman, Principles of Color Technology, 2nd ed., John Wiley and Sons, New York, NY. 1981.
2. Datacolor, Instrumental Color Control, Seminar Papers.
3. Diano Corporation, Color Technology and Its Applications in Industry, Diano Corporation, Foxboro, MA, 1970.
4. Gohl, E.P.G., and L.D. Vilensky, Textile Science, 2nd ed., Longman Cheshire, Melbourne, Australia, 1983.
5. Hardy, A.C., Handbook of Colorimetry, Massachusetts Institute of Technology, Cambridge, MA 1936.
6. Kuehni, R., Computer Colorant Formulation, D.C. Heath and Company, Lexington, MA, 1975.

Dyeing Principles

Color is a major consideration in selection of textile products by the consumer. The human eye is an excellent detector of small color differences in textile products so color application by the textile manufacturer must be very uniform in most cases. Uniform application is usually much more critical for color than it is for most chemical finishes. For example, even if a softener is applied nonuniformly, the fabric may still be acceptable to the consumer, because he will never know that it was applied unevenly. On the other hand, if a dye is applied unevenly, even the untrained observer knows. Furthermore, control of color from one dye lot to another or along the length of a fabric in continuous dyeing is important because color differences in different panels of a sewn product or garment will be obvious and unacceptable in almost all cases. Absence of metamerism is also important in most colored materials.

Color fastness properties of colored products have a direct impact in the every day use of textile products by the consumer. The color must be durable for the life of the product in many cases or in other cases must fade in a predictable and pleasing manner with use. Colorfastness of the dyed material to washing, laundering, dry cleaning, light, perspiration, rubbing (crocking), atmospheric contaminants, weathering, and other conditions are all important. The end use of the product determines the level of importance and what particular type of fastness properties a textile product must have. For example, colorfastness to dry cleaning may not be very important for fabrics going into automotive seat covers, but lightfastness requirements might be very high for this application.

Uniformity and colorfastness requirements are major determining factors in selection of dyes and dyeing methods for textile materials. Many variables must be controlled in dyeing of textile materials. In order to better understand control of variables in the

Figure 4-1. Dyeing as a mass transfer process

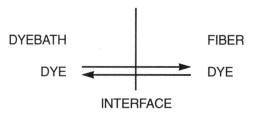

dyeing process, consider the model of a dyeing system shown in Figure 4-1.

This model describes dyeing as a mass transfer process. The model is applicable to virtually all dyeing systems; continuous or batch, cotton or synthetic fibers, fiber or fabric or garments. The task that must be accomplished in dyeing is to transfer dye from the dyebath to the fiber. The term "exhaustion" is used to express the degree of dye transfer from dyebath to fiber. Exhaustion is usually expressed as a percentage of the amount of dye originally placed in the dyebath. For example, if ¾ of the dye originally added to the dyebath transfers to the fiber, the exhaustion is 75%. The depth of color achieved depends mainly on how much dye is added to the fiber. The location of dye on the fiber influences the apparent depth of color. Dye near the surface of the yarn or fabric contributes more to the apparent depth than does deeply penetrated dye. Thus, the apparent darkness of the dyeing is not necessarily the same for two fabrics containing exactly the same amount of dye.

For economic and environmental reasons, a high degree of exhaustion is desirable. Dyes are expensive, and dye which is left in the bath is wasted. Furthermore, dye left in the dyebath is a pollutant which must be controlled and disposed of along with the wastewater from the plant. Often, auxiliary chemicals are added to the dyebath to improve exhaustion.

Dye exhausts gradually from the dyebath to the fiber as time passes, but there is usually a diminishing return in exhaustion as time of dyeing increases. After some finite dyeing time, the additional time and chemicals required to produce higher exhaustion may be more expensive than savings achieved in dye and waste treatment costs.

Most dyeing processes are reversible. That is, as dye molecules transfer from the dyebath into the fiber, other dye molecules desorb from the fiber and reenter the dyebath. The number of dye molecules in the fiber will increase with dyeing time until the rates at which dye molecules enter and leave the fiber are equal. When these rates become equal, the amount of dye in the fiber does not change with additional dyeing time. An equilibrium or steady state condition has been established. The time required to reach equilibrium depends on many things such as temperature, type of dye, type of fiber, and presence of dyeing auxiliaries. Equilibrium dyeing time may range from a few minutes to many hours. Typically, the equilibrium dyeing time is longer than is commercially feasible so commercial dyeing systems often do not reach equilibrium. If a dyeing is not carried to equilibrium, the exhaustion of dye is less than it would be at equilibrium.

Dye distributes between the dyebath and the fiber because it has an inherent attraction for both of these phases. The attraction of dye to the fiber is often referred to as the "affinity" of the dye. Actually, the dye has affinity for both the fiber and the dyebath. The driving force for transfer of a dye molecule from one phase to the other (dyebath to fiber or fiber to dyebath) is the *concentration* of dye in the two phases. Since dye adsorption is *concentration* dependent, the relative amounts of dyebath and fiber used influences the exhaustion.

The term "liquor-to-fiber ratio" or just "liquor ratio" is used to express the relative amounts of dyebath and fiber. The liquor ratio is the mass of dyebath used per unit mass of material being dyed. If one (1) kilogram of dyebath is used per one-tenth (0.1) kilogram of material being dyed, the liquor ratio is 10 to 1 (10–1). Liquor ratio varies over a wide range depending on the type of dyeing process and equipment used. Typical values range from about 50–1 for some batch processes to as low as 0.3–1 for some continuous processes. Low liquor ratio, smaller amount of bath relative to the amount of fiber being dyed, gives higher dyebath exhaustion other factors being equal. Therefore, utilization of dye is usually better under lower liquor ratio dyeing conditions. Many factors determine the optimum liquor ratio for a given dyeing process.

Interaction of Components in a Dyeing System

Fiber, water, dye, and dyeing assistants (additives) usually comprise a dyeing system. Each of these four (or more) components can affect every other component in the system as is illustrated in Figure 4-2.

Figure 4-2. Interactions between components in a dyeing system

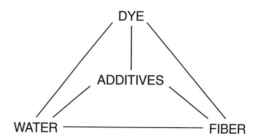

The influence of the interactions of some of the components in a dyeing system have been studied in detail and are well understood. Sometimes interactions between components are not so well understood, and the influence of some substance in the dyebath may have an unpredictable effect. Let us examine some of these interactions between dyebath components.

Dye/Water Interactions

The two general types of dyes with regard to their behavior in water are ionic dyes and nonionic dyes. Ionic dyes may be either anionic or cationic. In anionic dyes the part of the molecule primarily responsible for color has a negative charge, Dye^-Na^+. In cationic dyes, the colored part of the dye molecule is positively charged, Dye^+Cl^-. The situation is actually more complex than this because some dyes are ionic at one stage of the dyeing process and nonionic at another stage. These situations will be discussed later. Ionic dyes dissociate into positive and negative ions in water forming a solution. The solution formed by many dyes in water is colloidal as is illustrated in Figure 4-3.

Although the solution formed may be clear and transparent, the dye molecules may be aggregated in water. Degrees of aggregation of dyes can be measured, and aggregation numbers for several dyes have been published. Generally, higher dyebath temperature decreases the aggregation number of a dye. Since smaller aggregates should diffuse into fibers more easily, this lower degree of aggregation is one of the reasons cited for the greater dyeing rate observed at higher dyeing temperature.

Addition of salts such as sodium chloride is believed to increase the degree of aggregation of ionic dyes in water. This is sometimes

Figure 4-3. Schematic showing colloidal behavior of dyes in water

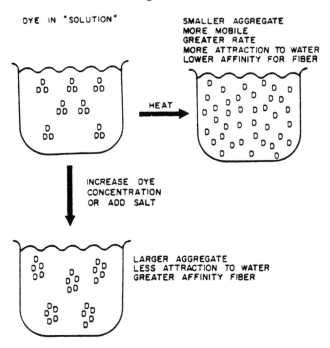

called the "common ion effect." Since larger aggregates will be less attracted to water, the dye may transfer to the fiber more easily. This "salting out" effect may be one of the reasons why addition of salt causes increased exhaustion of dye in some dyeing systems.

Nonionic dyes do not interact strongly with water and are usually used as dispersions in water. Although nonionic dyes are usually thought of as being insoluble in water, they often are very slightly soluble in water. This solubility, although small, may be vital to adsorption and diffusion of dye in the fiber. Nonionic dyes are manufactured to have very small particle size and are formulated with surfactants so that they are easily dispersible in water.

Fiber/Water Interactions

Water is usually the dyeing medium. Interaction between water and the fiber has a major role in application of many types of dyes. Hydrophilic fibers like cotton, rayon, and wool attract water. Water molecules diffuse into the amorphous regions of the fiber and break internal hydrogen bonds. Swelling of the fiber results. Swelling of the fiber by water may also be important in dyeing of some of the more hydrophilic synthetic fibers such as nylon. Swelling increases the size of openings and increases the mobility of the polymer molecules in the amorphous regions of the fiber making possible the diffusion of dye into the fibers. Swelling of the fiber in water is enhanced by higher temperature. The effect of temperature on swelling of fibers in water is probably a major reason why increasing dyeing temperature increases dyeing rate.

Hydrophobic fibers like polyester and some polyamides do not swell much in water. Water plays a less active role in the dyeing of these fibers. Water may still be needed as the medium to dissolve the dye so that the particles or molecules of dye are small enough to diffuse into the fibrous polymer. Water may also serve as the heat transfer medium in dyeing of polyester which is often dyed at temperatures of about 130°C. In continuous dyeing of polyester, water is simply the medium through which dye is deposited on the surface of the fibers and serves no active role in transporting dye into the fibers.

Dye/Fiber Interactions

Dyes and the fibers to which they are applied usually have an inherent attraction for one another. This natural attraction promotes transfer of dye from the dyebath to the fiber and is sometimes important in holding the dye in the fiber. Dyes are attracted to fibers because of chemical interactions between the dye molecule and the fiber. The bonding between the dye and fibers may result from weak secondary interactions such as hydrogen bonding or van der Waals forces.

<pre>
                          Fiber
                            |
 polar   A^δ- - - - - - - -D^δ+   polar
 group | | group
                          B^δ+ - - - - - - C^δ-
                            |
                          Dye
</pre>

Secondary Forces

Since each individual secondary bond is relatively weak, multiple interactions between a single dye molecule and the fiber are needed for good bonding to occur. Therefore, dyes which bond to fibers mostly by secondary forces are usually relatively large, high molecular weight structures which can have a large area of interaction with a fiber molecule. Diffusion of large molecules in the fiber is also hindered giving them the potential for better fastness properties than smaller molecules, other factors being equal. Fibers which bond dyes mainly by secondary forces do not have any specifically identifiable "dyesites". As a result, there is usually no specific limit to the amount of dye the fibers can absorb. That is, the fiber does not become "saturated" with dye.

Ionic bonding is important in dyeing of fibers which have strong acidic or basic character. An ionic bond can form between a fiber having acidic groups and a dye having basic groups or a fiber having basic groups and a dye having acidic groups. The bond formed is a salt linkage which is stronger than secondary interactions such as hydrogen bonds and van der Waals forces discussed above. Fibers which bond dyes by forming salt linkages may absorb only a limited amount of dye because the dye is attracted to a specific chemical group in the fiber. When these groups, "dyesites", are occupied by a dye molecule, they are no long available to other dye molecules. Fibers of this type are mainly synthetic, and the fiber manufacturer builds the required number of dyesites into the fiber during the fiber manufacturing process.

$$DYE-SO_3H + H_2N-FIBER \longrightarrow DYE-SO_3^- \quad H_3^+N-FIBER$$

acidic group   basic group   salt linkage (ionic bond)

Although individual dyes vary greatly, dyes which form salt linkages with the fiber usually have good washfastness characteristics. Since the strength of bonding between the dye and the fiber depends mainly on the strength of one or two ionic bonds between the dye and the fiber, dyes which bond by this mechanism can be smaller than dyes depending on secondary bonding. Since smaller molecules usually have narrower light absorption bands, they are often brighter in color than very large, high molecular weight dyes.

A third type of interaction between dyes and fibers is covalent bonding. Dyes which form covalent bonds with fibers depend on secondary forces for their initial attraction to the fiber. After the dye is adsorbed on or in the fibers, a chemical reaction is induced to cause covalent bond formation between the dye and the fiber. Since the covalent bond is very strong and resistant to cleavage, dyes which form covalent bonds with fibers have excellent washfastness. As is true with dyes forming ionic bonds with the fiber, dyes forming covalent bonds with the fiber can be relatively small, brightly colored structures.

$$DYE-X \ + \ HO-FIBER \ \longrightarrow \ DYE-O-FIBER \ + \ HX$$

Group capable   active   covalent
of displacing   hydrogen   bond
active hydrogen

Some types of dyes are water soluble during the application stage but are converted to pigments in the final stages of dyeing. These colorants in their pigment form do not have inherent affinity for the fiber and are simply mechanically trapped in the fiber. Although the fixation mechanism of these types of dyes on textiles is sometimes described as physical entrapment of dye inside the fiber, the extreme insolubility of the dye in water contributes to the fastness of the color. It is possible for these dyes to have good wash fastness even when the dye is mainly on or near the surface of the fiber. Crockfastness (fastness to rubbing) of pigments deposited on the fiber surface can be poor even though washfastness is good.

Variables in Dyeing

Because of the complex interactions of the components in a dyeing system, many variables must be controlled in order to produce high quality dyeings. Variables in dyeing may be of several types including substrate variations, variations in chemicals (including water), variations in preparation of the substrate for dyeing, and procedural variations.

Substrate variations

Several types of substrate variations may cause variations in dyeability of textiles. Cotton maturity is an excellent example of a variation in raw material that can have a major effect on dyeability. The secondary wall in the immature cotton fiber is not completely developed. Since dyes adsorb on the cellulose molecules in the fiber, immature fibers do not dye the same as mature fibers. Different dyes are adsorbed to different degrees on very immature cotton fibers. Defects due to the presence of immature cotton fibers range from the presence of clumps of white, undyed fibers to off shade materials resulting from differential uptake of the different dyes in the dye formulation. More subtle fiber differences than gross differences in cotton maturity can also affect dyeability of the fiber. Minor differences in dyeability of cotton fiber should not be a problem where appropriate blending of fiber is done in the yarn manufacturing processes.

Although the synthetic fiber manufacturer has more control over the manufacturing process than does the manufacturer of natural fibers, synthetic fibers are also subject to variations which affect dyeability. For example, the manufacturer of synthetic fibers such as nylon and acrylics builds-in a specific number of dyesites during polymer synthesis. A small variation in the number of dyesites in these fibers can affect the dyeability of the fibers with certain types of dyes. Variation in dyeability resulting from differences in number of dyesites in the fiber come from differences in affinity of the fiber for the dye. Such differences cannot be corrected by dyeing for longer times or at higher temperatures. By judicious dye selection, the dyer can sometimes compensate for these fiber differences that are related to affinity for dyes.

Variation in yarn and fabric structure can also cause dye defects. For example, wetting and dye uptake in highly twisted yarns will usually be slower than that in soft twist yarns. In continuous dyeings or nonequilibrium batch dyeings, these differences can cause streaks or other dye defects. Incorrect blend level in a blended yarn can cause dyeing differences. Contamination by either fibrous or nonfibrous substances can also cause dyeing defects.

Variations in chemicals

Variations in water or auxiliary chemicals used in the dyeing process can cause dyeing defects. The dye itself is probably the best example of a possible chemical variation that can affect dyeing. Dyes can vary in strength, a measure of the color depth per unit of dye used, or in hue.

Residual chlorine in the water supply has been known to react with and decolorize some of the dye in the dyebath. Any variation in a chemical used in the dyeing process is a potential source for dyeing defects.

Variations in preparation

Consistent preparation of the substrate for dyeing is critical to consistent dye application. Variations in preparation often cannot be corrected in dyeing and cause defects or off-quality product. Thermoplastic synthetic fibers such as nylon and polyester are subject to variation in dyeability resulting from differences in the "heat history" or "energy history" of the fibers. Just a few degrees of difference in temperature of heat setting or small changes in tension on fibers, yarns, or fabric in manufacturing can cause dyeing rate differences. Differences in dyeability due to differences in rate of dye uptake can sometimes be overcome by increasing dyeing time or by adding auxiliary chemicals to the dyebath.

Inconsistent desizing, incomplete desizing, size material redeposition, and inconsistent scouring are common causes of dye defects. The size may cause a difference in the wettability of the textile material which affects dye uptake. The residual size material may also have strong attraction for the dye causing increased dye uptake where the size is present. Residual oils will repel water and resist dye uptake. Oil may appear as dark spots because of differences in light reflectance from the spots.

Bleaching variations can also cause dye defects. Since the base color of a fabric contributes to the color of the dyed fabric, variations in whiteness achieved in bleaching can affect the color of the dyed material. Furthermore, oxidation of cellulose, which sometimes occurs if the material is bleached too severely, can increase the electronegativity of the fiber and cause decrease in affinity for anionic dyes.

$$\text{Cell}-\text{CH}_2\text{-OH} \quad \xrightarrow{\text{Oxidation}} \quad \text{Cell}-\overset{\displaystyle \overset{\text{O}}{\|}}{\text{C}}-\text{OH}$$

cellulose   oxidized cellulose
                                 (higher electronegativity)

Mercerization has a dramatic effect on dyeability of cellulose and usually improves markedly the dyeability of immature fibers. Since mercerization affects the dyeability of cotton fibers, mercerization must be done uniformly in order for the fabric to be dyed uniformly.

Even the way the material is batched for dyeing may affect dyeability. For example, cones or tubes for package dyeing must be uniformly wound so that dye liquid can be forced uniformly through the package. If winding tension on dye packages varies a lot, the dye liquid will take the path of least resistance through the package, and uneven dyeing will occur.

Procedural variations

Procedural variations must be closely controlled in dyeing. Obviously, dye and chemical computations and weighings must be correct. Reproduction of dyeing cycle time, dyeing temperature, rate of temperature rise, and agitation of the substrate and dyebath must all be controlled for dyeing to be successful.

Adsorption of Dye from the Dyebath

Several distinct identifiable events take place in the dyeing of a textile material. The events are as follows:

Diffusion in solution—Dye must move or diffuse through the dyebath in order to establish contact with the textile material being dyed.

Adsorption on fiber surface—Dye molecules are attracted to the fiber and are initially deposited on the fiber surface.

Diffusion in the fiber—Dye deposited on the surface creates a concentration gradient which is the driving force for movement of dye from the surface toward the interior of the fiber. During diffusion, dye molecules migrate from place to place on the fiber. This migration tends to have a levelling effect on the dye application. Dyes which migrate readily are easy to apply uniformly. However, dyes which migrate and level easily also tend to have poorer washfastness than dyes which do not migrate and level well.

Dissolution of dye in the dyebath—Dyes which are only sparingly soluble in water may have to dissolve from a dispersion of highly aggregated particles in order to be small enough to diffuse into the fiber.

Figure 4-4. Hypothetical dyeing profile

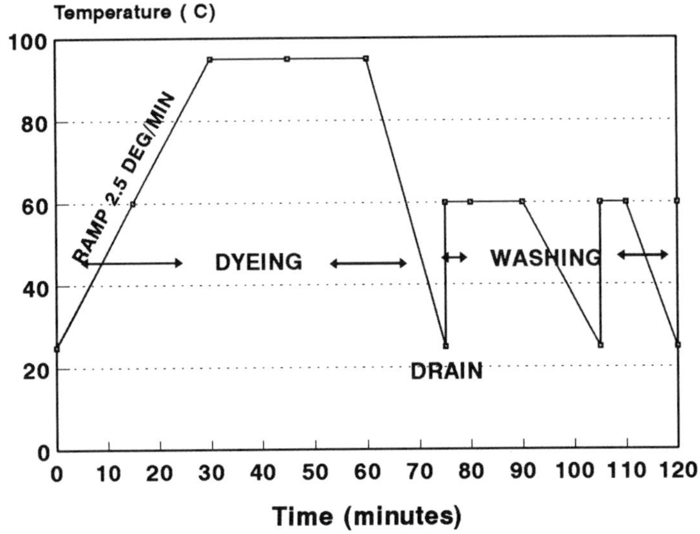

A hypothetical dye cycle is shown schematically in Figure 4-4. Actual dye cycles vary greatly depending on the type of dye and fiber as well as the type of equipment used. In a typical dyeing procedure, the dyebath and the material to be dyed are placed in contact. The system is then gradually raised to some predetermined temperature over a predetermined period of time.

The system is held at this elevated temperature for some period of time after which the dyebath is drained or washed away. The system may be cooled some before the dyebath is drained. Required aftertreatments are then done to the dyed material.

If dyeings with a given dye were done under different isothermal conditions, a series of curves similar to those in Figure 4-5 would be obtained. These curves are sometimes called rate of dyeing isotherms.

Rate of dyeing isotherms show some inherent characteristics of dyeing systems. First, an increase in dyeing temperature causes an increase in the initial rate at which dye is taken up by the fiber. The slope of the curve varies depending on the temperature, type of fiber, type of dye, amount of agitation of the dyebath, amount and type of dyeing auxiliaries used, and other factors. As the amount of dye on the fiber increases, the slope of the rate of dyeing isotherm

Figure 4-5. Rate of dyeing isotherms

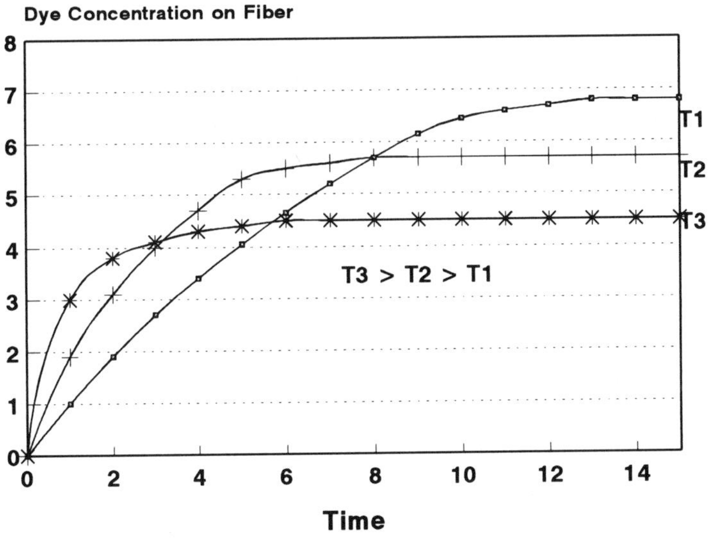

Dye Concentration on Fiber

decreases, i.e. less dye is adsorbed per unit of time as the amount of dye on the fiber becomes greater. This occurs because the fiber surfaces or dyesites become occupied, and dye must leave the surface and diffuse toward the interior of the fiber before additional dye molecules can be adsorbed from the dyebath.

The optimum rate of dyeing is that which yields the greatest, uniform deposition of dye on the fiber in the shortest period of time. A slow dyeing rate means that the dyeing time must be long. A greater dyeing rate reduces the time required to complete the dyeing. However, if the dyeing rate is too fast, the dye may be adsorbed nonuniformly. Dyeing time and dyeing uniformity requirements must be balanced in a commercial dye process.

After some period of time, the slope of the isotherm becomes flat indicating that the system has reached equilibrium. The time required to reach equilibrium is always shorter at higher dyeing temperature. Notice that, at higher temperatures, the fiber contains more dye in the early stages but less dye in the latter stages of dyeing. Thus, higher temperature increases the dyeing rate but decreases the ultimate exhaustion if the dyeing time is long enough. Dye adsorbs to a greater degree at a lower temperature because the dyeing is exothermic.

Dye + Fiber   ⇌   Dyed Fiber + heat

At higher dyeing temperature more heat is added to the system driving the equilibrium position to the left. Since the amount of fiber in the system is constant, this means that some dye must leave the fiber and enter the dyebath if the system temperature is raised.

It is possible to take advantage of the effects of temperature on both dyeing rate and exhaustion by using high temperature in early stages to achieve rapid adsorption followed by cooling in the later stages of dyeing to achieve higher dye exhaustion.

References

1. Peters, R.H., Textile Chemistry, Volume 3, Elsevier Scientific Publishing Company, New York, NY, 1975.
2. Trotman, E.R., Dyeing and Chemical Technology of Textile Fibres, 6th Edition, John Wiley and Sons, New York, NY, 1984.
3. Vickerstaff, Thomas, The Physical Chemistry of Dyeing, Oliver and Boyd, London, England, 1954.

Chapter 5

Dyes

Colorants for textile materials may be classified as either dyes or pigments. The terms dye and pigment, while almost interchangeable in common use, have distinctly different meanings in coloration of textiles. A dye is a substance which at least during some stage of its application has inherent affinity for the textile material. Dyes are soluble in the dyeing medium during or at least in some stage of the dyeing process. A pigment is simply a substance used to impart color and which does not have inherent affinity for the textile material. Both dyes and pigments can be used to color textile materials. Dyes can diffuse into fibers and interact with the polymer structure of the fiber. Pigments are simply bonded to the surface of the fiber, fabric, or yarn by other chemical agents. Pigments can be either organic or inorganic substances. All textile dyes are organic chemicals.

Dyes may be classified according to chemical structure or according to their method of application. Classification of dyes according to chemical structure is most useful to the dye chemist who may be interested dye synthesis and the relationship between chemical structure and properties of the dye. Classification according to method of application is most useful to the technologist concerned with coloration of textile products. Understanding of both of these methods of classification is useful to the textile engineer or textile chemist.

Dye Classes by Application Method

Eight major dye classes according to method of application are commonly used in textiles. The five (5) classes used mainly on cellulose fibers are direct dyes, sulfur dyes, azoic dyes, reactive dyes, and vat dyes. The three (3) classes used mainly for protein and synthetic fibers are acid dyes, basic dyes, and disperse dyes. All of these dyes are synthetic organic compounds that have been discovered since the synthesis of the first synthetic dye by W.H. Perkin in 1856. Several important synthetic dyes produced today have natural counterparts, but synthetic manufacture of the products is more economical than collecting the naturally occurring dyes. Following is a brief introduction to these eight (8) major classes of dyes. Each of these classes is discussed in more detail later in this chapter.

Direct dyes are so named because they have natural affinity for cellulose and can be applied without using any auxiliary chemicals. In practice, the dyeing rate and color yield can be greatly improved by adding inorganic salts such as sodium chloride or sodium sulfate to the dyebath. The direct dyes are widely used on cotton and rayon. The greatest advantage of direct dyes is simplicity of application. The greatest limitation of direct dyes is that their fastness to washing is not good enough for some purposes. Washfastness of direct dyes is improved by resin treatment of dyed fabrics or by various aftertreatments.

Sulfur dyes are complex organic compounds synthesized by heating simple amines or phenolic compounds in the presence of sulfur. Sulfur dyes exist as a pigment form which does not have affinity for cellulose. They are converted to a water soluble form having affinity for cellulose by treatment with a reducing agent under alkaline conditions. After application to the fiber, sulfur dyes must be oxidized back to their pigment form. The greatest advantage of sulfur dyes is relatively low cost. The biggest limitation of sulfur dyes is that they are not bright enough in color for many uses.

Azoic dyes are pigments that are synthesized inside the fiber by coupling of two components neither of which is a dye itself. The two components are an aromatic diazonium salt and an aromatic hydroxy compound, often a naphthol. Because of the use of naphthol as a component in the reaction, this class is sometimes called the "naphthol dyes." Although the colored material produced in azoic dyeing is a pigment, the azoics are classified as dyes because the naphthol component has affinity for cellulose and is applied like a dye before the diazo component is added. The greatest advantage of azoic dyes is that they provide an economical way to obtain certain shades, especially red. The greatest limitation of azoic dyes is that they sometimes possess poor fastness to crocking.

Reactive dyes are relatively new, having been developed in the 1950s. They are sometimes called "fiber reactive dyes." As the name implies the reactive dyes chemically react with the fiber forming covalent bonds. Since the covalent bonds between the dye and the fiber are strong, reactive dyes have excellent washfastness. Outstanding washfastness is the greatest, but by no means the only, advantage of reactive dyes. Limitations of reactive dyes include higher cost than some other classes.

Vat dyes are like sulfur dyes in that they are pigments which must be reduced and oxidized during application. However, the similarity between sulfur and vat dyes ends there. Vat dyes have outstanding washfastness and lightfastness as a class. An exception to this rule is the vat dye indigo which has very poor washfastness. The biggest disadvantage of vat dyes is their relatively high cost.

Acid dyes are so called because they contain acidic groups in their structure. The acidic groups react with basic groups in protein and polyamide fibers forming organic salts. Individual acid dyes vary greatly in properties and are sub grouped according to properties and compatibility.

Basic dyes are sometimes called cationic dyes because the chromophore in basic dye molecules contains a positive charge. These basic or cationic groups react with acidic groups in acrylic, cationic dyeable polyester, cationic dyeable nylon, or occasionally protein fibers. The salt linkages formed are similar to those formed between acid dyes and fibers containing basic groups. A limitation of basic dyes is that their fastness to light is sometimes not satisfactory, especially on protein fibers.

Disperse dyes are used mostly for polyester, nylon, and cellulose acetate although they will dye some other fibers. The name disperse dye comes from the fact that these dyes are almost insoluble in water and have to be dispersed in water to make the dyebath. Disperse dyes were developed when cellulose acetate was first marketed. Disperse dyes are the only acceptable dye class for acetate and unmodified polyester fibers.

The application and properties of each of these classes of dyes will be covered in more detail in later sections.

Dye Classes According to Chemical Structure

Gregory (5) classifies dyes according to chemical structure into the thirteen groups shown in Table 5-1.

Azo dyes

Azo structures account for over half of all commercial dyes. The azo group is a powerful chromogen so the azo dyes typically have

Table 5-1. Dyes by structural classes

Structural Class	Description	Application Classes
Azo dyes	Contain one or more azo, –N=N–, group	direct, azoic, reactive, acid, basic, disperse
Anthraquinone dyes	9,10–anthraquinone substituted at one or more of the four alpha positions (1,4,5, and 8)	vat, reactive, disperse, acid
Benzodifuranone dyes	Contain benzodifuranone (BDF) chromogen	disperse, (maybe others)
Polycyclic aromatic carbonyl dyes	Contain one or more carbonyl groups linked by a quinonoid system	vat
Indigoid dyes	Contain indigoid chromogen	vat (only indigo and tetrabromo indigo are of commercial importance)
Polymethine and related dyes	Contain conjugated system of double bonds not in aromatic rings	basic
Styryl dyes	Contain styryl, C=C, group	disperse
Di- and tri-aryl carbonium dyes	Contain di- or tri-aryl substituted carbon atom	basic, related structures found in direct and reactive classes
Phthalocyanine dyes	Contain metal complex phthalocyanine chromogen	direct, reactive, acid
Quinophthalone dyes	Contain quinophthalone chromogen	disperse
Sulfur dyes	Contain sulfur atoms bridging aromatic ring structures	sulfur
Nitro and nitroso dyes	Contain nitro group on aromatic ring	acid, disperse
miscellaneous dyes	stilbene, formazan structures	direct, reactive

*Table derived from Waring, 1990.

high tinctorial strength. The azo dye structure contains one, two, three, four, or occasionally more azo groups. The monazo types are most important followed by the disazo types. The azo groups are attached to at least one but most commonly two aromatic groups in trans configuration about the azo group.

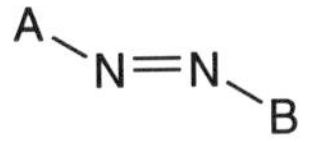

General structure of azo dyes
(A and/or B aromatic)

The groups A and B may be either identical or different and typically contain substituent groups which affect the color and properties of the dye. The nitrogen atoms are sp^2 hybridized, and the bond angles are approximately 120°. The general shape of the molecule is linear. Azo dyes are purely synthetic and have no natural counterparts. The number of azo dye structures theoretically possible to synthesize is enormous.

Anthraquinone dyes

Anthraquinone dyes are second only to azo dyes in importance. They are made by step wise addition of electron donating groups such as amino or hydroxyl substituents to 9,10-anthraquinone, which itself is essentially colorless. While anthraquinone dyes are brighter in color than azo dyes, they are more expensive and weaker in tinctorial strength.

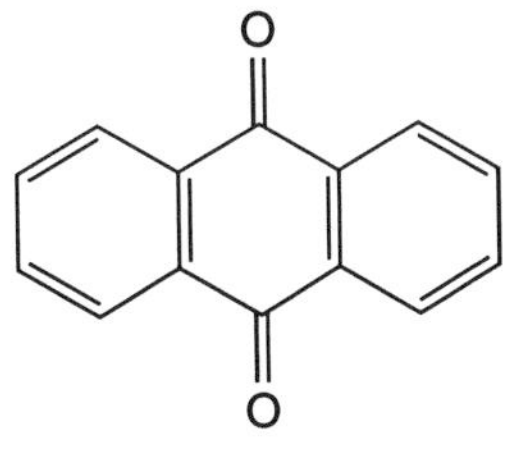

9, 10-anthraquinone

Although positions 1–8 are all available for possible substitution, the most common substitution patterns are 1,4–, 1,2,4–, and 1,4,5,8–. Since only eight positions are available for substitution, the number of variations possible for anthraquinone dyes is much more limited than is the case with azo structures. Various colors can be produced in anthraquinone dyes with different substituents and substitution patterns.

Benzodifuranone dyes

Benzodifuranone (BDF) dyes are competitive with anthraquinone dyes.

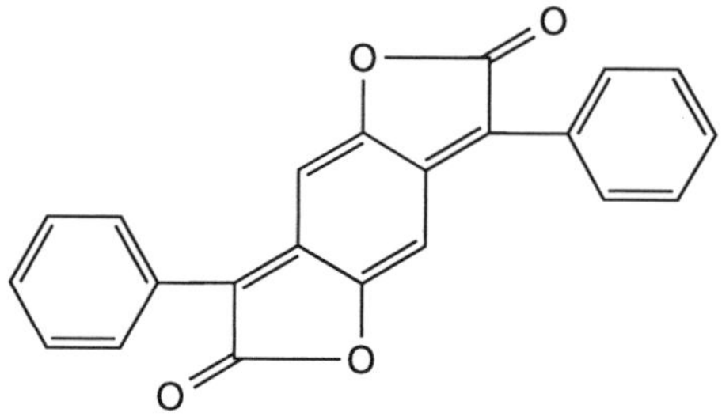

benzodifuranone

BDF's can be made in all hues from yellow to red to blue, and they have much greater tinctorial strength than anthraquinone dyes.

Polycyclic aromatic carbonyl dyes

Polycyclic aromatic carbonyl dyes have been used for many years as vat dyes. They have outstanding fastness to washing and light on cellulose. Many of them are made up of anthraquinone units bridged together by nitrogen or other atoms.

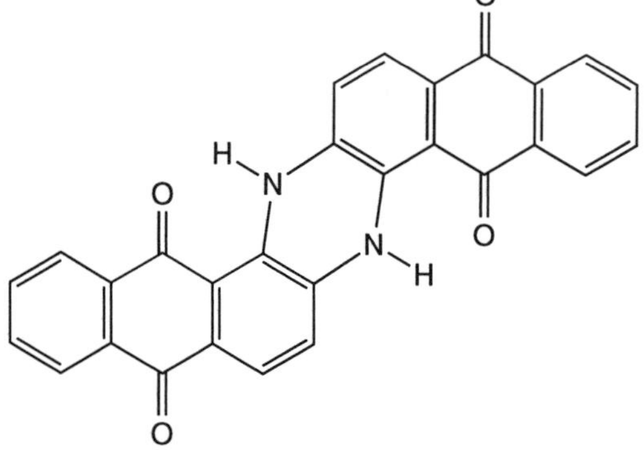

indanthrene blue

Although almost all hues can be made in this class, only blues, browns, greens, and blacks are common.

Indigoid dyes

Indigoid dyes have been used for thousands of years. Indigo is the parent dye of this class.

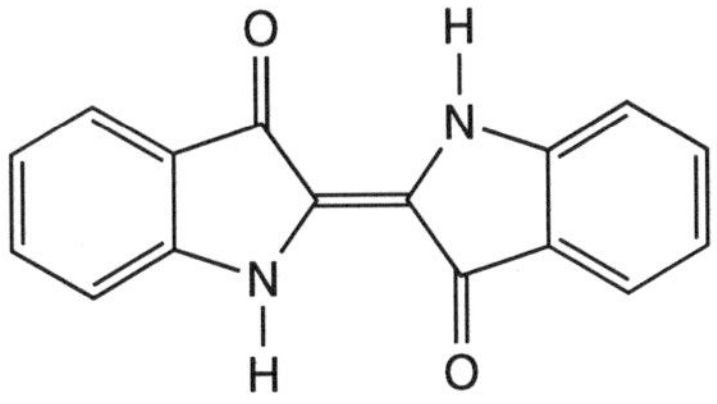

indigo

The ancient dye, Tyrian Purple, is dibromoindigo. The only indigoid structure other than indigo itself that is of commercial importance today is tetrabromo indigo, which produces a redder shade on cellulose than indigo. Although indigo is a vat dye, it does not possess the outstanding fastness properties typical of vat dyes. In fact, the appeal of indigo as a dye is because of the novel way in which garments dyed with it fade with use. Indigo fades readily when washed, but garments dyed with indigo retain the beautiful blue hue characteristic of indigo throughout the life of the garment.

Polymethine dyes

The Colour Index defines polymethine dyes as those containing a conjugated chain of carbon atoms terminated by an ammonium group and containing a nitrogen, sulfur, or oxygen atom, or equivalent unsaturated group. Polymethine dyes containing a quaternary nitrogen atom are important basic dyes for acrylic fibers.

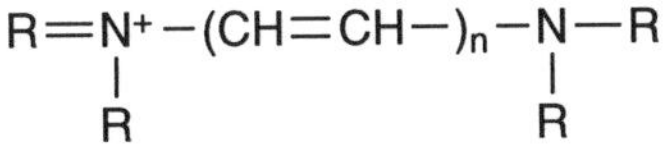

a polymethine dye

Styryl dyes

Styryl dyes contain various substituents on the ethylene group. Often a substituted aromatic group is present. Exceptionally bright red and blue dyes can be made by having cyano groups as the alkene substituents.

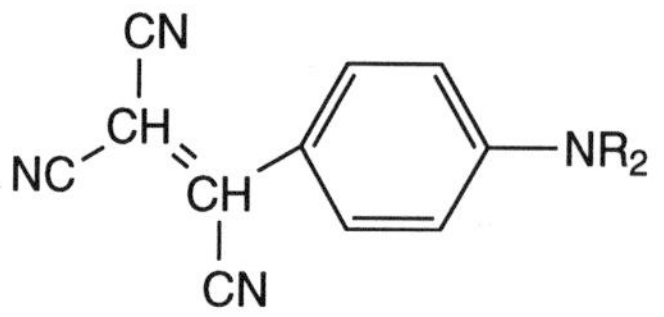

NR_2

$R = Alkyl\ group$

Aryl carbonium dyes

Arylcarbonium dyes are important as basic dyes. They are very bright in color but usually not very fast to light. As the name of the class implies, the positive charge on the dye ion can occupy the carbon atom in one of the possible resonance structures.

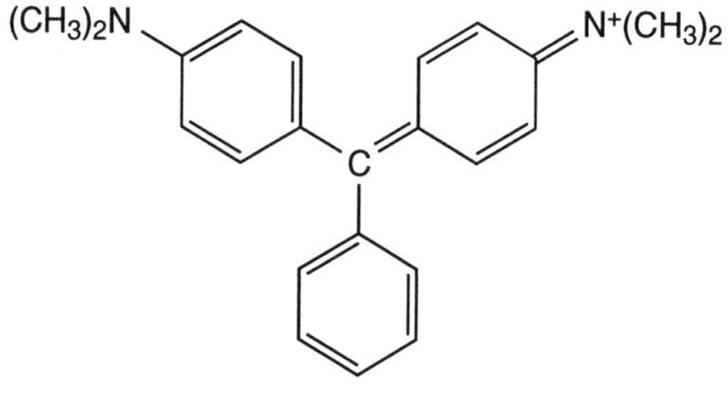

an aryl carbonium dye

Phthalocyanine dyes

Phthalocyanine was discovered in 1928. It is the metal complex of the following structure. Various metal complexes are possible, but copper is the most common metal used. Since substituent groups do not affect the color much, the phthalocyanine hues are all blue or green. The phthalocyanine structure is used in direct dyes. Phthalocyanine pigment is widely used in inks and paints.

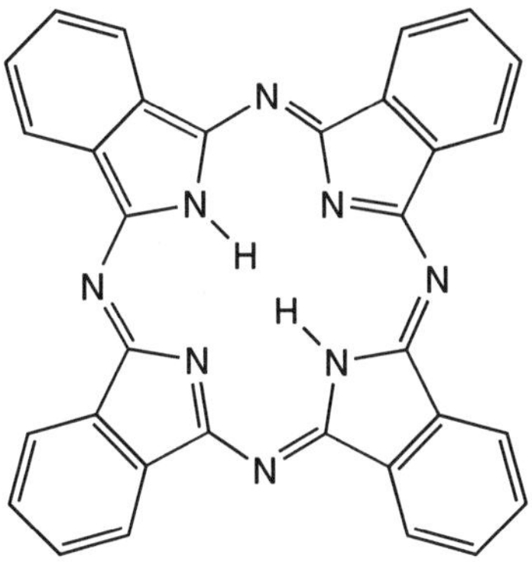

Phthalocyanine

Quinophthalone dyes

Quinophthalone structures are found in disperse dyes as well as pigments for plastics.

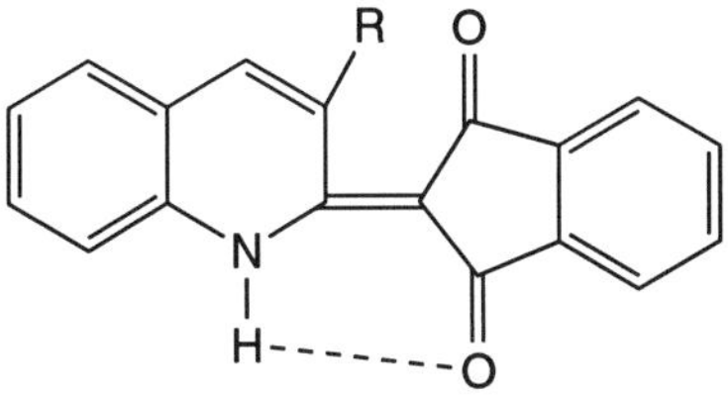

a quinophthalone dye

These dyes owe their intense color to the formation of the internal hydrogen bond shown in the structure above.

Sulfur dyes

The term sulfur dye is used to refer to both a structural class and to an application class. In both of these cases the reference is to the same dyes. The exact structure of the chromogen in sulfur dyes is difficult to determine. Sulfur dyes are made by heating aromatic amines, phenols, or nitro compounds in the presence of sulfur. Complex ring structures containing carbon, nitrogen, oxygen, and sulfur are formed.

$$Ar-S_x-Ar \qquad Ar = aromatic\ ring$$

general structure of sulfur dyes

The ring structures are bridged by groups of sulfur atoms. The oxidation state of the sulfur atoms in the bridges affects the brightness of the color in the sulfur dye. Sulfur dyes are economical to use and are important dyes for cellulose.

Nitro and nitroso dyes

Nitro and nitroso dyes are of minor commercial importance. Aromatic nitro structures are found in a few yellow disperse dyes.

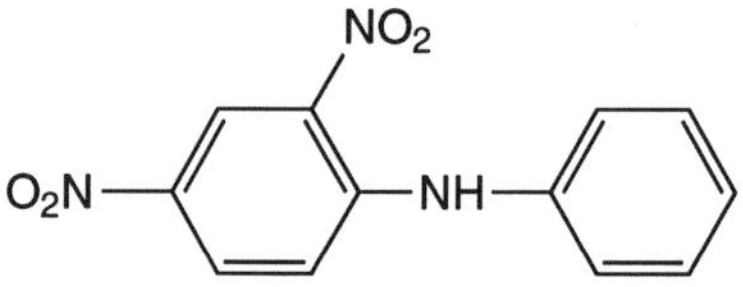

Colour Index Disperse Yellow 14

Picric acid is the most interesting dye in this class. Picric acid is a yellow substance which will dye wool because the electron withdrawing nitro groups make the phenolic hydrogen atom very acidic. Picric acid is an unstable compound which is explosive when shocked or heated.

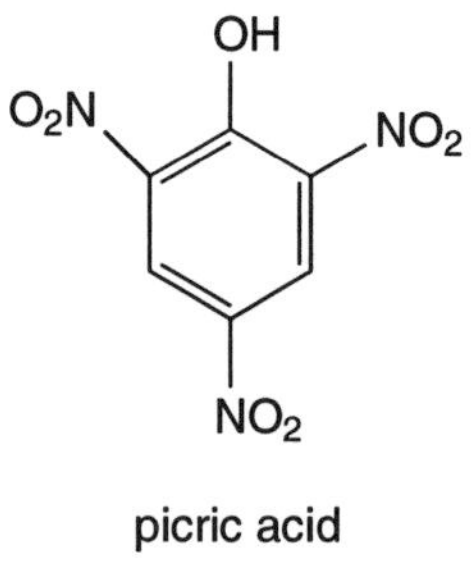

picric acid

Dye Classes According to Application

Direct dyes

Direct dyes have been used to dye cellulose for over 100 years. Because of the simplicity of application and great choice of products available, direct dyes are a popular dye class. Direct dyes range from moderate to poor in washfastness. Lightfastness varies from poor to excellent depending on the particular dye.

Structural Characteristics

Direct dyes depend on secondary forces such as hydrogen bonds and van der Waals forces to bond with cellulose fibers. Since secondary forces are relatively weak, the interaction between the dye and fiber is greater if the dye molecule is large. Therefore, direct dye molecules have relatively high molecular weights, typically about 400 to 1200.

The great majority of direct dyes are azo structures. A few direct dyes are monazo types, but disazo and trisazo structures are more common because the higher molecular weight structures have better washfastness.

C.I. Direct Blue 78 is a good example to show the important structural characteristics of direct dyes.

C.I. Direct Blue 78

The trans configuration of the azo groups gives the molecule a generally linear shape. Linearity in the structure is important so that the dye molecule can align and interact well with the cellulose chains in the fiber. The aromatic rings in the structure must also have the capability to rotate into a coplanar arrangement with one another.

Coplanarity of the aromatic rings is vital for two reasons. First, coplanarity of the rings makes the molecular shape generally flat allowing good interaction between the dye and fiber. Also, coplanarity of the rings is required for overlap of the pi orbitals and delocalization of electrons (resonance). Resonance is an important factor in light absorption and color of organic molecules.

Direct dyes must be soluble in water. The presence of sodium sulfonate groups makes the dye molecule polar enough to dissolve in water. Degree of exhaustion of dye from the dyebath to the fiber depends on the relative attraction of the dye molecule for these two phases. Therefore, direct dye molecules are sulfonated just enough to make them soluble in water but not so much that excessive attraction for water causes the dye to exhaust poorly. Many direct dyes have two sulfonate groups, some have four sulfonate groups, and a few have more. The solubility of direct dyes in water increases dramatically with an increase in temperature, and hot water is usually required to dissolve the dye in the dyebath. The sulfonate groups on direct dye molecules are salts formed by the reaction between a sulfonic acid group and a strong base.

$$DYE-SO_3H \ + \ NaOH \ \longrightarrow \ DYE-SO_3^-Na^+ \ + \ HOH$$

free acid form   sodium salt form of dye

Although the sulfonic acid group is strongly acidic, many direct dyes precipitate if the pH of the bath is lowered. On the other hand, raising the pH of the dyebath will increase the solubility of the dye and may decrease dye exhaustion.

Direct dyes also generally contain groups such as amino or hydroxyl which are capable of forming hydrogen bonds with hydroxyl groups in the cellulose fiber.

Dyeing Methods

Direct dyes may be applied by either batch or continuous methods. Details of the procedure vary according to the equipment used and the particular dyes selected. Exhaust dyeing procedures consist of the following steps:

1. Dye is dissolved in water and added to the dyebath containing the fabric which has been appropriately prepared for dyeing.

2. The temperature of the dyebath is gradually increased to near the boiling point of water and held at this temperature for some period of time. The temperature may be decreased in the latter stages of dyeing to enhance exhaustion. In a commercial dye cycle (not dyed to equilibrium) some dyes exhaust better near the maximum dyeing temperature while others exhaust better at lower temperature.

3. Common salt or Glauber's salt is added to enhance exhaustion of the dye. The timing of salt addition depends on the particular dyes selected. In some cases, salt can be added at the beginning of the dye cycle. Some dyes are very sensitive to salt in the dyebath, and require that the salt be added gradually after heating of the dyebath commences.

4. The fabric is rinsed to remove residual salt and dye that did not exhaust.

5. An aftertreatment to improve colorfastness of the dyed material may be done at the end of the dye cycle or during a subsequent finishing process.

This description of the dyeing process for direct dyes makes it obvious that not all direct dyes behave exactly the same way during application. Therefore, the dyer must be concerned about compatibility of the individual dyes used in a formulation and must use techniques that are acceptable for the particular dyes being used. Dye suppliers usually provide procedural recommendations and compatibility information about their products.

Continuous and semi-continuous dyeing methods include a padding step. The concentration of dye in a pad formulation must be much higher (as much as 50 times) than the concentration of dye in a batch process. Therefore, the solubility of the dyes in water must be very high for the dye to be applicable by continuous methods. Many direct dyes are not soluble enough to be applied by padding. However, selected direct dyes can be applied by padding followed by a fixation stage to allow the dye to diffuse into the fibers. Padding methods that can be used for direct dyes include pad-jig, pad-batch on hot roll, and pad-steam.

Effect of Salt

Electrolytes in the dyebath promote the exhaustion of direct dyes. Tetra sulfonated dyes are affected more by the presence of salt than

Figure 5-1. Donnan model for dye adsorption.

Interface

Dyebath

Fiber

DYE $\rightleftharpoons$ DYE

External
solution

Internal
solution

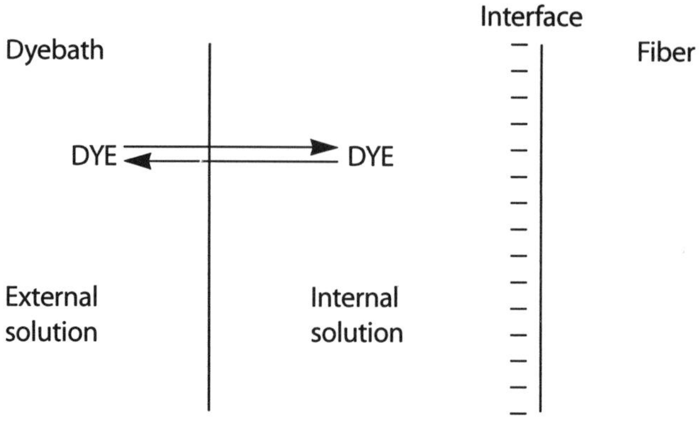

are dibasic dyes. This fact supports the theory that the effect of salt is electrical. Cellulose assumes a negative charge when in contact with water as indicated in Figure 5-1. Since the direct dye chromophore is also negatively charged, the dye and the fiber repel one another. In order for dyeing to occur, this electrical repulsion must be overcome by other forces of attraction between the dye and the fiber.

The Donnan model for dye adsorption on cellulose is based on the concept that the water layer very close to the fiber surface, called the internal solution, is influenced by the charge on the fiber. The bulk of the solution, called the external solution, is not affected by the charge on the fiber. According to the Donnan model, dyeing occurs by transfer of dye from the external to the internal solution. When salt (sodium chloride) is added to the dyebath, the ions distribute between the external solution and internal solution so that the surface charge of the fiber is neutralized or shielded. This neutralization of charge allows the dye molecules to approach the fiber closely enough for the forces of attraction between the dye and fiber to take effect.

Although electrical effects are generally believed to be at least partially responsible for the influence of salt in direct dyeing, the common ion effect discussed earlier may also be important. That is, the salt being very soluble in water may "salt out" or increase the degree of aggregation of dye molecules so that the dye is held less tenaciously by water. This less soluble dye could transfer more easily to the fiber surface from where it could diffuse into the fiber interior.

Aftertreatments for Direct Dyes

Fastness properties of direct dyes can be improved by aftertreating the dyed material. Aftertreatments sometimes affect the color of the dye so the aftertreatment being used must be considered at the color matching stage of the manufacturing process. Aftertreatments to enhance washfastness generally work on the principle of increasing the size of the dye molecule or decreasing its solubility in water. Either or both of these effects should restrict the ability of the dye to diffuse out of the fiber during washing. A treatment to enhance a particular property may in some cases have a detrimental effect on some other property of the product.

Treatment of the fabric with a resin finish usually improves fastness of direct dyes to washing. The improvement in fastness probably results mostly from the crosslinking effect of the resin on cellulose. Crosslinking decreases the tendency of cellulose to swell in water which restricts diffusion of the dye out of the fabric. It is also possible that chemicals in the resin finish react with the dye molecules increasing their size and restricting their ability to diffuse out of the fiber.

Direct dyes which contain a primary amino group attached to an aromatic ring can be diazotized and coupled to a naphthol component. The naphthol component is called the developer, and dyes which have this capability are called direct-developed dyes.

Diazotization

$$Ar-NH_2 \; + \; NaNO_2 \; + \; 2\,HCl \; \longrightarrow \; Ar-N\equiv N^+\,Cl^- \; + \; 2\,H_2O \; + \; NaCl$$

Coupling

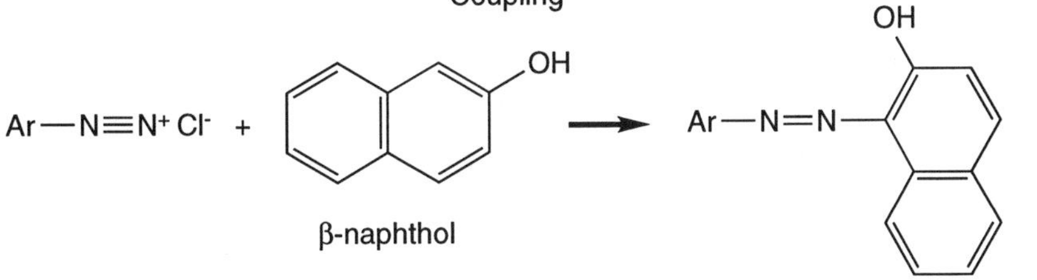

β-naphthol

Aftertreatment by diazotizing and developing actually adds an azo group to the dye structure so the color of the dye is usually affected. The final color of the dye also depends on the structure of the developer used. Primuline, a bright yellow direct dye, is a classic example of a direct-developed dye. It becomes various shades of orange and red when diazotized and developed with different developers. Primulene is reddish yellow when developed with phenol and bright red when developed with β-naphthol.

Aftertreatment of direct dyes with cationic fixation agents can improve their washfastness. Care must be exercised in doing this because lightfastness of the dye is sometimes decreased. Cationic agents which improve washfastness of direct dyes are actually surface active agents.

$$C_xH_y\ N^+(CH_3)_3\ +\ DYE-SO_3^-Na^+ \longrightarrow C_xH_y\ N^+(CH_3)_3\ SO_3^- - DYE$$

| cationic fixing agent | anionic dye | organic salt |

C_xH_y = long hydrocarbon chain

The cationic agent is believed to combine with the sulfonic acid groups in the dye to produce a large organic salt which is insoluble in water and therefore more difficult to wash from the fabric. The effect of cationic agents on direct dyes can be demonstrated by adding the cationic agent to a solution of the dye in water. Generally the dye will precipitate. Some dyes will even transfer from water to a water-immiscible organic solvent when treated with a cationic surfactant. This transfer test is sometimes used to detect or identify a substance as a cationic surfactant.

Direct dyes which have atoms containing unshared electron pairs at certain positions in the dye molecule will form complexes with metal ions such as copper and chromium. The treatment with metal salts improves washfastness and lightfastness. Improvement in lightfastness is generally associated with copper while improvement in washfastness is usually associated with chromium. The electron donating groups must be in such position that the metal ion can be a part of a five or six member ring when the complex forms. Examples of dyes having this capability are those having hydroxyl, methoxyl, or carboxyl groups o– and o'- to an azo linkage as shown below. Dyes containing two electron donating groups ortho to one another are also aftertreatable with metal salts.

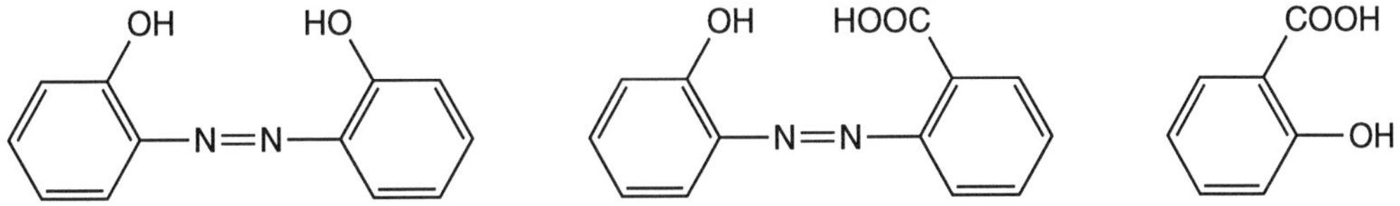

Heavy metals such as copper and chromium are water pollutants. They are also toxic to microorganisms in biological wastewater treatment systems. Therefore, use of these heavy metals is undesirable in most cases.

Sulfur dyes

Sulfur dyes are widely used on cotton mainly because they are economical to use. They have good to excellent washfastness and good lightfastness in dark shades. Lightfastness of pale shades is poor. Sulfur dyes are usually dull in shade since the molecular structures are complex. As a class, the sulfur dyes are not resistant to chlorine-containing bleaches.

Structural Characteristics

Although the exact structure of sulfur dye molecules cannot usually be determined, the features responsible for their properties and behavior in application are known. Ring systems of conjugated double bonds are bridged by chains of sulfur atoms. The ring systems in the following reactions are denoted Ar while the sulfur bridges are shown as disulfide groups.

$$Ar-S-S-Ar \underset{}{\overset{reduction}{\rightleftharpoons}} 2\,Ar-SH$$

a disulfide   a thiol

$$Ar-SH + OH^- \rightleftharpoons Ar-S^- + HOH$$

salt of thiol

Sulfur dyes in the oxidized (disulfide) form are pigments which have no affinity for cellulose. The pigment form of sulfur dyes may be very high in molecular weight since the sulfur bridges can link many ring systems together. The disulfide linkages may be reduced by alkali polysulfides to thiol groups. The acidic thiol groups react with alkali in the reduction medium forming salts. The reduced form of the dye is soluble in water and is sometimes referred to as the "leuco" form. The reduced form is much lower in molecular weight than the pigment form because reduction of the disulfide linkages severs the molecule into smaller pieces.

Dyeing Methods

Sulfur dyes are usually supplied as solutions of the reduced form in water. The dyebath can be made by diluting the sulfur dye product to the concentration required for dyeing. The presence of dissolved oxygen or other oxidants in the water may require that more reducing agent be added to keep the dye reduced when it is diluted. The reduced form of a sulfur dye has affinity for cellulose and adsorbs on cellulose much like a direct dye does. Salt serves as an exhausting agent as it does with direct dyes.

After the reduced sulfur dye is adsorbed by the cellulosic fiber, it must be oxidized to the pigment form to make it insoluble in water and to produce the desired color. Oxidation is a critical step in sulfur dye oxidation. The desired reaction in oxidation of sulfur dyes is conversion of the thiol groups to disulfide groups.

$$Ar-S^- \underset{}{\overset{oxidation}{\rightleftarrows}} Ar-S-S-Ar$$

The residual alkali and reducing agent should be rinsed from the dyed material before oxidation to conserve oxidizing chemicals. The oxidation will occur in air, but chemical oxidizing agents such as hydrogen peroxide are usually used to lower the time required for oxidation. Some sulfur dyes, mainly the red-brown shades, are not oxidized satisfactorily by hydrogen peroxide. Dichromate salts are the preferred oxidizing agents for sulfur dyes but are not used much because of the pollution and water treatment problems associated with use of heavy metals.

Since sulfur is subject to oxidation to higher oxidation states, the oxidation step must be controlled. Over-oxidation of sulfur dyes can produce sulfones and sulfoxides which are more polar than disulfides.

Higher oxidation states of sulfur dyes

$$Ar—\overset{\overset{O}{\|}}{S}—S—Ar \qquad Ar—\overset{\overset{O}{\|}}{\underset{\underset{O}{\|}}{S}}—S—Ar \qquad Ar—SO_3H$$

a sulfone   a sulfoxide   a sulfonic acid

Over-oxidation of sulfur dyes usually decreases washfastness of the dye, makes the shade brighter, and makes the sulfur-dyed fabric feel softer.

The preferred method to apply sulfur dyes is continuous pad-steam. The reduced form of the dye is padded on the fabric. The fabric may be immediately steamed after which rinsing, oxidation, and soaping is done. Alternatively, the padded fabric may be dried and then padded again with a reducing agent before steaming. The latter method tends to give a more uniform shade and is often used on 100% cotton fabric. Because most continuous dye ranges have only two padders, the former method is usually used for dyeing blends where the first pad must be used for the polyester dyes. Since sulfur dyes in their reduced form rapidly adsorb on cellulose, tailing of the dyebath can be a problem. Overfeeding of the dye to compensate for dye exhaustion from the pad may be required. The exhaustion rate increases dramatically at higher temperature so tailing is accentuated by elevated temperature in the dye pad. The temperature of a sulfur dye pad should be no higher than is required for the fabric to be wetted by the dye formulation.

Sulfur dyes may also be applied by batch methods. Care should be taken to exclude air to prevent premature oxidation of the dye which causes deposition of dye on the surface of the material being dyed.

Bronzing and Tendering in Sulfur Dyeing

Two problems sometimes encountered with sulfur dyes are bronzing and tendering. Bronzing is a shiny appearance on the surface of the fabric caused by surface deposits of dye. Bronzing can be caused by premature oxidation of the dye or by application of too much dye. Bronzy fabric may be salvaged by reworking to remove some of the surface color.

Tendering of sulfur-dyed fabric is caused by acids formed from decomposition of the sulfur dye or other sulfur containing components. When tendering occurs, it is usually in fabrics which have been stored in warm, humid conditions. Tendering can be prevented by insuring that the fabric is finished on the alkaline side so that residual alkali in the fabric will neutralize the acid as it forms.

Azoic Dyes

Azoic dyeing consists of reacting two components, neither of which itself is a dye, with one another inside the fiber to form an azo pigment. Azoic dyeing is sometimes called naphthol dyeing because one of the components used to make the pigment is often a naphthol. Azoic dyeing is common only on cotton although other cellulosic fibers, wool, and even synthetic fibers can be dyed using azoic dyeing principles.

Technically, azoic dyes may be classified as ingrain dyes. In ingrain dyeing, a colorant is formed in the fiber by reaction between intermediate compounds. The Colour Index uses the classification Ingrain for a small group of phthalocyanine compounds once used for textile printing. The term "ice colors" is also sometimes used to refer to azoic dyes because ice can be used to produce the low temperature required in their application.

The two components used to form azoic dyes are a diazonium salt and a coupling component.

$$\text{Diazotized base} \quad + \quad \text{Coupling component} \quad \longrightarrow \quad \text{Azoic dye (pigment)}$$

The azo compound formed inside the fiber by this reaction is a pigment which is fast to washing mainly because it is extremely insoluble in water. Since the pigment is not chemically bound to the fiber, poor crockfastness results if the azoic pigment is formed on the fiber surface during azoic dyeing.

Structural Characteristics

Azoic coupling components are designed to have affinity for the fiber so that they can diffuse into the fiber prior to the reaction which forms the azo pigment. A series of derivatives of 3-hydroxy-2-naph-

Table 5-2. Chemical Names of Some Azoic Coupling Components

C.I. Azoic Coupling Component Number	Chemical Name
2	3-hydroxy-2-naphthoic anilide
4	3-hydroxy-2-naphthoic 1'-naphthanilide
7	3-hydroxy-2-naphthoic 2'-naphthanalide
8	3-hydroxy-2-naphthoic 4'-chloro-2'-methylanilide
12	3-hydroxy-2-naphthoic 5'-chloro-2',4'-dimethoxy-anilide
14	3-hydroxy-2-naphthoic 2'-ethoxyanilide
18	3-hydroxy-2-naphthoic 2'-methylanilide
19	3-hydroxy-2-naphthoic 2',5'-dimethoxyanilide

thoic acid (β-oxynaphthoic acid; BON acid) comprises an important group of azoic coupling components. The first members of this group were marketed in 1912 under the trade name Naphtol AS. The general structure of these compounds is as follows:

AR = benzene or naphthalene ring (usually substituted)

Table 5-2 shows the chemical names and C.I. numbers of some of these coupling components.

The colors obtained using naphthol derivatives as the coupling component are usually orange, red, violet, or blue. Coupling components of various structures can be used to make other hues including yellow, brown black, and dull green. Bright greens in the azoic range proved difficult to find. C.I. Azoic Coupling Component 108, a metal phthalocyanine-based substance of undisclosed structure produces bright green.

The diazonium salts used in azoic dyeing are diazotized bases made from substituted aromatic amines. The bases are usually marketed in the hydrochloride form and are called Fast Bases. Some examples of aromatic amines used as bases in azoic dyeing are shown in Table 5-3.

Table 5-3.   Chemical Names of Some Azoic Bases

C.I. Azoic Diazo Component Number	Chemical Name
2	3-chloroaniline
4	2,3'-dimethyl-4-aminoazobenzene
5	1-amino-2-methoxy-4-nitrobenzene
11	4-chloro-2-methylaniline
20	4-benzoylamino-2,5-diethoxyaniline
32	5-chloro-2-methylaniline
34	2-methyl-4-nitroaniline
44	2-chloroaniline

Dyeing Methods

Azoic dyes are applied in two steps. A schematic of the process follows.

Steps in Azoic Dye Application

Vessel 1	Vessel 2
Dissolve naphthol	Dissolve base
Apply naphthol to fiber	Diazotize the base
Salt rinse naphtholated fiber	
Rinse	
Wash	
Rinse	

The coupling component is applied first because it has affinity for the fiber and will diffuse into the fiber much like a dye. Before the coupling component can be applied, it must be dissolved in water to make a dyebath. Most coupling components are insoluble in water and must be converted to their salt form to make a water soluble substance. Dissolving the coupling component and applying it to the fiber is called naphtholation, referring to the formation of the naphtholate salt, even though not all coupling components are naphthols.

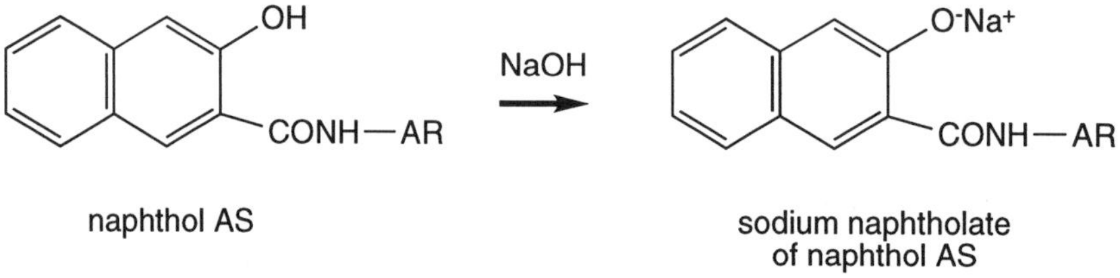

naphthol AS →(NaOH) sodium naphtholate of naphthol AS

Dissolving the coupling component is an art. Recommendations of the naphthol supplier about dissolving particular coupling components are helpful.

Addition of salt improves exhaustion of the solubilized coupling component as was also the case with direct and sulfur dyes. Heating the bath increases rate of exhaustion of the coupling component. However, the coupling components are relatively small molecules so very high temperature is not usually required for diffusion into the fiber. Rinsing of the material after application of the naphthol is important in prevention of the formation of pigment on the fiber surface. A solution of salt is used for these intermediate rinses so that only naphthol on the surface will be removed. Salt discourages loss of naphthol from within the fiber during rinsing. These intermediate salt rinses improve the crockfastness of azoic dyes.

The diazonium salt is made in a separate vessel. The fast base is dissolved or dispersed in water. A mineral acid such as hydrochloric acid is added to dissolve the base and to facilitate the diazotization reaction. Even though the base is often provided in its water soluble hydrochloride form, excess acid is required for diazotization. Diazotization consists of reaction of the primary amino group with nitrous acid.

$$AR-NH_2 + HONO \longrightarrow AR-N\equiv N^+ \ (X^-) \quad \text{(from mineral acid in bath)}$$

| primary amine | nitrous acid | diazonium salt of the amine |

AR = aromatic ring (usually substituted)

Since nitrous acid is not stable, it is prepared by adding sodium nitrite to the aqueous fast base solution. Diazonium salts are not very stable so the solution must be cooled to prevent decomposition of the diazonium salt prior to the coupling reaction.

The material containing the naphthol is entered into the diazonium salt solution. The naphthol and diazonium salt couple forming the azo pigment in the fiber.

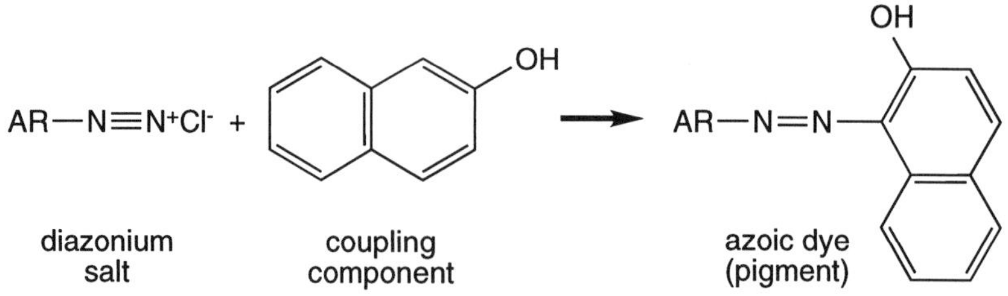

The number 1 position on the naphthol ring is the primary coupling point in the naphthol type coupling components because it is the most negative position on the ring.

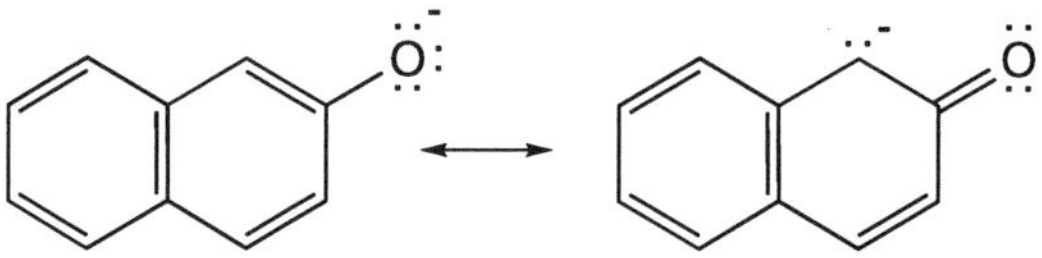

resonance structures of naphtholate ion

The diazonium salt is a weak electrophile which will react only with electron-rich substances. Thus diazonium salts react well only with the salt form of the naphthol. Low pH converts the naphthol to its free acid form making it less reactive with the diazonium salt. High pH favors the salt form and makes the naphthol more reactive.
The effect of pH on reactivity of the diazonium compounds is the opposite of its effect on reactivity of the coupling component. Diazonium salts tend to form stable diazotates at high pH. This makes them less reactive in coupling.

$$AR{-}N{\equiv}N^+\,Cl^- + OH^- \longrightarrow AR{-}N{=}N{-}OH + Cl^-$$

diazonium salt base a diazotate (stable)

The characteristics of the diazonium component rather than the coupling component usually determine the pH used. Coupling is usually done using acidic, neutral, or very slightly alkaline conditions. Fortunately, the coupling reaction is very fast and takes place before the acidic medium can convert the naphthol to its less reactive free acid form. Dye suppliers provide information about the best coupling conditions for particular diazonium compounds.

After coupling is completed, excess diazonium salt is rinsed from the material with warm water, and the dyed material is washed in a hot detergent solution. Many azoic dyes undergo significant change in color during soaping. The soaping treatment develops the true hue of the dyeing. Soaping also removes loosely bound colorant. This improves the crockfastness and other fastness properties of the dyeing.

Azoic dyes may be applied using either batch or continuous methods. Since the process requires separate baths for application of the coupling component and coupling with the diazonium component, both pads in a continuous dye range are needed. Therefore, dyeing of a blend such as polyester-cotton requires running the fabric twice, once to dye the polyester with disperse dyes and again to dye the cotton with the azoic dye.

Stabilized diazonium compounds

Since the diazotization process and the instability of the diazonium salts tend to present problems in azoic dyeing, stabilized diazonium compounds have been developed to make azoic dyeing simpler. Several different types of stabilized diazonium compounds have been marketed. Some of these are available while others are only of historical interest. Stable diazonium compounds called Fast Color Salts have been made by incorporating certain counterions into the diazonium compound. The most successful have been the zinc chloride double salts.

$$(AR-N\equiv N^+)_2 \ ZnCl_4^=$$

zinc chloride double salt (stable)

These stabilized diazonium salts can be isolated and stored in solid form. A reactive diazonium salt is formed when the stabilized salt is dissolved in water.

Stabilized diazonium compounds formed by reaction of the diazonium salt with alkali metal hydroxide have been made and marketed. The substance formed is a diazotate.

$$AR-N=N-OH$$

a diazotate (stable)

Mixtures of a diazotate and a naphthol were used as compositions for printing on fabric after which the fabric was steamed to cause coupling and color development. In a similar method, diazonium salt was treated with sodium sulfite to produce diazosulfonates which regenerate the reactive diazonium compound when treated with an oxidizing agent. Diazotates such as these are no longer used commercially.

Reaction of diazonium salts with primary or secondary amines produces stable triazines. Several compounds have been used to make this type of stable diazonium salt. An example is sarcosine.

$$AR-N\equiv N^+ Cl^- + CH_3NHCH_2COOH \longrightarrow AR-N=N-N \begin{array}{c} CH_3 \\ \diagdown \\ CH_2COOH \end{array}$$

diazonium salt   sarcosine

a triazine (stable)

The best-known trade name associated with compounds of this type is Rapidogen. Rapidogen colors are mixtures of a stable triazine with a naphthol. Coupling occurs when the formulation is acidified. Versions of this technique have been marketed for both printing and exhaust dyeing applications.

Reactive Dyes

Reactive dyes contain groups that react with the hydroxyl groups in cellulose. Reactive dyes for protein fibers and nylon have also been offered by dye manufacturers, but dyeing of cellulose is the major use for dyes in the reactive classification. The reaction between a reactive dye and the fiber produces a covalent bond. By their nature, reactive dyes also react with water. Dye which reacts with the fiber is said to be "fixed" to the fiber. Dye which reacts with water is said to be "hydrolyzed."

The reaction between the dye and the fiber is a nucleophilic displacement. The electron-rich oxygen atom in the hydroxyl group of cellulose (or water) attacks an electron-deficient carbon atom on the reactive group in the dye displacing a leaving group such as a chlorine atom. Since the by-product of the reaction is an acid and because alkali increases the negative nature of the oxygen atom on cellulose, the above reactions are catalyzed by alkali.

Fixation reaction

Cell—CH$_2$—OH + DYE—X ⟶ Cell—CH$_2$—O—DYE + HX

cellulose   reactive dye   dyed fiber   acid
           X = reactive group

Hydrolysis reaction

H—O—H + DYE—X ⟶ DYE—OH + HX

Dye molecules which react with the fiber and become fixed have excellent fastness to washing because of the high strength of the covalent bond. Dye molecules which are hydrolyzed may be weakly attached to the fiber and if not washed out at the end of the dye cycle have very poor washfastness.

Hydrolysis is an undesirable side reaction. Hydrolyzed dye cannot react chemically with the fiber but may be weakly attached to the fiber by secondary forces. Hydrolyzed dye must be completely washed from the fabric before the dyeing process is completed to achieve the excellent washfastness properties for which the reactive dyes are known. Reactive dyes can be designed to have low substantivity so that hydrolyzed dye can be easily washed from the fabric at the end of the dyeing process. Hydrolyzed dye is discharged in the wastewater from the dye house and represents both an economic loss and a potential pollutant which must be treated.

Structural Characteristics

Reactive dyes consist of a chromophore attached to a reactive group through a –NH– group. The chromophore is responsible for the color of the molecule. The reactive group provides capability for the dye to react with the fiber and has little or no influence on the color.

CHROMOPHORE—NH—REACTIVE GROUP

reactive dye structure schematic

Since the dye is fixed to the fiber by covalent bonds, the chromophore can be a small, simple structure with limited attraction to the fiber. Small molecular structures in reactive dyes provide advantages such as high solubility in water, easy removal of hydrolyzed dye, easy cleanup, rapid diffusion in the fiber at low temperature, and bright colors. Therefore, the chromophore is usually a relatively small structure containing sulfonate groups to make the dye soluble in water. Typical chromophores in reactive dye structures are monazo, anthraquinone, phthalocyanine (for bright turquoise hues), triphenodioxazine, and formazan. The azo group is sometimes metallized with copper, cobalt, or chromium to produce a bathochromic shift.

Reactive dye chromophores   X = reactive group

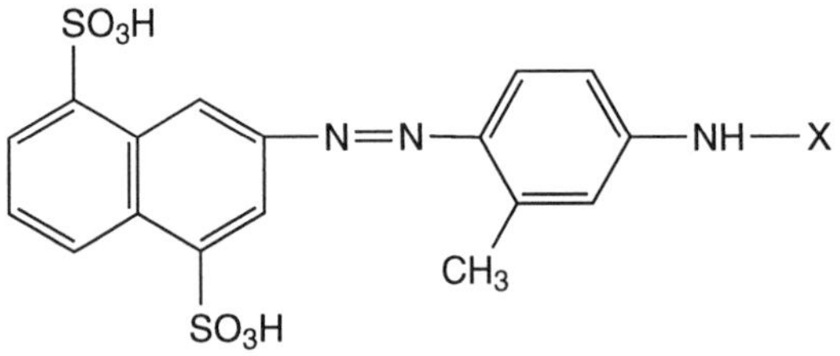

monazo type

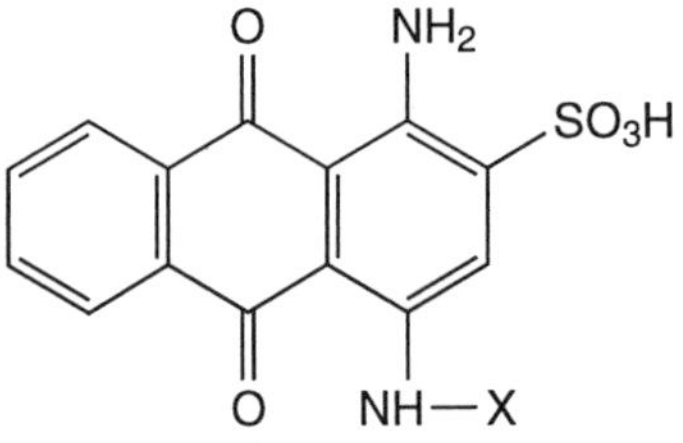

anthraquinone type

Several types of reactive groups are found in reactive dyes. The first reactive dyes contained triazine reactive groups. This type of reactive group is important in reactive dyes today. The dyes are made by attaching a chromophore to trichlorotriazine (cyanuric chloride).

trichlorotriazine
(cyanuric chloride)

dichlorotriazine
reactive dye

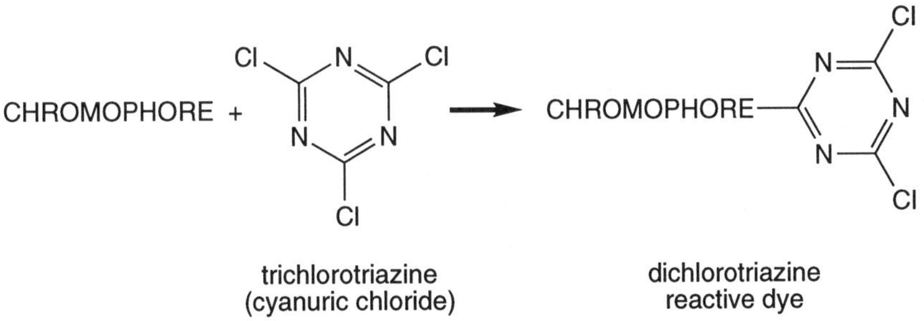

Dichlorotriazine type reactive dyes contain two displaceable (reactive) chlorine groups. Monochlorotriazine type reactive dyes are made by substituting one of the remaining chlorine atoms with an unreactive group leaving only one reactive group on the dye molecule. Dichlorotriazine reactive dyes are more reactive and are usually applied at lower temperatures than monochlorotriazine reactive dyes. Both types are widely used.

Cyanuric chloride is a chromophoric blocking group. Attachment of two chromophores through the triazine ring structure produces a dye with the color that would be produced by physically mixing the two chromophores. Thus, attachment of a blue and a yellow chromophore through a triazine ring produces a green dye. Although the structures produced by this method are too large to be good reactive dyes, the technique is used in making direct dyes. C.I. Direct Green 26 is an example of a dye produced by this method.

Diazine reactive groups are also used in reactive dye molecules. Pyrimidine and quinoxaline are the most important of the diazines in commercial reactive dyes.

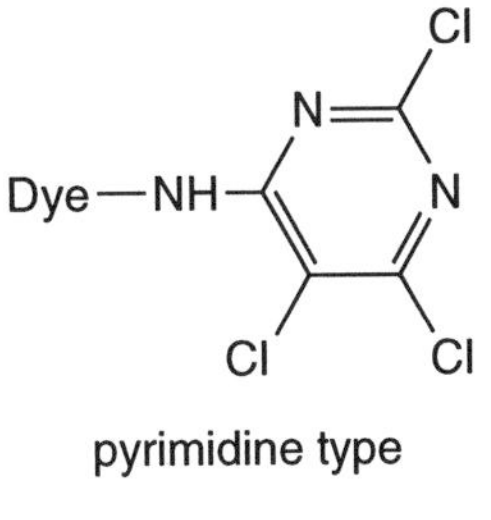

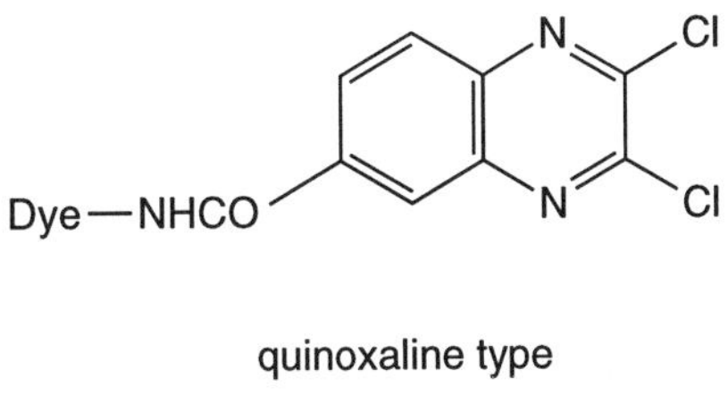

pyrimidine type

quinoxaline type

The leaving groups (chlorine or other) on diazine rings are less reactive than those on triazine rings. The quinoxaline dyes are the most reactive of the diazine types, but even these are less reactive than dichlorotriazine reactive dyes. Even though they may contain more than one labile halogen atom, the reactivity of the other diazine types is similar to that of the monochlorotriazine types.

Although chlorine is the most common leaving group on reactive dye molecules, many other leaving atoms and groups have been described in patent literature. Three leaving groups other than chlorine that are found on commercial dyes are fluorine, quaternary ammonium, and methyl sulfonyl. Following are examples of dyes with these leaving groups.

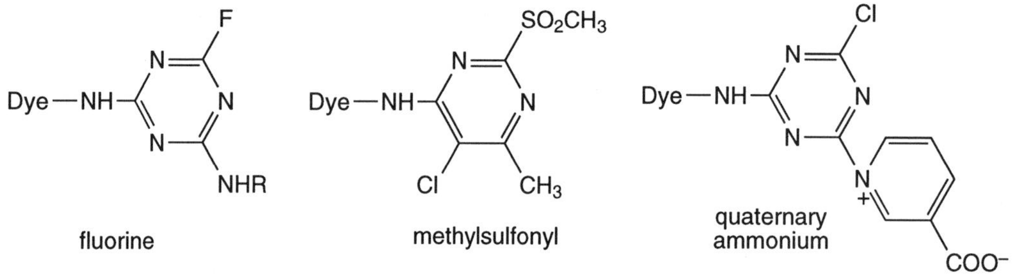

fluorine   methylsulfonyl   quaternary ammonium

All three of these groups are effective leaving groups which make the dyes more reactive than dyes with reactive moieties containing chlorine leaving groups. The nicotinic acid leaving group shown in the quaternary ammonium example above produces dyes which react with cellulose under neutral conditions. This allows them to be applied simultaneously in the same dyebath with disperse dyes on polyester-cotton blend fabrics.

Vinyl Sulfone Type Reactive Dyes

Vinyl sulfone reactive dyes react with cellulose by nucleophilic addition to a carbon-carbon double bond rather than by nucleophilic displacement as was the case for the azine type reactive dyes.

$$Dye-SO_2-CH_2=CH_2 + Cell-CH_2OH \longrightarrow Cell-CH_2-O-CH_2CH_2SO_2Dye$$

vinyl sulfone   cellulose   dye bonded to fiber
reactive dye

The sulfone group (or some other electron attracting group) bridging the chromophore and the alkene group is required to activate the alkene. This group makes the alkene group reactive enough to participate in the addition reaction with the hydroxyl group of cellulose.

The reactive group in commercial vinyl sulfone reactive dyes is usually the sodium salt of the sulfuric acid ester of a β-hydroxyethyl sulfone group.

$$Dye-SO_2-CH_2-CH_2-O-SO_3^-Na^+$$

reactive group on commercial vinyl sulfone dye
(β-sulfatoethylsulfone group)

This group ionizes in water and makes the dye soluble in water. This type of dye is soluble in water even without additional solubilizing groups. However, textile dyes of the vinyl sulfone type usually have additional solubilizing groups on the chromophoric part of the molecule. These additional solubilizing groups make the dyes more soluble in water so more concentrated solutions can be made for padding and printing. The additional solubilizing groups also make removal of hydrolyzed dye easier.

In the presence of alkali in the dyebath, the β-sulfatoethylsulfone groups convert to vinyl sulfone groups which react with cellulose. Vinyl sulfone dyes are usually intermediate in reactivity between dichlorotriazine dyes and monochlorotriazine dyes.

Bifunctional Reactive Dyes

Reactive dyes with more than one type of reactive group in the same molecule are claimed to give improved fixation. This is a reasonable expectation since the dye can bond with cellulose through reaction with either of the reactive groups, and hydrolysis of one of the groups should not prevent the other from reacting. Commercial dyes containing both a monochlorotriazine and a vinyl sulfone type reactive group are available. Since these two groups differ in reactivity and temperature sensitivity, these bifunctional reactive dyes appear to be less sensitive to dyebath temperature variation than reactive dyes containing only a single type of functional group.

Dyeing Methods

Reactive dyeing is usually done in two stages, the adsorption stage and the fixation stage. Reactive dyeing methods are designed to optimize the effects of time, temperature, and pH (or alkalinity) on the behavior of the dye in these two stages. Dyebath pH and temperature affect the various types of reactive dyes differently. A particular type of reactive dye is generally designed and recommended for one or a few specific applications. Reactive dyes can be applied by a great variety of methods by judicious selection of the type of reactive dye and dyeing time, temperature, and pH.

Goals in reactive dyeing include achieving a high level of fixation and minimizing the amount of dye hydrolysis. Exhausting the dye into the fiber under conditions where the dye reactivity is low helps to accomplish these goals. Generally, the rate of reaction of reactive dyes with cellulose and water increases at higher pH and higher temperature in the dyebath. Therefore, the pH may be near neutral in the early stages of dyeing when most of the dye is still in the dyebath. The reactivity of the dye may be increased by adding alkali later in the process when most of the dye is on the fiber. The type and amount of alkali required also depends on the particular type of reactive dye being used. Various alkali systems using sodium bicarbonate, sodium carbonate (soda ash), sodium hydroxide (caustic soda), sodium silicate, and other alkalies are used commercially in reactive dyeing.

The temperature used is that which is consistent with the type of reactive dye selected and the dyeing process being used. Generally, the optimum dyeing temperature is very specific for each particular type of reactive dye. Dyes having high inherent reactivity are usually applied at higher temperature than dyes with inherently low reactivity. If the process being used dictates that the alkali be added at the beginning of the dyeing, then low temperature and long dyeing time may be required for dye fixation.

Salt is often used to drive the dye into the fiber in exhaust dyeing methods for reactive dyes. The amount of salt required may be many times that required for direct or sulfur dyeing because the reactive dyes, by design, have low affinity for the fiber. Padding methods usually do not require salt because the low liquor ratio used in padding results in good transfer of dye to the fiber.

Whatever method of application is used, reactive dyeings must be thoroughly washed at the end of the dye cycle to remove hydrolyzed dye. Multiple washes with surfactants at elevated temperature are usually required to adequately remove hydrolyzed dye.

Vat Dyes

Vat dyes are used mainly on cellulosic fibers, but some can be applied to protein fibers. They usually have outstanding color fastness properties. Vat dyes are more expensive and difficult to apply than other classes for cellulose such as directs, sulfurs, and reactives. Indigo is a special case in the vat dye class. Indigo is attractive for its pleasing blue color and for the unique fading characteristics of garments dyed with it. Color fastness properties of indigo are poor.

Vat dyes are characterized by the presence of a keto group that can be reduced to an alcohol.

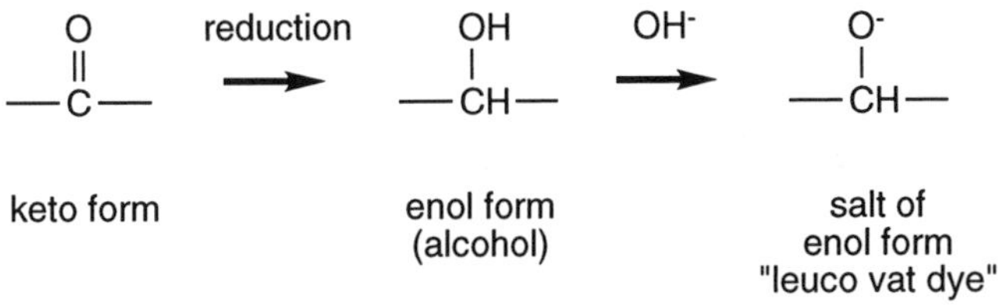

Vat dyes in keto form are water insoluble pigments. The enol form is a strong enough acid to form a water soluble salt when reacted with strong alkali. The reduced, water soluble form is usually called the "leuco" form of the dye.

Structural Characteristics

Vat dyes are usually classified into the following three groups:

1. Indigoid
2. Anthraquinone
3. Fused ring polycyclic

There are only a few members in the indigoid group. The parent member of the group is indigo (C.I. Vat Blue 1).

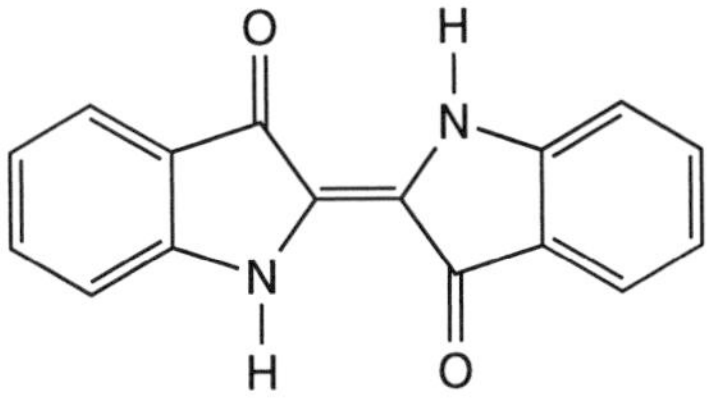

Indigo is an ancient dye which was extracted from cultivated plants for hundreds of years. Synthetic indigo, identical in structure to natural indigo, is widely used to dye yarn for denim fabrics. Tetrabromo indigo is also used today. It is redder in hue than indigo itself. Tetrabromo indigo is a synthetic product that is similar to Tyrian Purple (dibromoindigo), which was extracted from sea snails in ancient times.

Thioindigo has exactly the same structure as indigo except that sulfur atoms occupy the positions occupied by the N-H groups in indigo. Thioindigo is a red dye (C.I. Vat Red 41). Addition of substituents to the rings produces different hues and fastness properties. Other hues including violet, brown, and black are produced with structures containing a nitrogen atom in one ring and a sulfur atom in the other ring.

Anthraquinone vat dyes contain one or more substituted anthraquinone groups. Introduction of electron donating groups produces a bathochromic shift. A full range of hues can be made by modifying the anthraquinone structure. Many of the anthraquinone vat dyes contain two or three anthraquinone rings bridged together by nitrogen atoms or various chemical groups.

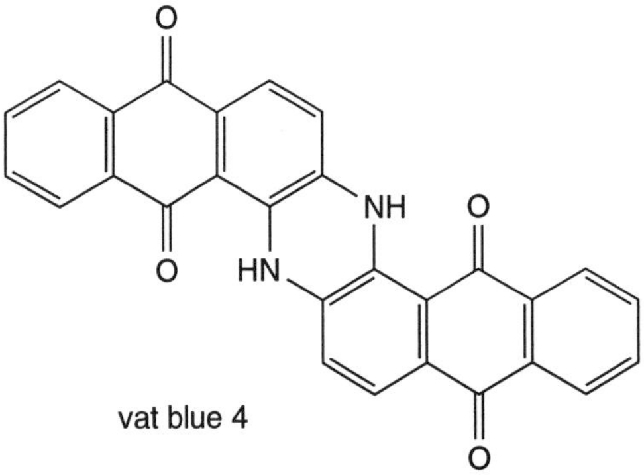

vat blue 4

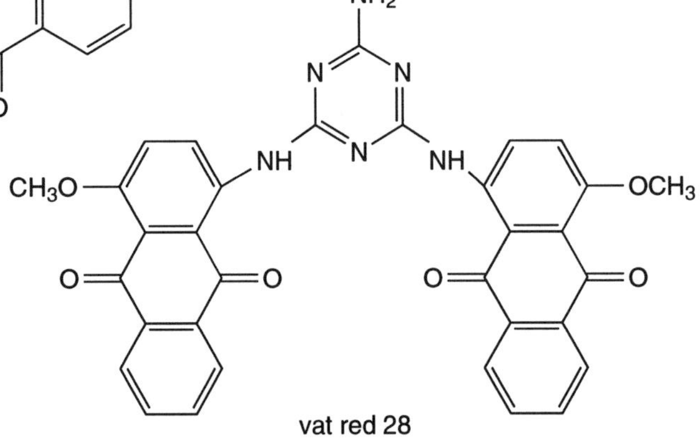

vat red 28

Many vat dyes are the fused polycyclic type. The suffix "anthrone" in the name denotes this type of structure.

R = —OCH₃

substituted dibenzanthrone
(C.I. Vat Green 1)

pyranthrone
(C.I. Vat Orange 9)

Dyeing Methods

Vat dyes are usually categorized according to the temperature at which they perform best in dyeing. Some dyes are applicable at ambient temperature while others dye better at higher temperatures of 50°C or 60°C. The recommended temperature for a few dyes, notably blacks, is about 90°C. The amounts of caustic, hydro, and salt recommended for the various groups may also differ somewhat.

Application of vat dyes requires the following steps:

1. Preparation of dye dispersion in water
2. Reduction
3. Adsorption of dye on fibers
4. Oxidation
5. Rinsing and soaping

The order in which these steps are performed depends on the dyeing method employed. The two general dyeing methods are called the pigment method and the reduced method. In the pigment method, the vat dye dispersion in pigment form is distributed in the material to be dyed. After the pigment is uniformly distributed in the material, the dye is reduced so that the dye can be adsorbed by the fibers. In the reduced method, the dye is reduced to the soluble, leuco form before coming in contact with the material to be dyed. The material is then contacted with the reduced dye, and the dye is adsorbed by the fibers. The dyeing process may be either batch or continuous. The dye manufacturer provides the product as either a powder or paste containing additives to aid in dispersion of the dye in water.

Application of vat dyes using pigment methods or in printing requires that the dye particles be finely dispersed and uniform in size. Coarse particles may be filtered by the material in package dyeing or deposited unevenly on the material by the printing machine giving nonuniform coloration. Particle diameter of vat dyes today is typically less than 1 micron.

Reduction (Vatting)

Vat dyes in pigment form are insoluble in water and do not have affinity for cellulosic fibers. They must be converted to a water soluble state so that they can be absorbed by fibers. The process of dissolving the dye is called vatting. The term vatting dates to ancient times when indigo was applied by a laborious process in a deep "vat." Vatting consists of reduction of keto groups on the dye structure using sodium dithionite (sodium hydrosulfite). The name "hydro" is commonly used for sodium hydrosulfite in the dyehouse. Reduction is done in the presence of sodium hydroxide which is usually called caustic in the dyehouse.

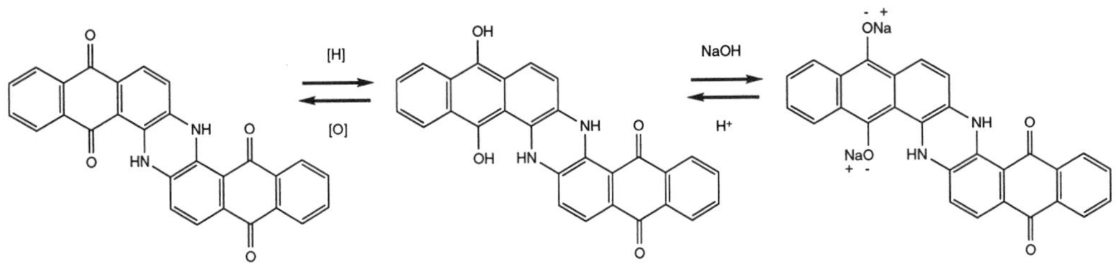

Although the vatting of C.I. Vat Blue 4 is shown above as consisting of two reactions, all of the chemicals are usually in one bath, and the process consists of only one step. Rate of reduction of the vat dye depends on size of the particles in the dye dispersion, concentration of caustic and hydro used, and temperature used. A finely divided, well-dispersed vat dye usually undergoes reduction in just a few seconds. The quantities of caustic and hydro required depend on how many keto groups in the dye molecule are reduced. One mole of hydro is required to reduce two keto groups to the enol form. Theoretically, one mole of caustic is required to convert each enol group to its salt form. In practice, the quantities of hydro and caustic used are several times the theoretical amounts. Excess hydro must be present because oxygen in the atmosphere and in the dyebath will consume some of the hydro. Excess caustic is required to drive the neutralization reaction to the right to fully produce the soluble, leuco form. Usually, the dyebath pH must be above 12 to ensure complete solubility of the leuco compound.

The temperature used in vatting is important, and the optimum temperature depends on the particular dye. If the temperature is too low, reduction may be incomplete. If the temperature is too high, over-reduction can occur. Over-reduction affects shade and fastness of the dyeing. An example of over-reduction is the reduction of all four keto groups on an indanthrone dye giving a brown leuco product rather than the blue leuco product which forms when only two of the keto groups are reduced. Another example of over-reduction is the formation of anthrol and anthrone rather than the desired anthrahydroquinone in anthraquinone type vat dyes.

Hydrolysis of vat dyes can occur if caustic concentration or vatting temperature is too high. An example of hydrolysis is the displacement of halogen atoms by hydroxyl groups.

Reactions of this type may affect the hue of the dye or reduce its colorfastness properties. If the caustic concentration is too low, molecular rearrangements may occur in the reduced dye causing unsatisfactory dyeings.

Reduced vat dyes are sometimes sensitive to light. The displacement of bromine from the reduced vat dye is a photochemical reaction which results in a change in shade of the dye. Some reduced vat dyes are also sensitive to calcium and other ions in hard water. C.I. Vat Blue 6 is particularly sensitive to hard water, and precipitates in the presence of a relatively small concentration of calcium ions.

Adsorption of Dye

Vat dyes exhaust rapidly in the early stages of the dyeing process

Figure 5-2.   Dyeing rate isotherm for a vat dye

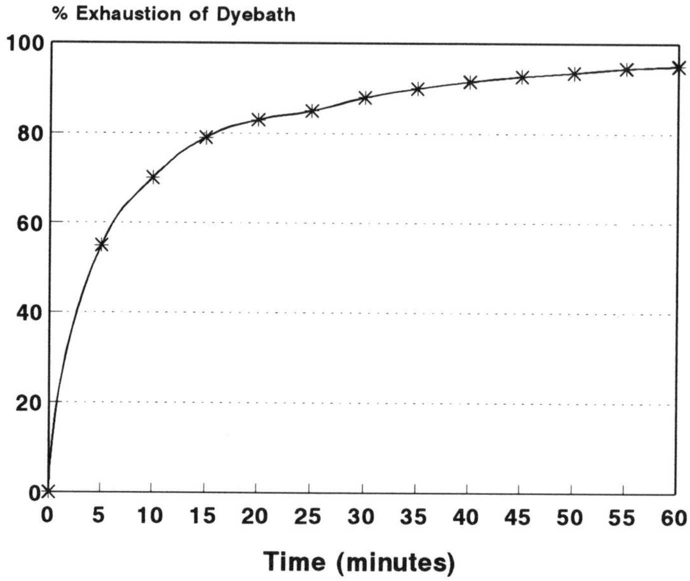

% Exhaustion of Dyebath

Time (minutes)

as shown in the rate of dyeing isotherm in Figure 5-2. The rapid exhaustion rate makes uniform application of the dye difficult. Initially, a high concentration of dye builds up near the fiber surface. High temperature, low liquor ratio, and low dye concentration accentuate the rapid initial exhaustion. As the dyeing proceeds, the dye molecules diffuse toward the center of the fiber. Higher temperature greatly increases the diffusion rate and levelling tendency of the dye. However, high dyeing temperature may be undesirable because lower dye affinity and undesirable reduction and hydrolysis reactions are also favored by high temperature.

Oxidation

After the dye is exhausted and diffused into the fiber, the material is rinsed to remove most of the residual caustic and hydro. The dye is then oxidized to its insoluble pigment form in the fiber. Oxidation may be done with any of several agents including air, hydrogen peroxide, perborates, hypochlorite, iodates, bromates, persulfates, and chromates. The most common agent used today is peroxide. The oxidation is done in acidic medium to neutralize residual alkali and convert the dye to the acid form. Acetic acid is the most common acid for this purpose.

Soaping Aftertreatment

Soaping is the term used for a high temperature detergent wash at the conclusion of vat dye application. Soaping removes loosely adhering dye and residual chemicals and is often accompanied by a dramatic change in shade. The cause of the shade change is not known with certainty but is believed to be the result of crystallization of dye within the fiber. The practical implication is that the dyeing must be soaped to develop the final shade before leaving the dyehouse so a color change will not occur when the material is washed by the consumer.

Vat dyes may be applied by batch or continuous methods. In batch methods, the dyeing is done in one vessel which is drained between the various steps required for dye application. Salt is often used to assist exhaustion. Padding methods are also common. In continuous dyeing, the dye in pigment form is usually padded followed by drying. The dry fabric is then padded with a solution of caustic and hydro and steamed to cause reduction and diffusion of dye into the fiber. Alternatively, the reduced dye can be padded followed immediately by steaming of the wet fabric. Vat dyes can also be applied by semi-continuous methods such as padding and drying using a continuous applicator followed by reduction, adsorption, and washing using a jig.

Application of indigo requires the same steps as other vat dyes. However, the most common use of indigo is to dye warp yarn using an indigo dye range. Long chain indigo dyeing, as this process is sometimes called, is discussed elsewhere in this text.

Soluble Vat Dyes

Vat dyes in a water soluble form are available. They are the sulfuric acid esters of reduced vat dyes.

The advantage of soluble vat dyes is that the reduction step in the application procedure is not needed. The dye is simply dissolved in the dyebath, exhausted by the addition of salt, and oxidized to its pigment form. The preferred oxidation method for soluble vat dyes is acidified sodium nitrite solution.

Acid Dyes

Acid dyes contain acidic groups, usually $-SO_3H$, and are used on fibers containing basic groups that can interact with these acidic groups. The fibers that are dyeable with acid dyes are polyamides containing some free amino, $-NH_2$, groups. Nylon is the most important synthetic fiber having this characteristic. Wool, silk, and other protein-based natural fibers also have amino groups that can bond with acid dyes. The bonds formed between the dye and fiber are salt linkages.

$$\text{Fiber}-NH_2 \ + \ HSO_3-\text{Dye} \ \longrightarrow \ \text{Fiber}-NH_3{}^+{}^-SO_3-\text{Dye}$$

Fiber with basic amino group

Dye with acidic sulfonic acid group

Dyed fiber with salt linkage between dye and fiber

Acid dyes are manufactured as the sodium salt of the sulfonic acid form shown above.

The color fastness properties of various acid dyes range from good to excellent. Fastness to light is exceptional in the case of transition metal-containing acid dyes.

Structural Characteristics

The most common structural types of acid dyes are monazo and anthraquinone.

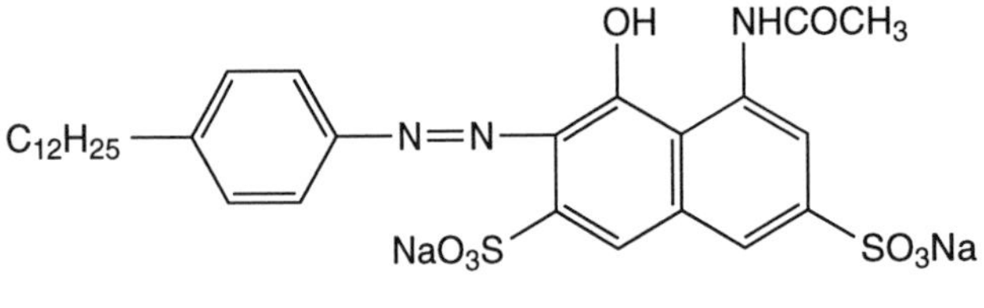

C.I. Acid Red 138

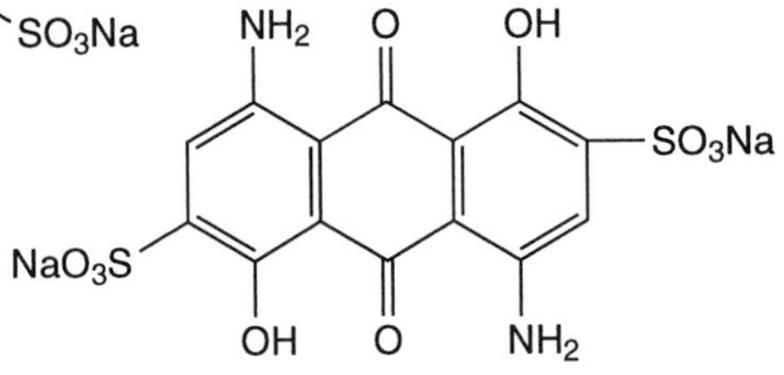

C.I. Acid Blue 45

Metallized acid dyes are also common. These contain chromium or cobalt ions complexed with the dye molecule. The dye must have electron donating groups located so that 5- or 6-member ring complexes can form between the dye molecule and the metal ion. Typical types of metallized acid dyes are the 1:1 complexes containing 1 dye molecule per metal ion and the 2:1 complexes containing 2 dye molecules per metal ion. Note that the 2:1 metal complex dye shown does not contain the sulfonic acid groups usually characteristic of acid dyes. Although some metal complex acid dyes do contain sulfonic acid groups, other polar groups such as sulfonyl and sulfonamide provide sufficient polarity to make these dyes water soluble.

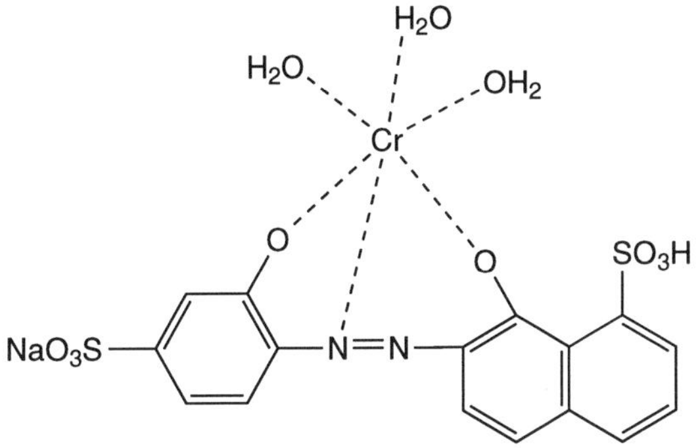

C.I. Acid Blue 159
(1:1 metal complex)

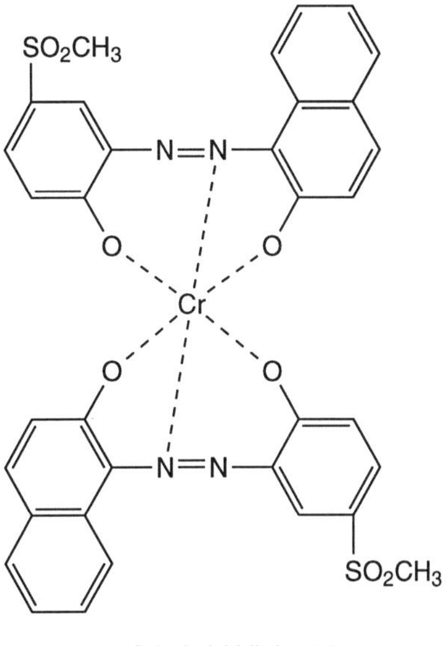

C.I. Acid Violet 78
(2:1 metal complex)

Other common structural types of acid dyes are triphenylmethane, nitro, diazo, and phthalocyanine.

Dyeing methods

Acid dyes are usually categorized into three or four subgroups according to their dyeing behavior. Table 5-4 shows the general properties of acid dyes categorized into three subgroups.

The term "leveling" is derived from the fact that the acid dyes in this subgroup are not firmly attached to the fiber and can move about

Table 5-4.   Comparison of Acid Dye Subgroups

Property	Leveling Acid Dye	Milling/Supermilling Acid Dye	Premetallized Acid Dye
Color brightness	Good	Less than leveling dyes	Lowest of acid dyes
Leveling tendency	Very good	Poor to fair	Poor
Wet fastness	Poor to fair	Good to very good	Excellent
Light fastness	Good	Good	Excellent
Dyebath pH requirements	Very acidic; pH= 2–4	Acidic to neutral; pH= 4–7	Neutral to very acidic
Dyebath additive requirements	Sulfuric or acetic acid; sodium sulfate (optional)	Acetic acid; rate retarder	Sulfuric acid; acetic acid; acidic salts
Solubility in water	High (40–80 g/l)	Lower than leveling dyes (3–30 g/l)	Varies depending on dye
State of dye in water	Molecularly dispersed solution	Colloidal	Varies
Molecular weight	Low (200–400)	High (500–900)	High (500–900)
Affinity for polyamides	Lowest of acid dyes	High to very high	Very high

and become more uniformly distributed on the fiber if applied unevenly in the early stages of dyeing. The term "milling" is derived from the durability, or wet fastness, of the dyes in this subgroup to milling, a vigorous scouring process in the felting of wool.

The milling/supermilling subgroup is sometimes shown as two separate groups, but there is no sharp line of demarcation in the behavior of these dyes.

Several of the properties in the table are related to one another. For example, color brightness, solubility in water, and fastness properties are all partially dependent on the molecular weight of the dye. Leveling acid dyes are easier to apply than milling or premetallized acid dyes because of their ability to move from one place to another on the fiber. This same characteristic makes them less fast to washing than milling dyes. Premetallized dyes do not migrate once adsorbed on the fiber. Extreme care must be used in the exhaustion stage to ensure that the dye is applied uniformly. The low tendency to migrate results in very good fastness properties in premetallized dyes. The milling/super milling dyes are intermediate between leveling and premetallized dyes in fastness properties and difficulty of applying uniformly.

The subgroups of acid dyes differ so greatly from one another in properties that individual acid dyes from different subgroups are usually incompatible with one another for mixture dyeings. For example, super milling dyes may completely block the adsorption of leveling dyes. Furthermore, supermilling dyes may even displace leveling dyes from previously dyed material.

Acid dyes may be applied using either batch or continuous methods. Batch methods are commonly used for carpets, knit fabrics, and woven fabrics. Nylon carpets are sometimes dyed using a continuous pad-steam method.

Dyeing Mechanism on Wool

Wool consists of the protein keratin which is made up of the imino acid proline and eighteen α-amino acids. The eighteen amino acids differ from one another according to the structure of the R– group in the general structure.

general structure of α-amino acids in wool

The amino acids are combined in polypeptide chains with the pendant R– groups. The R– groups which differ in size and chemical composition are responsible for many of the properties of wool including dyeing behavior. As shown in Table 5-5, some of the amino acid groups contain acidic and basic groups.

These acidic and basic groups are vital in the dyeing mechanism of acid dyes on wool. Since wool is amphoteric, it can absorb either acid or basic substances and can be either electrically positive or negative depending on pH. The pH range of about 4.7 to 7.2 is the isoelectric region for wool. In this pH range wool exists in a Zwitterionic form.

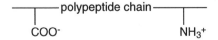

Wool at isoelectric point

Table 5-5. Some Amino Acids in Wool

Amino Acid Name	Side Group (R–)
Glycine	–H
Alanine	$-CH_3$
Serine	$-CH_2OH$
Tyrosine	$-CH-\langle\bigcirc\rangle OH$ 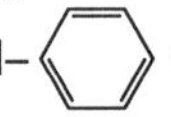
Aspartic acid	$-CH_2COOH$
Glutamic acid	$-CH_2CH_2COOH$
Lysine	$-CH_2CH_2CH_2CH_2NH_2$
Arginine	$-CH_2CH_2CH_2NH_2-C-NH_2$ $\qquad\qquad\qquad\quad \overset{\|\|}{N}H$
Cystine	$-CH_2S-SCH_2-$

When the pH is above the isoelectric point, the amino group is neutral, and wool has a net negative charge.

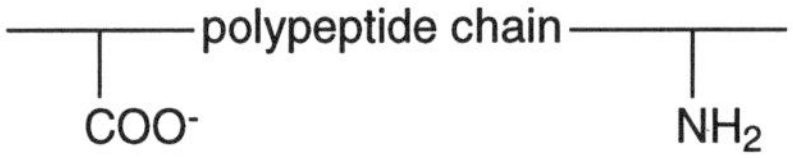

$$\text{———}\overset{\|}{\underset{COO^-}{}}\text{—polypeptide chain—}\overset{\|}{\underset{NH_2}{}}\text{———}$$

Wool at pH higher than isoelectric point

When the pH is below the isoelectric point, the carboxyl group is protonated, and wool has a net positive charge.

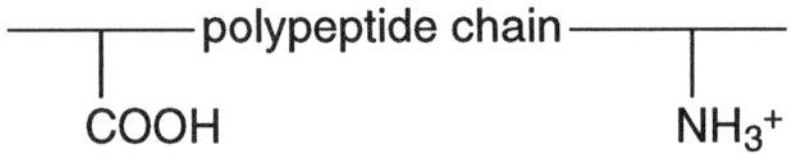

$$\text{———}\overset{\|}{\underset{COOH}{}}\text{—polypeptide chain—}\overset{\|}{\underset{NH_3^+}{}}\text{———}$$

Wool at pH lower than isoelectric point

Since acid dyes contain negatively charged sulfonate groups, the positively charged amino group is the main dye site for acid dyes. Wool contains many amino groups which serve as sites for adsorption of acid dyes. Furthermore, wool is mostly amorphous because of the bulkiness of the R– groups and is easily penetrated by dyes. Therefore, wool can absorb large amounts of acid dye and can be easily dyed to dark shades. Amino and carboxyl groups also terminate the polypeptide chains in wool, but the number of these end groups is small compared to the number of acid and basic groups on the pendant side chains.

The main sites for absorption of acid dyes on wool are believed to be amino groups, and salt linkages are the main mode of bonding between the dye and fiber. While this model explains many of the observations about acid dyeing of wool, other mechanisms such as secondary interactions and physical entrapment of dye are also of some importance.

Acid dyes can migrate and level somewhat if applied nonuniformly in the early stages of dyeing. However, uniform application from the beginning of the dyeing is preferred. Control of temperature and rate of heating of the dyebath is important in acid dyeing of wool. Dye absorption begins at temperatures of 40–60°C depending on the particular dye, and dyeing becomes very rapid around 70°C. The temperature is gradually raised to near the boiling point of water and held for some period of time.

Uniformity of application can also be enhanced by use of dyeing rate retarders. Sodium sulfate, Glauber's salt, serves this function for leveling dyes and some milling dyes which are applied at dyebath pH below the isoelectric point of wool. The sulfate ion from the Glauber's salt competes with the acid dye ion for the positively charged dye sites in the fiber. Since the sulfate ions are small, they diffuse quickly into the fiber and occupy dye sites. This reduces the attraction between the dye and dye sites and decreases the rate of dyeing. Since the large dye anions have greater affinity for the dye sites than do the sulfate ions, the dye eventually diffuses into the fiber and displaces the sulfate ions from the dye sites. Sodium sulfate serves as a dyeing rate retarder only if the dyebath pH is low. At high pH, sodium sulfate behaves as an exhausting agent for acid dyes on wool by the same mechanism that salt increases exhaustion rate of anionic dyes on cellulose.

Supermilling acid dyes exhaust on wool under neutral or slightly acidic conditions. These dyes have greater affinity for wool and do not migrate and level as well as leveling and milling dyes. Therefore, care must be taken to apply the supermilling dyes uniformly. A slow rate of temperature rise and gradual lowering of the dyebath pH are usually used to promote uniform exhaustion. Salts such as ammonium acetate, ammonium sulfate, and ammonium chloride produce neutral or slightly acidic solutions at room temperature. As the temperature of the dyebath containing one of these salts is increased, the pH drops gradually causing the fiber to become more positive and attractive to the dye.

Organic rate retarding agents are also used to promote uniform exhaustion of supermilling dyes. Anionic surfactants containing sulfonic acid groups retard the rate of absorption of acid dyes on wool. They are believed to function by competing with the anionic dye ions for available dye sites. Retarding agents containing both quaternary ammonium cationic groups and polymeric ethylene oxide chains have also been introduced.

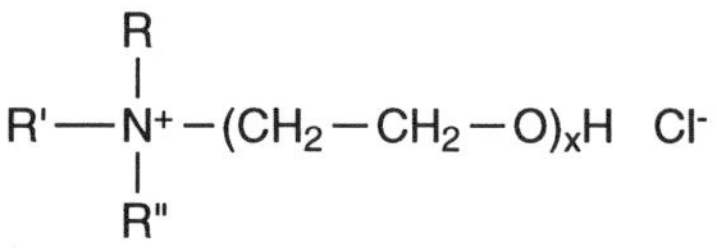

$$R'—N^+—(CH_2—CH_2—O)_xH \quad Cl^-$$

with R above N and R'' below N

retarder for acid dyes

The cationic groups in these products are believed to complex with the dye ions. The polar ethylene oxide chains hold the dye in solution at low dyebath temperature. As the dyebath temperature increases, the dye/surfactant complex breaks (decreases in solubility) allowing the dye ions to be absorbed by the fiber.

Dyeing Mechanism on Nylon

Nylon fibers are polyamides. The molecular chains in nylon are linear and, unlike wool, have no side chains with dye sites.

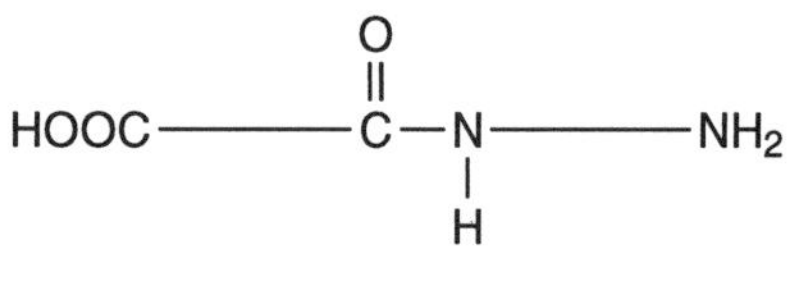

$$HOOC———C(=O)—N(H)———NH_2$$

Schematic representation of polyamide chain in nylon

The dye sites in nylon for acid dyes are amino groups which terminate the molecular chains. One sulfonic acid group on a dye molecule can interact with one amino group in the fiber. Once the amino group is occupied by a sulfonic acid group it is blocked and is not available for attachment to another sulfonic acid group. Dyes with more than one sulfonic acid group can occupy more than one dye site. Therefore, monosulfonated dyes buildup up darker shades on nylon than do disulfonated and higher sulfonated dyes which occupy more than one dye site.

Since the maximum number of end groups is two per chain and the actual number is usually about one per chain, nylon has only a small number of sites for absorption of acid dye. Therefore, competition between dyes and dye compatibility problems can be severe when dyeing nylon with acid dyes. Dyeing of dark shades can also be difficult because of the small number of dye sites available.

Some acid dyes may also be absorbed by hydrogen bonding on the amide groups, but this mechanism is believed to be confined mostly to acid dyes having very high molecular weight. At pH of 2.0 or lower, nylon absorbs much more dye than the amount required to occupy only amine end groups. At very low pH, amide groups in the polymer backbone are protonated and become sites for absorption of acid dye molecules. Since nylon is subject to chemical damage at low pH, dyeing below pH of about 3.0 is not practical.

The nylon manufacturer can make nylon fibers having different levels of dyeability since the dyeability of nylon depends greatly on the number of amine end groups in the polymer. In regular nylon about one half of the chain ends are amino groups while the other half are carboxyl groups.

$$HOOC \underline{\quad\quad polyamide\ chain \quad\quad} NH_2$$

Representation of nylon with one amino group per chain

Acid dye-resist nylon is made by blocking most of the amine end groups or terminating the polymerization reaction so that most of the chain ends are carboxyl rather than amine groups.

$$HOOC \underline{\quad\quad polyamide\ chain \quad\quad} NHCOCH_3$$

Nylon with amino group blocked to limit dyeability

Deep dyeing nylon is made by terminating the polymerization reaction so that most of the chain ends are amine groups.

$$H_2N \underline{\quad\quad polyamide\ chain \quad\quad} NH_2$$

Nylon with two amino groups per chain

Cationic dyeable nylon is made by incorporating acidic groups in the polymer backbone.

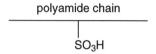

Nylon modified to incorporate sites for cationic dyes

These modifications of nylon provide special styling capabilities in nylon products. Tone-on-tone and multicolor patterns can be produced from a single dyebath by using textile products containing nylon fibers of more than one dyeability type. This technique of producing multicolored products is commonly used in carpet manufacturing and may be used in flat fabrics as well.

Since the dyeability of nylon with acid dyes depends greatly on the number of end groups in the polymer, the fiber manufacturer must control this characteristic of the fiber. The number of end groups in a given weight of fiber depends on the molecular weight of the polymer. Therefore, molecular weight variations can cause dyeability variations in nylon.

Dyeability of nylon can also be affected by heat or mechanical treatments to which the fibers have been subjected prior to dyeing. The terms "energy history" or "heat history" of the fiber are sometimes used to refer to these effects. The term barré is used to refer to fabrics which exhibit a light and dark streaky appearance. Barré is usually associated with texturized yarns. Differences in tension on yarns in a woven or knit fabric can cause differences in dye uptake in the fabric during dyeing giving a streaky dyeing. Products which contain yarns which were heat-set prior to fabrication of the product can have dye defects if the heat setting temperature varies from one yarn to another. Care must be taken to avoid this type of defect in products such as tufted carpet. Fabrics which are heat-set in open width continuous ranges may dye nonuniformly if heating is not uniform across the width or along the length of the fabric.

Dyeing of nylon with acid dyes is similar to dyeing of wool. Generally, the affinity of an acid dye for nylon is greater than for wool. Extreme care must be taken to apply acid dyes uniformly to nylon since levelling of nonuniform dyeings is difficult. Uniform dyeing is accomplished by pH control, slow uniform heating of the dyebath, and judicious use of retarding agents just as is the case in dyeing of wool. The dyebath pH does not have to be as low to dye nylon as to dye wool with acid dyes because of the greater affinity of nylon for the dye. Since nylon contains fewer dye sites for acid dyes than does wool, dye compatibility problems are accentuated.

Nylon is a thermoplastic fiber. The rate of dyeing of thermoplastic fibers is very dependent on dyeing temperature. Acceptable rate of dyeing is achieved only at temperatures well above the second order transition temperature of the polymer. In the case of nylon, the absorption of dye by the fiber begins as low as 40°C and is rapid at temperatures below the boiling point of water. Therefore, dyeing can be done at temperatures below 100°C and pressurized dyeing equipment is not required. Although nylon is readily dyeable at temperatures below 100°C, higher dyeing temperature increases the migration and levelling tendency of the dye. Nylon containing physical irregularities which cause nonuniform dyeing at 100°C may dye uniformly at higher temperatures of around 115°C. High dyeing temperature and prolonged dyeing time help to produce uniform dyeing of nylon with physical irregularities because these dyeing differences are caused by differences in the rate of dyeing. However, dye defects caused by variations in amine end group content in the nylon polymer are not corrected by extending the dyeing time or using higher dyebath temperature.

Dyeing with Premetallized Dyes

The premetallized dyes are widely used where wash and light fastness requirements cannot be achieved with other types of dyes. The 1:1 premetallized acid dyes are applied to wool using strongly acidic conditions. Since the low pH used for these dyes may degrade polyamides, nylon is usually not dyed with the 1:1 premetallized dyes. The 1:1 premetallized dyes migrate only slightly. Since some leveling can be achieved by prolonged boiling, the dyebath is usually held near the boil for an extended time near the end of the dye cycle.

The 2:1 premetallized acid dyes are usually applied at near neutral pH and are widely used on nylon. Prolonged boiling is not necessary because the 2:1 premetallized dyes do not migrate from one dye site to another. Therefore, the 2:1 premetallized dyes must be applied uniformly by control of dyebath temperature and use of retarding agents.

After Treatment of Acid Dyeings

Acid dyeings can be after treated to improve fastness of the dye to washing. The agents used for this purpose are called syntans. The term "syntan" is short for synthetic tanning agent which is derived from an antiquated treatment called "back tanning." Back tanning consisted of treating the dyed fabric with tannic acid followed by treatment with tartar emetic. Syntans are usually phenol/formaldehyde copolymers containing sulfonated aromatic rings.

The mechanism by which syntans work is somewhat obscure. It is postulated that the sulfonic acid groups in the syntan absorb on amino groups near the fiber surface and serve as a barrier to diffusion of dye from the interior to the surface of the fibers.

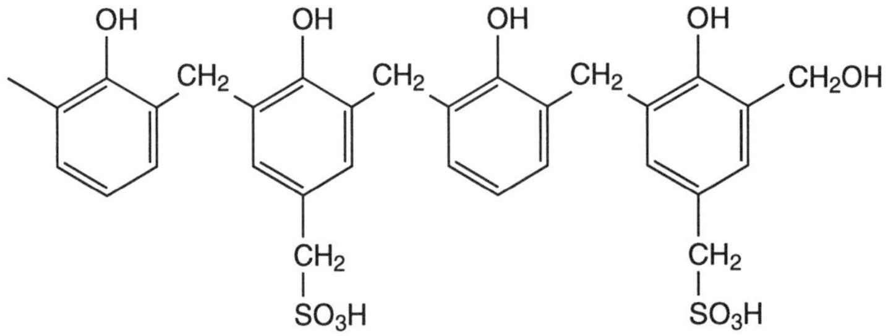

Basic Dyes

Basic dyes are sometimes called cationic dyes because the chromophore contains a positive charge. Basic dyes are used on fibers containing acidic groups that can interact with these cationic (basic) groups. The fibers that are dyeable with basic dyes contain either carboxyl, –COOH, or more commonly sulfonic acid, –SO_3H, groups. The bonds formed between the dye and fiber are salt linkages.

$$Fiber—SO_3H \quad + \quad R_3N^+—Dye\ Cl^- \quad \longrightarrow \quad Fiber—SO_3^-\ R_3N^+—Dye$$

Fiber with acidic sulfonic acid group	Dye with basic group; R usually CH_3	Dyed fiber with salt linkage between dye and fiber

Basic dyes are manufactured as the salt of the basic form, typically the chloride as shown above.

The color fastness properties of basic dyes vary greatly from one dye to another and depend on what fiber they are used on. As a general rule, wash fastness and particularly light fastness of basic dyes are poor on wool and other protein fibers. On the other hand, wash fastness and light fastness are very good to excellent on acrylic fibers.

Because of poor colorfastness properties on protein fibers, basic dyes are used to dye these fibers only in cases where exceptional brightness is needed and good color fastness is not a requirement. The largest consumption of basic dyes is for coloration of acrylic fibers.

Structural Characteristics

Basic dyes may be classified into the following two general types:
1. Localized charge or pendant cationic types where the charge is localized on one atom, usually a nitrogen atom, and
2. Delocalized charge types where the positive charge is distributed over the entire molecule.

Localized charge basic dyes are mainly azo and anthraquinone dyes to which a pendant cationic group has been attached.

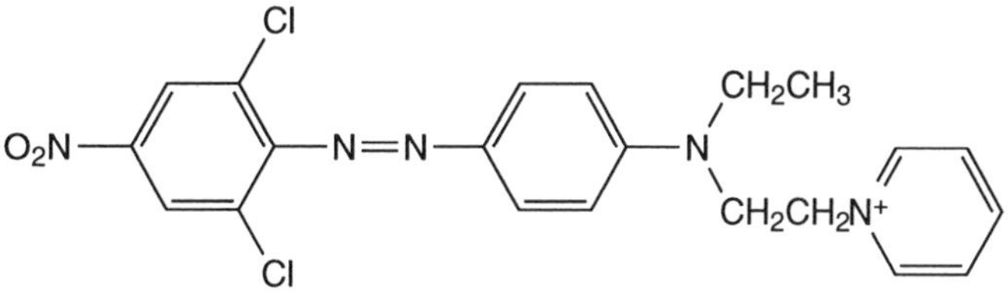

C.I. Basic Orange 30:1

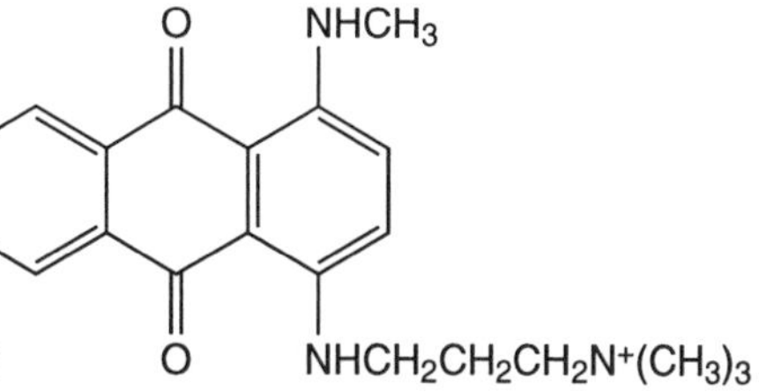

C.I. Basic Blue 22

Delocalized charge basic dyes have much greater tinctorial strength and are usually brighter in color than pendant charge types. Although many delocalized charge type basic dyes have been available for decades, they have very poor light fastness on protein fibers and were not used much. Many of these dyes have very good fastness on acrylic fibers and became popular when acrylic fibers were discovered. Many new basic dyes were also developed specifically for application to acrylic fibers.

Many delocalized charge basic dyes are azo or triphenyl methane structures in which the charge on the molecule is shared by all of the nitrogen atoms in the structure.

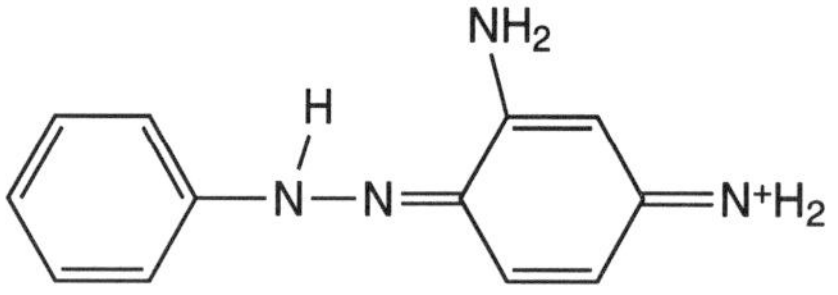

Chrysoidine (yellow)

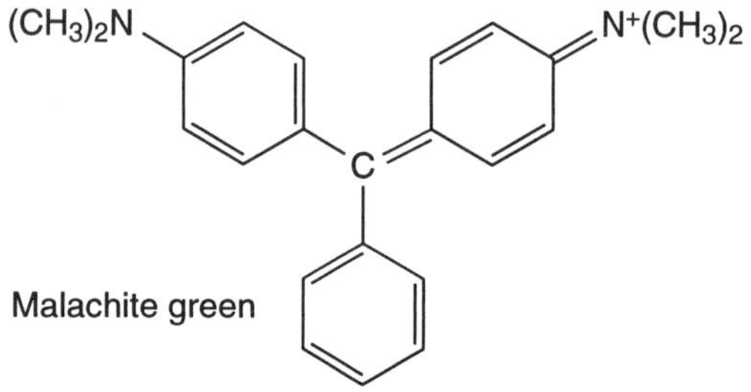

Malachite green

Other delocalized cationic dye structures include cyanines, oxazines, and thiazines.

Dyeing Methods

Although they can be applied to other fibers, the major use of basic dyes is on acrylic fibers. This discussion of application of basic dyes is restricted to acrylic fibers. Acrylic fibers are copolymers where at least 85% of the polymer consists of acrylonitrile units. Up to 15% consists of units provided by other vinyl monomers. The polymerization of acrylonitrile can be initiated by redox catalysts such as potassium persulfate or sodium bisulfite. These initiators produce polymers having sulfonic acid end groups.

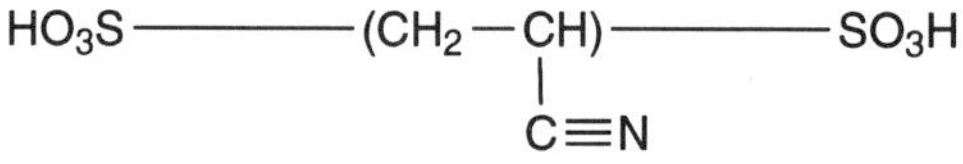

The fiber manufacturer can also incorporate sulfonic acid groups into the fiber by including a monomer such as styrene sulfonic acid in the polymerization.

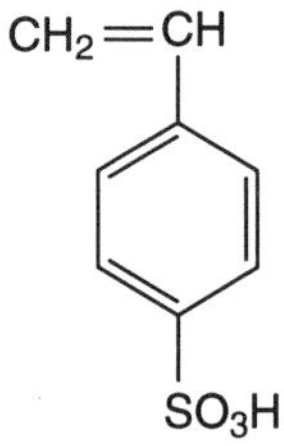

styrene sulfonic acid

Carboxyl groups which act as dye sites can also be incorporated into acrylic fibers.

The sulfonic acid groups and carboxylic acid groups serve as dye sites for basic dyes. Since the number of dye sites is limited, the amount of dye that can be absorbed by acrylic fibers is limited. Basic dyes in mixtures must be carefully selected to avoid incompatibility which may cause nonuniform or otherwise unsatisfactory dyeing. Compatibility of basic dyes is such an important issue that test methods to measure compatibility have been developed. In an AATCC test method to determine dye compatibility, basic dyes are assigned compatibility factors. A dye for which a compatibility factor is needed is applied in mixture with each of a series of basic dyes to acrylic fabric samples. The affinities of the test dyes vary over a wide range. Samples are dyed with the mixtures for various lengths of time. The compatibility factor assigned is the number of the test dye with which the unknown dye exhausts "on tone."

Acrylic fibers are mostly amorphous, but the molecules are highly oriented. Therefore, acrylic fibers do not absorb much water or dye at temperature below the glass transition temperature. When the dyebath temperature exceeds the glass transition temperature of about 60–85°C, the absorption rate of dye becomes very rapid. The sensitivity of dyeing rate to dyebath temperature changes makes control of dyeing temperature critical to uniform dyeing. Raising the temperature very slowly through the critical range is important since basic dyes do not migrate and level readily if applied non uniformly. Because they are mostly amorphous, acrylic fibers and fabrics are easily deformed at temperatures above the glass transition temperature. This tendency to deformation further complicates the dyeing process. Higher temperature promotes migration and leveling but increases susceptibility of the fabric to deformation and the fiber to degradation. The maximum dyeing temperature in most cases is 100°C.

Basic dyes are usually applied at pH values of 3.5–6.0. Basic dyes are most stable under slightly acidic conditions. Low pH retards the dyeing, and higher pH accelerates the dyeing. Use of low dyebath pH to retard the dyeing rate is desirable since the dyeing rate of acrylics is usually so rapid that uniform adsorption is difficult to achieve.

Rate of dyeing of acrylic fibers is difficult to control without auxiliary chemicals. Cationic retarders are commonly used to assist in applying the dye uniformly. Some cationic retarders are cationic surfactants which compete with the dye cations for dyesites in the fiber.

The key to using these cationic retarders is to achieve the required degree of rate retardation without blocking the dye molecules from being absorbed by the fiber. This is achieved by matching the cationic retarder with the particular dyes being used. Test methods have been developed to assist in matching cationic retarders and cationic dyes.

Another type of cationic retarder is polymeric. These high molecular weight polyquaternary ammonium compounds are too large to diffuse into the fiber. They occupy the fiber surface, and since they have multiple cationic groups, slow the initial absorption rate of basic dye molecules onto the fiber surface.

Anionic rate retarders for basic dyeing are also available. The anionic retarders function by forming a finely divided insoluble complex with dye molecules in the dyebath. The complex absorbs on the fiber surface in the early stages of dyeing. As the dyebath temperature is raised, the complex breaks up, and the evenly distributed dye molecules diffuse into the fiber leaving the anionic retarder in the dyebath.

Salts such as sodium sulfate also behave as rate retarders for basic dyes. The sodium ions are believed to function like the cationic retarders. The relatively small sodium ions diffuse into the fiber in the early stages of dyeing and occupy dyesites. Eventually, the dye ions which have greater affinity for the dye sites diffuse in and displace the sodium ions.

Dyeing methods based on dyebath temperature manipulation have been developed for dyeing acrylic fibers with basic dyes. One of these methods is based on increasing the dyebath temperature in small steps to 100°C over a period of about 90 minutes followed by boiling for 90 minutes. The dyebath is cooled before being drained. The method is not suitable for all dyes. In other methods, the dyes are added after the material and dyebath have been heated to 90–95°C. The bath is then heated to the boil and maintained at that temperature for some period. Dyeing at high temperatures (as high as 110°C) has also been shown to improve leveling of basic dyes on acrylic fibers. However, fiber degradation at these high temperatures particularly above 110°C may be unacceptable.

Acrylic materials are usually dyed using batch processes. The dyeings can be done on loose stock, yarn, or fabric.

Continuous pad-steam methods may also be used for certain types of material. However, long steaming times are required to give suf-

ficient diffusion of dye into the fiber. The extended steaming requirement makes continuous dyeing of acrylic fabrics or yarns impracti-
cal. Continuous dyeing of acrylics is usually restricted to tow or loose
stock dyeing.

Disperse Dyes

The disperse dye class is so named because these dyes are almost
insoluble in water and are used as finely divided aqueous dispersions. Disperse dyes can be applied to nylon, cellulose acetate,
acrylics and occasionally other fibers, but the major consumption
is for dyeing of polyester. Disperse dyes comprise the only dye
class generally acceptable for dyeing of polyester and cellulose
acetate. Wash fastness and light fastness of disperse dyes is generally good. Fastness to dry heat is deficient in some disperse dyes
because they sublime at relatively low temperature. Certain disperse dyes are susceptible to degradation by ozone and atmospheric contaminants. Some disperse dyes hydrolyze at high temperature especially under alkaline conditions. Therefore, dyeing
with disperse dyes is virtually always done using slightly acidic
conditions.

Structural Characteristics

The two most common types of disperse dyes are monazo and
anthraquinone.

C.I. (Colour Index) Disperse Blue 183   C.I. Disperse Blue 73

Other structural types of disperse dyes include diazo, nitrodiphenyl
methane, styryl, benzodifuranone, and quinophthalone. Development
work on disperse dyes is on-going, and new products and structures
are frequently introduced.

Disperse dyes are nonionic which accounts for their low solubil-

Table 5-6.   Solubility of Some Azo and Anthraquinone Disperse Dyes in Water

Disperse Dye C.I. Disperse-	Chemical Type	Water Solubility (mg/l at 80°C)
Orange 1	Azo	0.7
Red 9	Anthraquinone	8.2
Red 15	Anthraquinone	5.4
Orange 3	Azo	9.2
Red 11	Anthraquinone	9.3
Yellow 1	Azo	75.2

Data from Peters, 1975

ity in water. However, they do contain some polar groups and are very slightly soluble in water as indicated in Table 5-6.

Batch Dyeing with Disperse Dyes

The most widely accepted mechanism for disperse dyeing of hydrophobic fibers contends that the fiber absorbs dye molecules which are dissolved in the dyebath. When a dissolved dye molecule is absorbed from the dyebath, it is replenished by a molecule of dye from the dispersion of dye particles in the dyebath.

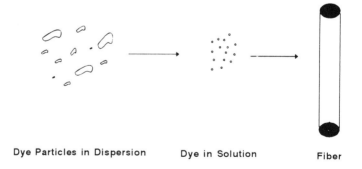

Dye Particles in Dispersion   Dye in Solution   Fiber

The addition of dispersing agent to the dyebath increases the rate of dyeing of disperse dyes. Since the dispersing agent is known to increase the solubility of dye in the dyebath, the effect of surfactant on dyeing rate is consistent with the proposed mechanism. The fact that higher temperature increases the solubility of the dye and also the rate of dyeing is also supportive of the proposed mechanism.

The nature of attachment of disperse dyes to hydrophobic fibers has been debated by various writers. The so called "solid solution

Figure 5-3. Linear equilibrium adsorption isotherm illustrating dyeing behavior typical of disperse dyes

DYE CONCENTRATION IN FIBER

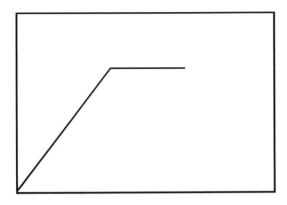

DYE CONCENTRATION IN DYEBATH

theory" is accepted by many. The solid solution theory proposes that the disperse dye molecule is simply dissolved by the hydrophobic fiber. If this is the case, then the dye should partition itself between the fiber and the dyebath in direct proportion to its solubility in these two phases. The resulting equilibrium absorption isotherms should be linear up to the limit of dye solubility in either the dyebath or the fiber as is shown in Figure 5-3. This linear absorption behavior has been observed with many disperse dyes.

The rate at which disperse dyes are absorbed by hydrophobic fibers is very dependent on dyeing temperature. The "free volume model" explains the effect of temperature on dyeing rate. The free volume model is based on the concept that a disperse dye molecule must have a certain size "hole" through which it can move in order to diffuse into the fiber. At low temperature the fiber molecules are frozen in place in the amorphous regions, there are few holes large enough for diffusion of dye molecules, and the dyeing rate is very slow. As shown in Figure 5-4, thermal expansion occurs as the temperature of the fiber is raised increasing the specific volume of the fiber, but molecular motion in the polymer is still restricted by inter-molecular forces. When the temperature exceeds a critical point (usually called the glass transition temperature), the slope of the specific volume-temperature plot increases. At temperature above the glass transition temperature, rotation of poly-

Figure 5-4.   Relation between specific volume and temperature of fibers

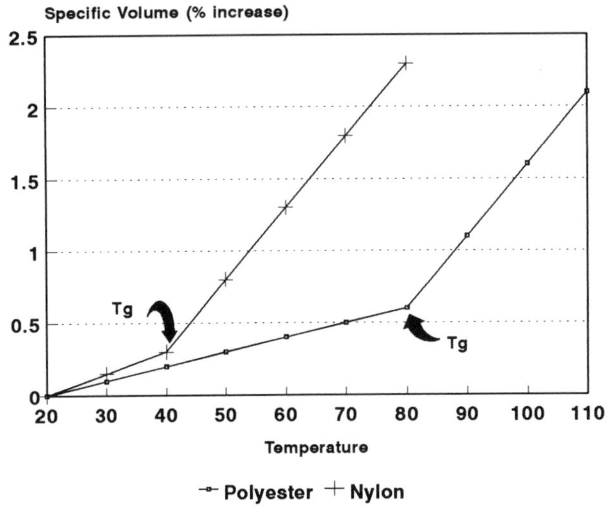

mer segments occurs. According to the free volume theory, movement of a polymer segment requires the presence of space (free volume) into which the segment can move. In turn, the rotating segment vacates a space making a hole through which a dye molecule can diffuse. As the temperature is raised further, the extent of segmental motion and free volume continue to increase. This increase in free volume improves the probability of a dye molecule encountering a hole large enough to diffuse through. Therefore, as higher dyeing temperature increases the free volume of the fiber, the dyeing rate increases.

As Figure 5-4 indicates, the increase in specific volume of the fiber with increase in temperature is much greater at temperatures above the second order transition temperature of the fiber. Therefore, the temperature required to dye synthetic fibers at an appreciable rate is always greater than the second order transition temperature. Since the second order transition temperature of nylon is lower than that of polyester, nylon can be dyed at lower temperatures than can polyester. Actually, the temperature required to achieve an acceptable dyeing rate is usually much above the second order transition temperature of the fiber. The term "dyeing transition temperature" is sometimes used to refer to the temperature at which the dyeing rate of a synthetic fiber becomes rapid. The following dyebath temperatures are typical in application of disperse dyes:

Fiber	Typical Dyeing Temperature
Polyester	100–140°C
Nylon	80–120°C
Cellulose Acetate (2°)	85–90°C
Cellulose Triacetate	115°C
Acrylics	95–110°C

The temperature required to dye with disperse dyes depends on the thermal characteristics of the fiber being dyed and the particular disperse dyes being used.

Dye suppliers usually classify disperse dyes as low, medium, and high energy dyes. These "energy" levels are indicative of the temperature required for the dyes to diffuse into the fibers. Low energy dyes are usually relatively small molecules which have high diffusion rates. They usually have poor sublimation fastness. High energy disperse dyes are usually large or awkward molecular structures. They have slow diffusion rates in polyester and require high dyeing temperatures but usually have very good color fastness properties. Medium energy dyes are intermediate in properties between low and high energy dyes.

Polyester dyes slowly at temperatures of 100°C or lower. The preferred dyeing temperature is about 130°C which requires a pressurized dyeing vessel. The dyeing rate of polyester can be increased by the addition of a "carrier" to the dyebath. Carriers are relatively small organic substances that usually have affinity for polyester. Chlorobenzenes, orthophenyl phenol, biphenyl, chlorinated benzene, aromatic esters, chlorinated hydrocarbons, and many other substances increase the rate of dyeing of polyester and have been used as carriers. Several theories have been proposed to explain the function of carriers. Carriers may

1. decrease the second order transition temperature of the fiber,
2. enter the fiber and cause it to swell,
3. increase the solubility of dye in the dyebath, or
4. be attracted to the fiber surface and dissolve dye forming a concentrated layer of dye on the surface of the fiber.

Many believe that more than one of these mechanisms may contribute to carrier function.

Many carriers are formulated products supplied to textile manufacturing plants by chemical vendors. These proprietary products usually contain several substances. Polyester can be dyed at 100°C if a carrier is added to the dyebath. Carriers are sometimes used even if the dyeing is done in pressurized equipment at temperature above 100°C. Carriers may stay in the fiber after dyeing or may be vaporized when the dyed material is dried. The greatest disadvantage in use of carriers is the potential for pollution of air.

Certain nonionic surfactants are beneficial in high temperature batch dyeing of polyester. These nonvolatile, ethoxylated materials improve the compatibility of mixtures of disperse dyes and have been promoted as substitutes for conventional carriers in high temperature dyeing of polyester.

Disperse dyes can also be applied using a continuous method called the pad/thermosol or pad/thermofix process. The process consists of padding, drying the fabric, and fixing the dye with heat. The key to this process is the property of disperse dyes to sublime. The dye is deposited uniformly on the fabric in the padding and drying steps, and the fabric is heated to a temperature of 190–230°C. At this temperature the dye sublimes, and the dye vapor is absorbed by the polyester fibers.

Disperse dyes are often used on hydrophobic fibers in a blend with a hydrophilic fiber like cotton. Although the hydrophilic fiber is not dyeable with the disperse dye, it may be stained by the disperse dye. This staining is undesirable because it is not fast to washing and may cause the wash fastness rating of the fabric to be unacceptable. Therefore, the stain must be removed by thoroughly washing the fabric before completion of the dye cycle. In a batch process this is sometimes done with a solution of a reducing agent and caustic soda and is called "reduction clearing."

Bibliography

1. AATCC Publications Committee, The Application of Vat Dyes, AATCC Monograph No. 2, American Association of Textile Chemists and Colorists, Research Triangle Park, NC, 1953.
2. Beech, W.F., Fibre-Reactive Dyes, SAF International, Inc., New York, NY, 1970.
3. Colour Index, 3rd Edition, The Society of Dyers and Colourists and the American Association of Textile Chemists and Colorists, 1971.
4. Datye, K.V. and A.A. Vaidya, Chemical Processing of Synthetic Fibers and Blends, John Wiley and Sons, New York, NY, 1984.
5. Gregory, P., in Topics in Applied Chemistry: The Chemistry and Application of Dyes, Plenum Press, New York, New York, 1990.

6. Johnson, K., Dyeing of Synthetic Fibers: Recent Developments, Noyes Data Corporation, Park Ridge, NJ, 1974.

7. Nunn, D.M., The Dyeing of Synthetic-Polymer and Acetate Fibres, Dyers Company Publications Trust, Society of Dyers and Colourists, Bradford, England, 1979.

8. Peters, R.H., Textile Chemistry, Volume III, Elsevier Scientific Publishing Company, New York, NY, 1975.

9. Preston, C., The Dyeing of Cellulosic Fibres, Dyers Company Publications Trust, Society of Dyers and Colourists, Bradford, England, 1986.

10. Shore, J. Ed., Colorants and Auxiliaries, Volume 1, Dyers Company Publications Trust, Society of Dyers and Colourists, Bradford, England, 1990.

11. Shore, J., Ed., Colorants and Auxiliaries, Volume 2, Dyers Company Publications Trust, Society of Dyers and Colourists, Bradford, England, 1990.

12. Trotman, E.R., Dyeing and Chemical Technology of Textile Fibres, 6th Edition, John Wiley and Sons, New York, NY, 1984.

13. Waring, D.R. and Geoffrey Hallas, Topics in Applied Chemistry: The Chemistry and Application of Dyes, Plenum Press, New York, New York, 1990.

Chapter 6

Dyeing and Printing Processes

Textile materials may be dyed using batch, continuous, or semi-continuous processes. The type of process used depends on several things including type of material (fiber, yarn, fabric, fabric construction, garment), generic type of fiber, size of dye lots, and quality requirements in the dyed fabric.

Machinery for dyeing must be resistant to attack by acids, bases, other auxiliary chemicals, and dyes. Type 316 stainless steel is usually used as the construction material for all parts of dyeing machines that will come in contact with dye formulations.

Batch Dyeing Processes

Batch processes are the most common method to dye textile materials. Batch dyeing is sometimes called exhaust dyeing because the dye is gradually transferred from a relatively large volume dyebath to the material being dyed over a relatively long period of time. The dye is said to exhaust from the dye bath to the substrate. Textile substrates can be dyed in batch processes in almost any stage of their assembly into a textile product including fiber, yarn, fabric, or garment. Generally, flexibility in color selection is better and cost of dyeing is lower the closer dye application is to the end of the manufacturing process for a textile product.

Some batch dyeing machines operate at temperatures only up to 100°C. Enclosing the dye machine so that it can be pressurized provides the capability to dye at temperatures higher than 100°C. Cotton, rayon, nylon, wool and some other fibers dye well at temperatures of 100°C or lower. Polyester and some other synthetic fibers dye more easily at temperatures higher than 100°C.

The three general types of batch dyeing machines are those in which the fabric is circulated, those in which the dyebath is circulated while the material being dyed is stationary, and those in which

Figure 6-1.   Dye beck

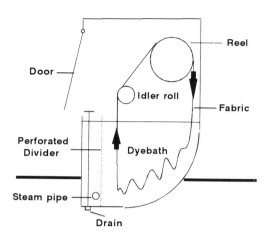

both the bath and material are circulated. Fabrics and garments are commonly dyed in machines in which the fabric is circulated. The formulation is, in turn, agitated by movement of the material being dyed. Fiber, yarn, and fabric can all be dyed in machines which hold the material stationary and circulate the dyebath. Jet dyeing is the best example of a machine that circulates both the fabric and the dyebath. Jet dye machines are excellent for knit fabrics but woven fabrics may also be dyed using jet machines. Following are examples of some batch dyeing machines.

Becks

Atmospheric becks may be used for dyeing at temperatures up to 100°C. Pressurized becks are used for dyeing at temperatures higher than 100°C. As shown in Figure 6-1, a dye beck consists of a reservoir or trough which contains the dye bath and a reel to move the loop of fabric through the dye formulation. The liquor ratio employed in becks is typically 15–1 or higher although becks using liquor ratio of as low as 4–1 are available.

The dye beck is sometimes called a winch because of the winch mechanism used to move the fabric. The ends of the fabric piece to be dyed are sewn together to make a continuous loop. The reel pulls the fabric out of the dye liquor in the trough and over an idler roll. After leaving the reel, the fabric slides down the back wall of the beck and gradually works its way from the back toward the front of the machine. Several loops of fabric of about the same length are dyed simultaneously. The individual loops are separated from one another by a dividing device called the peg rail extending the width of the machine. The peg rail contains smooth pegs spaced several cm apart to provide an opening through which the fabric rope can pass. Loops of fabric are typically 50 to 100 meters long depending on the weight of the fabric and other factors. The number of loops processed depends on the size of a particular machine and may vary from only one loop in a laboratory or sample machine to 50 or more loops in a large production machine.

The trough is slanted at its rear to allow the fabric layers to slide down into the dye liquor and move gradually toward the front of the machine. A deep trough and steep sloping back may work well for fabrics which do not crease easily while a shallower more gradual slope helps to prevent creasing. The idler roll presses some of the excess dye liquor from the fabric improving exchange of the liquid in the fabric with that in the trough.

Chemicals and dyes used in the dyeing are added to a compartment at the front of the beck. The divider separating the compartment from the trough is perforated allowing the added chemicals to gradually become mixed with the liquor in the trough.

Live steam is injected into the compartment to heat the liquor to the required temperature. The injection of steam vigorously agitates the compartment and aids in mixing the dyes and chemicals into the dye liquor. The steam injected into the beck condenses in the liquor so some dilution of the dye liquor must be tolerated.

The greatest advantages of becks are simplicity, versatility, and relatively low price. Becks subject fabrics to relatively low lengthwise tension and encourage the development of yarn crimp and fabric bulk. However, becks tend to use large amounts of water, chemicals, and energy. Becks may cause abrasion, creasing, and distortion of some fabrics.

A continuous strand instead of the usual multiple loops of fabric can be dyed if the beck has this capability. In this system a single long strand of fabric is gradually spiraled through the dye formulation from one side of the beck to the other. This method decreases the requirements for material handling, reduces waste, and eliminates the necessity for trimming and sewing of individual loops.

Figure 6-2.   Jet dye machine

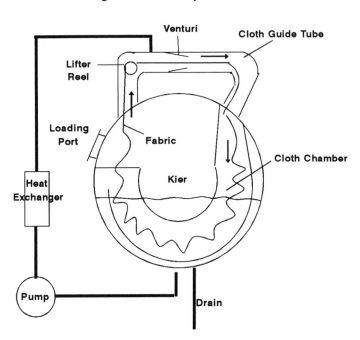

Jet Dyeing

Jet dye machines resemble becks in that the fabric is sewn into a continuous loop which is circulated through the machine. However, the cloth transport mechanism is dramatically different in these two types of machines. Figure 6-2 shows a schematic diagram of a jet dye machine. A high speed jet of dye liquid created by a venturi transports the fabric through the cloth guide tube of the jet machine. A jet machine has a cloth guide tube for each loop of fabric being processed. A powerful pump circulates the liquor through a heat exchanger outside of the main vessel and back into the jet machine. The fabric travels at high velocity of 200–800 meters per minute while it is in the cloth guide tube. The fabric leaving the cloth guide tube enters a larger capacity cloth chamber and gradually advances back toward the cloth guide tube.

Jet dye machines are usually pressurized to provide for high temperature dyeing capability. High temperature jet dye machines are especially suitable for delicate fabrics made of texturized polyester. The jet principle is also used in atmospheric machines designed for dyeing temperatures up to 100°C.

Jet dye machines provide the following advantages compared to atmospheric becks for dyeing fabrics made from texturized polyester.

1. Vigorous agitation of fabric and dye formulation in the cloth tube increases the dyeing rate and uniformity.
2. Rapid circulation of fabric through the machine minimizes creasing because the fabric is not held in any one configuration for very long at a time.
3. Lengthwise tension on the fabric is low so the fabric develops bulk and fullness of handle.
4. Dyeing at high temperature of about 130°C gives rapid dyeing, improved dye utilization, improved fastness properties, and makes possible the elimination of carriers which are required when dyeing at lower temperatures.
5. The lower liquor ratio used in jet dyeing allows shorter dye cycles and saves chemicals and energy.

Some disadvantages of jet dye machines compared to becks are as follows:

1. Capital and maintenance costs are higher.
2. Limited accessibility makes cleaning between dyeings and sampling for color during the dye cycle difficult.
3. The jet action tends to make formulations foam in partially flooded jet machines.
4. The jet action may damage the surface of certain types of fabrics.

Jet dyeing machinery evolved steadily after invention of the machine in 1961. The first machines were partially flooded. Fully flooded machines keep the fabric completely submerged during the dye cycle. This prevents the formation of longitudinal creases which occur when the fabric is lifted from the bath in a partially flooded machine. Fully flooding the machine also prevents formation of foam. The so-called "soft flow" machines use the same principle of a transport tube as a jet machine where the fabric is transported in a stream of dye liquor. However, transport of the fabric in soft flow jet machines is assisted by a driven lifter reel. These machines either eliminate the high velocity jet or use a jet having lower velocity than that used on conventional jet dye machines. The soft flow machines are more gentle on the fabric than conventional jet machines. Jet

Figure 6-3.   Dye jig

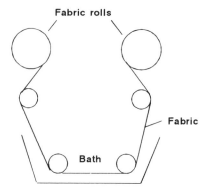

machines offering capability of very low liquor ratios of about 5–1 are also available.

Jigs

As shown in Figure 6-3, a jig consists of a trough for the dye or chemical formulation. The fabric from a roll on one side of the machine is run through the formulation in the trough and wound up on a roll on the opposite side of the jig. When the second roll is full, the drive is reversed, and the fabric is transferred through the formulation back to the first roll. Several passes are usually made.

The formulation in a jig is usually heated by injection of live steam into the bottom of the trough through a perforated pipe across the width of the jig. Closed coils containing high pressure steam can also be used to heat a jig. Live steam heats the formulation faster than closed coils but dilutes the formulation. Automatic devices control temperature and reverse the direction of the fabric when required on modern jigs.

A dye jig is usually used for dyeing at atmospheric pressure; however, high-pressure high-temperature jigs have been made. The top of a jig is usually covered to minimize heat loss to the atmosphere, keep the temperature uniform on all parts of the fabric, and minimize exposure of the formulation to air. Minimizing exposure to air is most important when using sulfur and vat dyes since these can be oxidized by atmospheric oxygen.

Maximum batch size on a jig may be up to several thousand meters of fabric. Jigs exert considerable lengthwise tension on the fabric and are, therefore, more suitable for woven than for knit fab-

Figure 6-4. Package dye machine

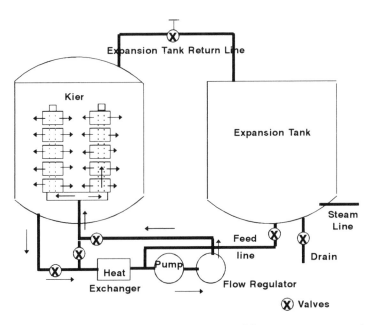

rics. Since the fabric is handled in open width, a jig is very suitable for fabrics which crease if dyed in rope form.

Package Dyeing

The term package dyeing usually refers to dyeing of yarn which has been wound on perforated cores so that dye liquor can be forced through the package. Packages may be tubes, cheeses, or cones. Cores for dye packages may be rigid stainless steel, plastic, or paper. Plastic and paper types are usually intended to be used only once while stainless steel cores may be reused indefinitely. Plastic cores as well as stainless steel springs are used as compressible cores. These compressible cores allow more packages to be forced into the dye vessel and increase the capacity of the machine.

As shown in Figure 6-4, the yarn packages are placed on perforated spindles on a frame which fits into a pressure vessel where dyeing takes place. The dye vessel is cylindrical and has domed ends. The top cover, which must be opened for loading and unloading, is secured during dyeing by bolts or a sliding ring which can be quickly locked. Most package dyeing machines are capable of dyeing temperatures up to 135°C. The number of packages may vary from as few as one in a laboratory machine to several hundred in a large production machine.

The dye formulation is pumped through the perforations in the spindles and package cores into the yarn. The flow of liquid can be either from inside to outside of the package or outside in. Periodic reversal of the direction of flow improves uniformity of dyeing.

A package dye machine has an expansion tank mounted alongside the dye vessel. The expansion tank accommodates the increased volume of dyebath resulting from thermal expansion when the bath is heated. Chemical and dye adds are made to the vessel through the expansion tank.

The dye liquor in a package dye machine is usually heated by a heat exchanger using high pressure steam as the energy source. The steam coils for heating the liquor are also usually used as cooling coils after the dye cycle is completed.

Liquor ratio in a package dye machine is typically about 10–1 when the machine is fully loaded. Use of lower liquor ratio can save water, energy, and chemicals. The liquor ratio can be lowered by only partially flooding the machine. If the liquor covers all of the packages but does not fill the top dome of the machine, the liquor ratio is only slightly lower than it is in a fully flooded machine. If only the base of the carrier is covered with dye solution, the liquor ratio may be as low as 4–1. However, the direction of liquor flow can only be inside-out using this arrangement. High quality dyeings may be more difficult to achieve at very low liquor ratio in package dye machines.

Raw stock, tow , and other materials can be dyed using the same principles as package dyeing. A basket (cage) is usually used to hold these materials during the dyeing.

Beam Dyeing

The principles of beam dyeing are essentially identical to those of package dyeing. Either yarn or fabric can be beam dyed. The fabric or yarn is wound on a perforated beam. A beam machine may be designed to hold a single beam or multiple beams in a batch. Beam dyeing of warps is practical in producing patterned fabrics where the warp yarn will be one color and the filling will be another color.

Figure 6-5. Side paddle dye machine (overhead view)

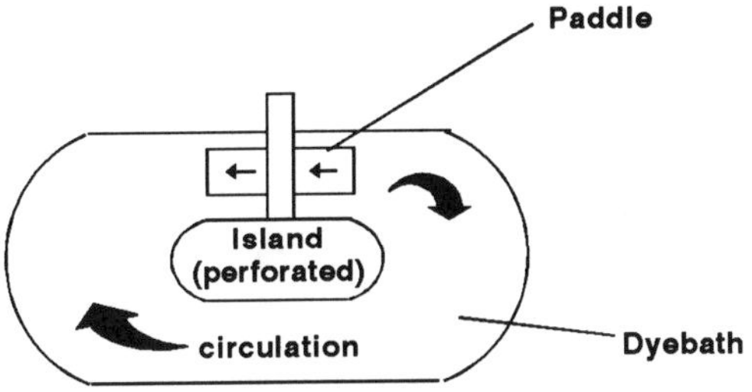

Skein Dyeing

In skein dyeing (also called hank dyeing), skeins of yarn are mounted on a carrier which has rods (sticks) at the top and bottom to hold the skeins. The skeins are suspended in the dye machine and dye liquor is gently circulated around the hanging skeins. Perforated plates may be used at the top and bottom of the machine to help provide uniform flow of the dye liquor. Alternatively, the dye liquor may be pumped through perforations in the sticks so that it cascades down over the hanging skeins. Skein dyeing produces good bulk in the yarn because of the low tension on the yarn in the dyebath. The method is used mainly for bulky yarns like acrylics and woolens for knitted outerwear and hand knitting. Woolen carpet yarn is sometimes skein dyed.

Skein dyeing uses a high liquor ratio and a lot of energy. Uniform dyeing is difficult to achieve in a skein dyeing machine. Slow winding and back winding requirements of the process make it labor intensive. Package dyeing has replaced some of the skein dyeing done in the past even though the yarn bulkiness achieved in skein dyeing is usually not matched in package dyeing.

Paddle Machines and Rotary Drums

Paddle machines and rotary drum machines can be used to dye textiles in many forms, but these two methods are used mostly to dye garments. Both of these types of machines are usually heated by injection of steam directly into the dyebath. Schematic diagrams of side paddle and overhead paddle dye machines are shown in Figures 6-5 and 6-6. The side paddle machine is shown from a top view since this gives the best view of the location of the parts of the

Figure 6-6.   Paddle dye machine

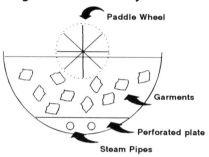

machine. The paddle circulates the bath and garments around a per-forated central island. Chemicals, steam for heat, and water are added inside the perforated central island. The overhead paddle machine is simply a vat with a paddle having blades the full width of the machine. The blades dip a few cm into the vat to stir the bath and push the garments down keeping them submerged in the dye liquor.

A rotary drum machine is a cylindrical vessel slightly larger than its internal perforated drum which holds the material to be dyed. The perforated drum is divided into several chambers each having its own door through which it can be loaded and unloaded. The drum rotates horizontally as is shown in the schematic diagram in Figure 6-7. Rotary drum machines are commonly used to dye hosiery.

Tumblers

Tumblers are very similar in principle to rotary dye machines

Figure 6-7.   Rotary drum dye machine

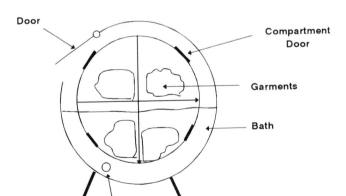

except that they are usually larger. They also resemble large commercial dry cleaning machines. Tumblers have a perforated drum which rotates inside a larger vat which contains the dye or chemical formulation. The drum can be divided into compartments to assist in agitating the garments, or baffles around the periphery of the drum may serve to tumble the garments in the dye formulation. These machines extract some of the water by centrifugal action after completion of the dyeing. Tumblers are used for dyeing garments and for wet processing (prewashing) garments dyed with indigo. Modern machines of this type are usually equipped with automatic controls, and some are designed to tilt forward to provide for easy loading and unloading of batches of garments.

Continuous Dyeing Processes

Continuous dyeing is most suitable for woven fabrics. Most continuous dye ranges are designed for dyeing of blends of polyester and cotton. Nylon carpets are sometimes dyed in continuous processes, but the design of the range for continuous dyeing of carpet is much different than that for flat fabrics. Warps can also be dyed in continuous processes. Examples of this are slasher dyeing and long chain warp dyeing usually using indigo.

Continuous Dyeing of Polyester-Cellulose Blend Fabrics

A continuous dye range is efficient and economical for dyeing long runs of a particular shade. Tolerances for color variation must be greater for continuous dyeing than batch dyeing because of the speed of the process and the large number of process variables that can affect the dye application. The process as shown in Figure 6-8 is often designed for dyeing both the polyester and cotton in a blend fabric in one pass through the range. The polyester fibers are dyed in the first stages of the range by a pad-dry-thermofix process. The cellulosic fibers are dyed in the latter stages of the range using a pad-steam process.

Fabric which was previously prepared for dyeing enters the dye range from rolls. A scray is used to accumulate fabric entering the range so that the range can continue to run while a new roll of fabric is sewn to the end of the strand being run. Uniformity of application of dye requires that continuous dyeing be done in open width. Typical line speed in continuous dyeing is 50 to 150 meters per minute.

Figure 6-8.   Schematic diagram of a continuous dye range

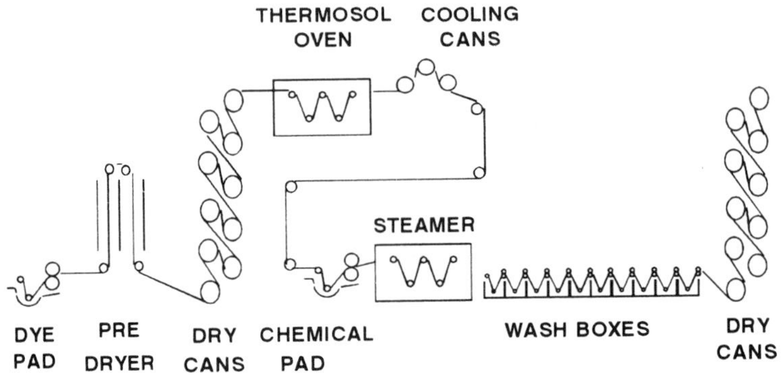

THERMOSOL   COOLING
OVEN   CANS

STEAMER

DYE   PRE   DRY   CHEMICAL   WASH BOXES   DRY
PAD   DRYER   CANS   PAD   CANS

Padding is a critical step in continuous dyeing. The disperse dye formulation (and sometimes the dyes for the cellulosic component) are applied in the first padder. The fabric is immersed in the dye formulation usually at room temperature and squeezed to give a uniform add-on of dye formulation across the width and along the length of the fabric. Low temperature in the formulation in the padder minimizes tailing. Higher temperature promotes wetting of the fabric in the short time the fabric dwells in the pad formulation.

The wet fabric leaving the padder enters a dryer to remove moisture and leave the dye uniformly deposited on the fabric. Radiant predrying using infrared energy inhibits migration of the dye. Drying is completed using steam-heated cylinders.

A thermal treatment called thermosoling fixes the disperse dye on the polyester fibers. The thermosol oven heats the fabric to a temperature of 390–430°F the exact temperature depending on the particular dyes being applied. The dye sublimes and diffuses into the polyester fibers during the thermosol treatment. The fabric dwells in the thermosol oven for about 1 to 2 minutes.

The cooling cans lower the fabric temperature so that it does not heat the solution in the chemical pad. The chemical padder applies the dyes (and sometimes chemicals) for the cellulosic fibers.

The steamer heats the wet fabric so that the dye can diffuse into the cellulosic fibers. The fabric usually dwells in the steamer for 30–60 seconds.

The washing section of the range is used for rinses, chemical treatments which may be required to complete the dyeing, and washing of the fabric to remove unfixed dye and auxiliary chemicals used in

Figure 6-9. Example of dye applicator for continuous carpet dye machine

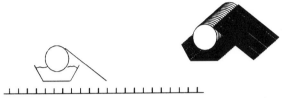

the dyeing. The dye and chemical formulations used in the padders and wash boxes depend on the particular classes of dye being applied.

Pad-Batch Dyeing

Pad-batch dyeing is a semi continuous process used mainly for dyeing of cotton fabrics with reactive dyes. Both woven and knitted fabrics can be dyed using this method. Fabric is padded with a formulation containing dye, alkali, and other auxiliary chemicals. The padded fabric is accumulated on a roll or in some other appropriate container and stored for a few hours to give the dye time to react with the fiber. Time, temperature, alkalinity, and reactivity of the reactive dye all influence the process. Pad-batch dyeing is usually done at ambient temperature, but heating of the fabric during batching decreases the time required in the batching stage. Higher alkalinity and selection of more reactive types of reactive dyes also shortens the time required to complete the reaction. Typical batching times range from 4 hours to 24 hours. The batch may be rotated to prevent settling of the formulation and nonuniform dyeing.

Pad-batch techniques have also been applied in preparation of certain types of fabrics for dyeing. Scouring and bleaching of cotton can be done using a cold pad-batch process.

Continuous Dyeing of Carpet

A continuous dye range for carpet consists of a dye applicator and steamer. The process is designed for application of acid dyes to nylon. Carpet manufacturers are innovative in application of dye to produce special color effects on their product. As a result, many variations of dye applicators exist. Very high liquor ratio is usually required to produce good quality dyeing of carpet. As shown in Figure 6-9, a typical application method is to meter the dye solution

Figure 6-10.   Festoon steamer for continuous carpet dye machine

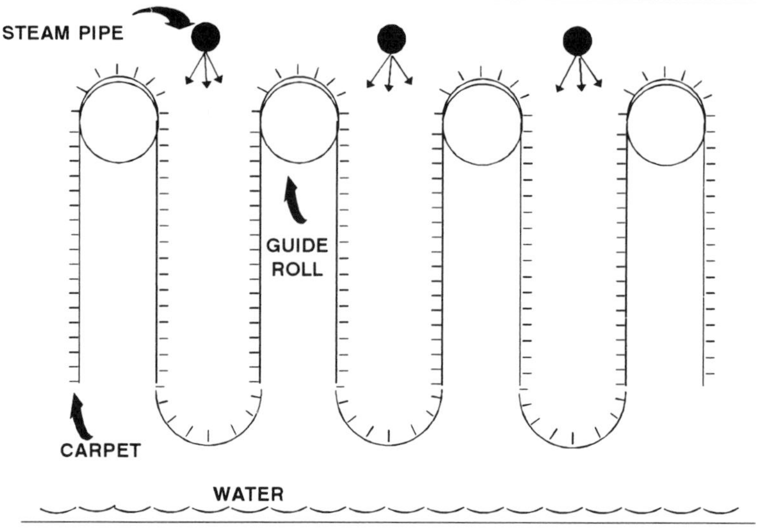

onto the surface of the carpet. The stream of dye being metered onto the carpet can be momentarily interrupted to produce patterned effects. Streams of different color dyes can be applied in different patterns to produce special effects.

Festoon steamers are used in continuous carpet dyeing so that the carpet always faces away from the guide rollers as shown in Figure 6-10. This prevents compression of the carpet pile by rollers in the steamer.

Long Chain Dye Range

Warp yarns are often dyed with indigo and sulfur dyes using a long chain dye range. The process is used where the warp will be one color and the filling another color or white, for example, in denim. A schematic diagram of the process is shown in Figure 6-11. Ball warps (sometimes called "logs" because of their cylindrical shape) are prepared as supply packages for the long chain dye range. A ball warp is a warp in which several hundred warp yarns are condensed into a rope and wound up as a single strand into a ball (log). The yarn from each ball warp constitutes a continuous rope (chain). A long chain dye range accommodates multiple ropes or chains side-by-side so that thousands of yarns are being dyed simultaneously. After exiting the long chain dye range, each rope is taken up in a separate container.

Figure 6-11.   Schematic diagram of long chain dye range

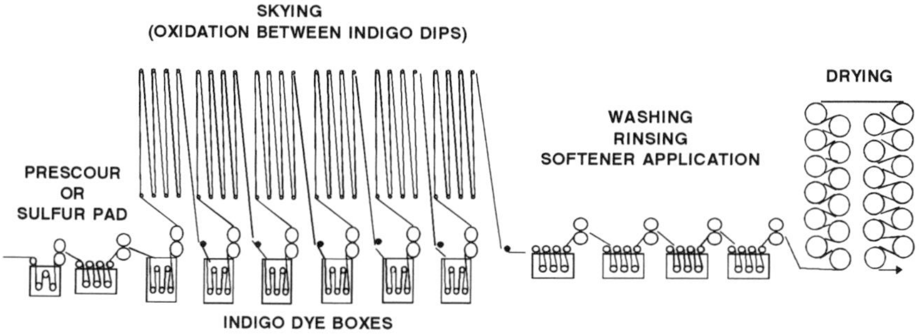

After dyeing, each individual warp is back wound onto a warper beam (section beam) and becomes a supply package for the slasher.

Long chain dye ranges usually have a wet-out box to wet and partially scour the yarn before it enters the dye application section of the range. The range contains a series of dye boxes which are designed to apply indigo. Indigo has low affinity for cellulose and must be applied in several stages called "dips." Each stage consists of immersing the yarn in a solution of the reduced indigo, squeezing to remove excess solution, and skying to allow air to oxidize the dye and make it insoluble. The shade gets progressively darker at each dip. The dye boxes are large and a circulation system involving all of the boxes is used to keep the indigo solution mixed well and prevent tailing of the shade.

A sulfur dye may be applied either before the indigo giving a "sulfur bottom" or after the indigo to give a "sulfur top." The use of a sulfur dye reduces the amount of the more expensive indigo needed to produce the shade and may also modify the fastness properties as required for a particular use of the fabric.

Printing Processes

Printing produces localized coloration of textile materials and is often used to produced colored patterns on fabrics or garments. Each color applied in a printing process must be applied in a separate step or position in the printing machine. Printing methods may be classified as direct, discharge, or resist.

Direct printing—Dye in a thickened formulation is applied to selected areas of the fabric producing a colored pattern.

Discharge printing—A discharging agent destroys dye on selected areas on a fabric which was previously dyed a solid shade. A white pattern remains where the dye was discharged. Alternatively, a discharge formulation containing dyes that are resistant to discharging produces a second color where the discharge is applied to the previously-dyed fabric.

Resist printing—Dye is applied to a fabric but not fixed. A resist formulation is printed on selected areas of the fabric. The resist agent prevents fixation of the dye in subsequent processing. The unfixed dye is washed away leaving a white pattern. If the resist agent is applied before the dye, the method is called a "preprint process." If the dye is applied first followed by the resist formulation, the method is called an "overprint process."

Resist and discharge printing have some similarities, but resist printing is more broadly applicable than discharge printing. Dyes that are fixed before discharging are difficult to destroy chemically, and only a few dyes can be discharged completely. On the other hand, unfixed dye can be removed relatively easily in resist printing processes.

The color in a printed design may be either pigment or dye. Pigments are applied using a binder in the print formulation to attach the pigment particles to the fabric. The pigment is physically attached to the surface of the fabric and does not penetrate into the fibers. Washing is usually not required after pigment application. One disadvantage of pigment printing is that the desired "hand" may be difficult to obtain. Improvements in hand and fastness properties of pigment prints with modern binders have increased the popularity of pigment prints. Fabric printed with dyes must be steamed or otherwise heated to effect fixation of the dye and must usually be washed after printing to remove unfixed dye.

Printing methods may also be classified according to the process used to produce the pattern. Screen printing and roller (gravure) printing are the two most common printing methods used in textiles. Ink jet printing, heat transfer printing, and methods based on reliefs are also practiced in textiles.

Figure 6-12.   Schematic diagram of rotary screen printing process

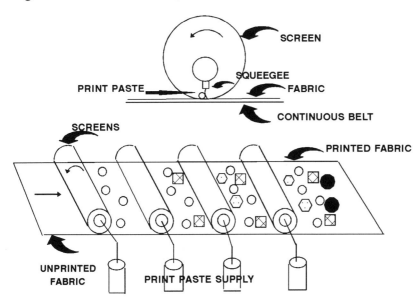

Screen Printing

Screen printing uses the principle of stencils. It is a "resist" method in the sense that the screen is made to resist penetration by the print formulation in areas where printing is not desired. Dye or pigment in a thickened formulation is forced by a blade or roller called a "squeegee" through a permeable screen onto a fabric underneath the screen. Screen printing may be done with either flat or cylindrical screens.

Rotary screen printing uses cylindrical screens as is shown in Figure 6-12. The cylindrical screens rotate allowing continuous printing of the fabric passing under the screens. Screens for rotary printing are made from very thin, perforated metal cylinders into which a pattern has been put. The pattern is made by blocking selected areas of the screen to passage of the print formulation. The squeegee may be either a flexible metal blade or a roller attracted by a magnet below the print belt. Rotary screen printing is a continuous, high production process. Rotary screen printing machines have a separate screen for each color in the pattern being printed as is shown in Figure 6-12. The fabric is transported on a continuous belt through the printing zone. The fabric is glued to the belt to keep it from sliding about so that the colors can be applied in the proper registration.

The pattern repeat is determined by the circumference of the screen. If the particular machine is designed to allow for it, discontinuous patterns can be printed by lifting the screens at predetermined intervals so that selected sections of the fabric are not printed.

The principle of flat screen printing is identical to that of rotary screen printing except that the screen is in a flat configuration. The screens are made from tightly woven fabrics usually of polyester or nylon monofilament yarn. The process is sometimes called "silk screen printing" because early screens were often made of silk fabric. The thin, permeable screen is mounted in a wooden or metal frame. Print formulation is pressed through the screen onto the fabric by moving the formulation across the screen with a flexible squeegee blade. Flat screen printing is a semi-continuous process since the screen must be lifted after printing a section in order to move a new area of fabric into position to be printed. Flat screen printing may be done on fabrics or garments and may be a manual (hand screen printing) or an automatic process.

Screens for Printing

A set of screens must be made in order to print a pattern. One screen is required for each different color in the pattern. Patterns for prints are conceived by designers and stylists. Artists do "color separations" , which are tracings of the areas occupied by each color in a pattern. These tracings or drawings are then used to make screens to print the various colors in the pattern.

Several different techniques can be used to make screens. The two most common methods are the lacquer method and laser engraving. Rotary screens provide a good example to describe the principles of screen making using these two methods. Both methods start with blank screens which are very thin metal cylinders perforated with many small holes. The holes are so small that they are not visible to the eye unless backlit so that light can pass through the screen. The size, shape, and number of holes in the screen are all important and affect the coverage and clarity of the print. The screens are first coated with a light sensitive emulsion (lacquer) to block all of the holes.

In the lacquer method, the tracings made in the color separation process are used to make films representing the colors in the pattern. The films are placed over the lacquered screens which are then

Figure 6-13.   Schematic diagram of roller printing process

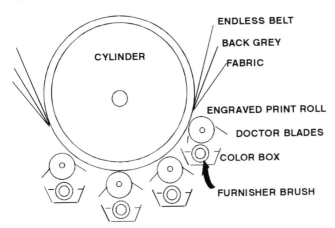

subjected to high intensity light to cure and harden the emulsion. The films prevent the patterned areas from being exposed to light so the emulsion is not cured where printing is desired. The emulsion is then washed out of the areas where it was not cured by the light. The perforations in the screen are thereby opened so color can pass through these areas of the screen during the printing process.

In the laser engraving method, the photo sensitive emulsion is cured over the entire screen. The tracings from the color separations are scanned into a computer which drives a laser beam to burn the emulsion from the areas of the screen where printing is desired.

Roller Printing (gravure printing)

The printing mechanism in roller printing is intaglio. A print roller is engraved with a pattern. Color deposited in the engravings is transferred to the fabric in the printing process. Figure 6-13 is a schematic of a roller printing machine.

A furnisher brush picks up print formulation from the color trough and transfers it to the print roll. A doctor blade scrapes color from the smooth, unengraved portions of the print roller and leaves the formulation in the engraved portions. The print formulation in the engraved portions of the print roller is transferred to the fabric. The lint doctor cleans the print roll of lint and trash as well as color picked up by the print roller from previously printed areas of the fabric. The cylinder supports the print blanket which provides a flexible surface which allows the fabric to be compressed into the engraved roll to accept the print formulation. The back grey prevents contamination of the blanket by print formulation which may pass through the fabric.

Printing with Reliefs

Block printing using wooden blocks with raised surface designs has been done for hundreds of years. Although block printing per se is not used commercially to print textiles today, a process using raised spongy surfaces on a roller is used to print carpets. Flexographic printing where the relief is produced by cutting designs into a rubber-covered roller is also used. Flexographic printing can also be used to print paper.

Ink Jet Printing

This technique is used mainly to produce patterns on carpets. It is fundamentally different from any of the techniques described previously. Patterns are produced on the carpet by impinging very small droplets of dye formulation on the carpet in a predetermined pattern. Two basic methods are used. In one method, droplets of color produced by nozzles that open and close quickly on command from a computer are fired onto the carpet passing beneath the nozzles. In another method, a stream of dye flows from a color bar and breaks into droplets as the stream falls toward the carpet passing underneath. Air jets mounted perpendicular to the stream of color deflect the color into a catch pan when printing is not desired. The air jets are controlled by computer so that a predetermined pattern of color droplets can be deposited on the carpet surface. Ink jet printing requires a color bar or series of nozzles for each color in the pattern.

Printing Formulations

Printing formulations contain color, binders, softeners, thickeners and other auxiliary chemicals. The rheology (flow characteristics) of a print paste is very important. The print paste must be fluid enough to pass through the screen without clogging the holes yet must not flow or wick once the formulation is on the fabric.

Print thickeners are water soluble polymers. Aqueous solutions of these polymers are high in viscosity (resistance to flowing) because of friction between the large molecules and by tangling and entrapping water in their structure. Under shear, such as stirring or being

Figure 6-14. Rheology of fluids

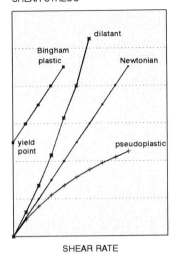

forced through a small opening, fluids may exhibit any of the behaviors exhibited in Figure 6-14. Shear rate can be thought of as stirring rate or velocity of movement of the fluid. Shear stress can be thought of as the force required to cause the fluid to move or to keep it moving at a certain velocity. A newtonian fluid is one in which the shear stress is directly proportional to the shear rate. By definition,

$$\text{viscosity} = \frac{\text{shear stress}}{\text{shear rate}} \, .$$

Therefore, the viscosity of a newtonian fluid is constant with change in shear rate as is shown in Figure 6-15. Non newtonian fluids either increase or decrease in viscosity when the shear rate changes. Pseudo plastic fluids decrease in viscosity when the shear rate is increased. Dilatant fluids increase in viscosity when the shear rate increases. Bingham plastics do not flow at all until the shear stress exceeds a certain level. Bingham plastics are said to have a "yield point." Catsup in a narrow-necked bottle exhibits Bingham plastic behavior.

Pseudoplastic behavior is often desirable in a print paste. A pseudoplastic print paste will decrease in viscosity and flow easily when it is pushed through the holes in a printing screen. After it is deposited on the fabric, the paste quickly increases in viscosity so that it stays where it was placed on the fabric. Since movement of the color is avoided, the print borders are sharp and well defined. Pseudoplastic

Figure 6-15.　Effect of shear on viscosity of fluids

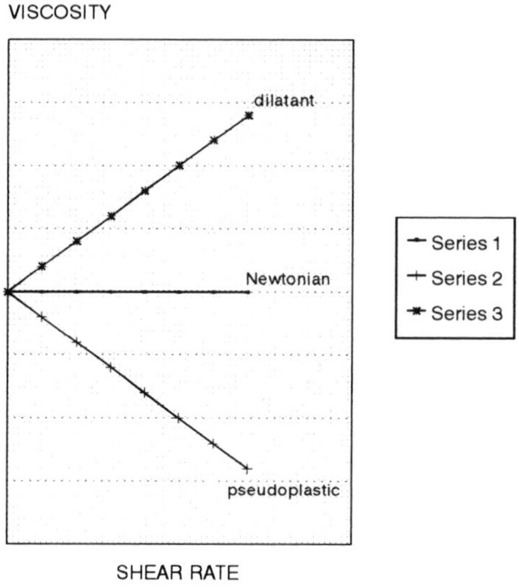

VISCOSITY

SHEAR RATE

behavior results from disentangling of polymer chains or decreased interaction of the polymer molecules with one another under conditions of shear.

Transfer Printing

In transfer printing, a design is transferred from preprinted paper to a textile fabric. Both woven and knitted fabrics can be transfer printed, but the major use of this method is on knitted fabrics. Woven and knitted fabrics can be transfer printed continuously while T-shirts, sweaters, or other partially or fully assembled garments can be printed using batch processes.

Both dry and wet systems have been developed for transfer printing. The most successful processes for transfer printing are dry methods which use heat to transfer the printing "inks" from paper to the fabric. The "inks" are actually disperse dyes which have sublimation temperatures around 200°C. The mechanism of transfer is sublimation of the dye from the paper which has low affinity for the dye to the fabric which has high affinity for the dye in the vapor phase. This is the same mechanism mainly responsible for fixation of disperse dyes on polyester in the thermosol process.

Equipment for heat transfer printing may be either continuous or batch. Batch processes use a flat bed press to hold the printed paper

Figure 6-16.   Calender type heat transfer printing machine

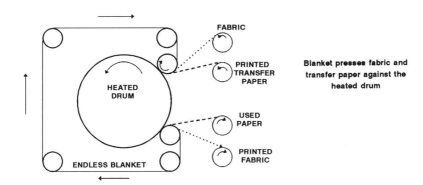

in contact with the fabric surface while heat is applied. This type of device is common for printing garments and can be used by the garment retailer at the point of sale of the garment.

Figure 6-16 shows a diagram of a continuous heat transfer printing machine. The machine is a calender with feeding devices for the fabric. Hot oil in the cylinder is usually the source of heat. A variation of this machine uses an external infrared heater as the energy source to heat the material and a slight vacuum to hold the fabric in position against the drum. The use of vacuum is said to improve the efficiency of dye transfer from the paper to the fabric.

Transfer printing requires a supply of paper with the appropriate design. The paper can be printed using any of the fabric printing methods described earlier including gravure, screen, and flexographic.

Dry thermal fixation of dye applies only to thermoplastic fibers such as polyester, nylon, acetate, and acrylic. Heat transfer printing is used most successfully on 100% polyester, but thermoplastic fibers in blends with nonthermoplastic fibers can also be heat transfer printed.

Fabrics of nonthermoplastic fibers such as cotton, wool, and silk require wet processes for fixation of dyes. Wet transfer printing processes have been developed to dye these fibers but are not nearly as common as heat transfer printing.

References

1. Gorondy, E.J., in Textile Printing: An Ancient Art and Yet So New, AATCC, Research Triangle Park, NC, 1975.
2. Kulkarni, S.V., C.D. Blackwell, A.L. Blackard, C.W. Stackhouse, and M.W. Alexander, Textile Dyeing Operations, Noyes Publications, Park Ridge, NJ, 1986.
3. Miles, L.W.C., Textile Printing, Merrow Publishing Company, Ltd., Watford, England, 1971.
4. Reichman, C., Transfer Printing Manual, National Knitted Outerwear Association, New York, NY, 1976.
5. Storey, J., Manual of Textile Printing, Van Nostrand Reinhold Company, New York, NY, 1974.
6. Trotman, E.R., Dyeing and Chemical Technology of Textile Fibres, 6th Edition, John Wiley and Sons, New York, NY, 1984.
7. Wyles, D.H. "Functional Design of Coloration Machines" in Engineering in Textile Coloration, C.W. Duckworth, Editor, Dyers Company Publication Trust, Bradford, England, 1983.

Chapter 7

Finishing

Finishing is a general term which usually refers to treatments on textile fabrics after dyeing or printing but before the fabrics are cut and sewn into garments, household textiles, or other products. However, many of the finishing principles covered in the following sections apply to treatment of yarns and garments as well.

Finishes have a wide variety of functions all of which are intended to make the fabric more suitable for its intended use. Functions of finishes include the following.

1. Accentuate or inhibit some natural characteristic of the fabric. Examples are softening, stiffening (firming), delustering, brightening, and changing surface characteristics.
2. Impart new characteristics or properties to the fabric. Durable press finishes, flame retardant finishes, and many other chemical treatments are examples of finishes which impart new characteristics.
3. Increase life and durability of the fabric.
4. Set the fabric so it maintains its shape and structure.
5. Set dyes.

Finishes may be categorized as mechanical or chemical. Often, mechanical finishing is thought of as modification of dry fabric by a machine and chemical finishing as treatment of fabric with aqueous solutions of chemicals. However, this distinction often fails because water and chemical formulations are often used in treatments that are best classified as mechanical finishes. Furthermore, most chemical finishes involve the use of machines which subject the fabric being finished to various degrees of mechanical action. Perhaps finishes can best be classified as mechanical or chemical depending on whether the mechanical treatment or the chemicals added are most responsible for imparting the desired characteristics to the fab-

Figure 7-1.   Schematic diagram of a five bowl calendar

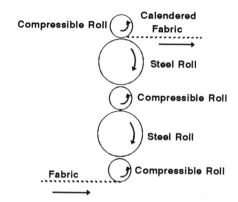

ric. Some overlap in classification of finishes as mechanical or chemical is inevitable.

Mechanical Finishes

Calendering

Calendering increases luster or otherwise changes the appearance of the fabric surface. Calendering consists of passing the fabric between rolls under pressure. Luster of the fabric is increased because the yarns are flattened making the fabric surface smoother and better able to reflect light. Adding moisture to the fabric and heating the calender rolls accentuate the effects of calendering. Calendered cotton fabrics have surface luster similar to that of mercerized cotton. However, much of the effect of calendering is lost when the fabric is washed while the luster of mercerized cotton is permanent. The durability of the luster achieved by calendering can be improved by adding resins to the fabric before calendering. Calendering to achieve luster is much less expensive than mercerization.

Calender rolls may be steel, paper-covered, rubber-covered, polished or engraved, cold or heated depending on the surface characteristics desired in the fabric. The rolls on a calendering machine are sometimes called bowls. A simple calender usually has three bowls while a more complex, high production calender may have several rolls allowing multiple nips of the fabric. Figure 7-1 shows a schematic diagram of a five bowl calender. One of the rolls at each

Figure 7-2. Engraved roll for schreiner calendering

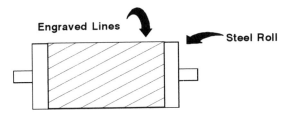

nip point in a calender must be a compressible material such as rubber or paper so that thick places in the fabric are not damaged.

In simple calendering the rolls run at the same speed and simply press the fabric. In friction calendering the surface speed of the rolls is different. Friction calenders polish the surface of the fabric producing a shiny effect.

Special surface effects can be achieved in calendering. Schreiner calenders give a very lustrous effect by impressing fine, parallel lines into the fabric surface. The fine lines are produced from shallow engravings in the surface of one of the calender rolls as is shown in Figure 7-2. Schreinering, as the process is sometimes called, embosses 300 or more fine lines per inch and produces very high luster.

Moiré luster finish is achieved by a concept similar to Schreinering. However, lines in the Moiré finish are produced by calendering two superimposed layers of fabric so that the yarns from one fabric make their impression on the other fabric. The luster in a Moiré calendered fabric is wavy rather than regular giving the appearance of water markings on the fabric.

Embossing raises figures or designs on the fabric. The fabric is pressed between heated engraved rolls to impress the pattern into the fabric. Adding a resin to the fabric improves the permanence of embossed patterns.

Mechanical Stabilization

Mechanical stabilization is most often done to prevent excessive shrinkage of fabrics when they are laundered or exposed to heat. Manufacturing processes create stresses and tensions in fibers, yarns, and fabrics. Water and heat provide the opportunity for these stresses to relax. Relaxation of stresses in the fabric and swelling of fibers in water usually cause contraction and shrinkage of the fabric.

Heatsetting of fabrics containing mostly thermoplastic fibers usu-

Figure 7-3.   Principle of compressive shrinking of woven fabric

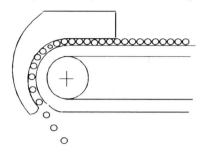

ally stabilizes these fabrics sufficiently. Principles of heatsetting are discussed in Chapter 2—Preparation for Dyeing and Finishing.

Woven fabrics containing nonthermoplastic fibers such as cotton can be mechanically stabilized by preshrinking the fabric. Since shrinkage in woven fabrics is mostly lengthwise (warp direction) rather than width wise, compressing the filling yarns closer together stabilizes the fabric against further shrinkage. The term "compressive shrinking" is used because the process mechanically pushes the yarns in the fabric closer to one another. Sanforizing is the best-known compressive shrinkage process. Figure 7-3 shows the principle of compressive shrinkage.

The thick rubber belt passes around a small guide roller which causes the rubber to stretch extending the belt on its outer radius. The heated shoe presses the previously wetted fabric against the stretched surface of the rubber blanket as the fabric enters the compressive shrinkage machine. When the belt straightens as it emerges from the compression zone, it relaxes and contracts. Since the fabric is held firmly against the belt, the filling yarns move closer together so the fabric conforms to the shorter length of the relaxed belt. The thickness of the blanket determines the degree of compression achieved. Fabric is dried on a cylinder before leaving the compressive shrinkage machine. The compressive shrinkage process must be controlled so that the residual shrinkage is slightly less than 1%. If compression of the fabric is excessive, the preshrunk fabric will stretch when laundered.

Knit fabrics may be preshrunk by overfeeding wet fabric into a pin tenter so that the fabric can relax and shrink during the drying process. The fabric is forced onto the pin tenter at a greater rate than the speed of the tenter providing some slackness to accommodate lengthwise shrinkage of the fabric during drying. Width wise

Figure 7-4. Schematic of principles of single and double action napping

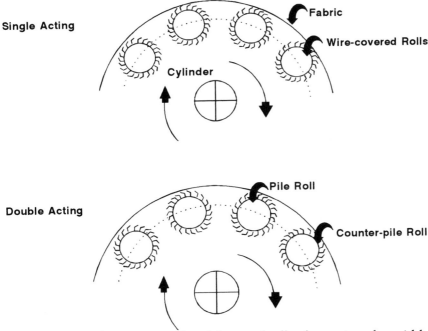

shrinkage can be accommodated by gradually decreasing the width of the frame as the fabric travels through the dryer.

Raising

Raising refers to the lifting of fibers from yarns near the surface of the fabric to produce a hairy or fuzzy surface. Teaseling, napping, sueding, and shearing are names commonly used for specific raising processes.

Napping uses small wires to pluck fibers from the yarns near the fabric surface. Figure 7-4 shows a schematic diagram of the principle of napping and a double action napping machine. Single action napping lays the fiber in one direct producing a fleece effect. Double action napping raises the pile to a more erect position.

Woven fabrics intended for napping may contain soft twist warp yarns which respond well to the action of the wires. Either one or both sides of a fabric may be raised in napping, and the fabric may be processed through the napper more than once to achieved the desired effect. Napping must be controlled well to prevent excessive strength loss in the fabric. Napping produces flannel fabric commonly

Figure 7-5.   Schematic diagram of a flocking process

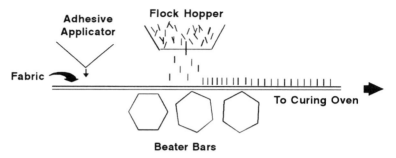

used in sleep wear and other garments. Napped fabrics are very soft. The air pockets between the raised fibers in a napped fabric produce a good insulating effect making napped fabrics warm to wear.

Sueding subjects the fabric to sandpaper covered rolls producing a surface resembling suede leather. Suede cloth may be raised on either one side or both sides.

Shearing is used to cut away a portion of the fibers on a fabric having a raised surface to produce a level fabric surface. Cut-pile carpet is commonly sheared to level the tuft length.

Mechanical Softening

Fabrics are stiff if the fibers and yarns are not flexible and able to move freely in the fabric structure. Drying of fabrics under tension tends to set fibers making them stiffer and chemical agents such as size materials, printing thickeners, film forming finishes, and durable press finishes bind fibers and yarns together making the fabric stiff.

Mechanical softening simply consists of bending, flexing, or pounding the fabric to cause adhesions between the fibers and yarns to break. A variety of machines can be used for mechanical softening.

Flocking

Flocked fabric is made by gluing short fibers to the surface of a base fabric. Flock can be applied to the entire surface of the fabric to produce a raised surface or to only certain areas to produce a pattern. As shown in Figure 7-5, flocking is done in a continuous process.

The adhesive is applied first, and then the fabric passes the flock applicator where the flock (short fiber) is sifted onto the fabric. Only a thin layer of adhesive is used so that the fabric does not become excessively stiff. Most of the flock must be perpendicular to the fabric surface in order to achieve the desired effect. In mechanical flocking, the fabric is vibrated by rotating beater bars beneath the fabric. This vibration helps the flock fibers which land vertically to become deeply imbedded in the adhesive. These vertical fibers then guide other fibers to land vertically. In electrostatic flocking, a charged field or air space is used to align the flock vertically. After the flock is applied, the adhesive is cured by convection, conduction, infrared, or dielectric heating to permanently bind the flock to the fabric.

Chemical Finishes

Easy-care Finishes

A severe limitation of fabrics made of all or mostly cellulosic fibers is their tendency to wrinkle. Wrinkling occurs when the fiber is severely bent. Hydrogen bonds between the molecular chains in the amorphous regions of the fibers break allowing the chains to slip past one another. The bonds reform in new places and hold creases in the fiber and fabric.

Resistance to creasing is imparted to cellulosic fibers by restricting the slippage of molecular chains. Chain slippage can be restricted by adding chemical crosslinks between the molecular chains in the amorphous regions of the fiber or by deposition of a polymeric substance in the amorphous regions. Permanent creases may be placed in a fabric by creasing the fabric at the desired location before the crosslinks are formed.

Durable press (DP), wash-and-wear, crease resistant, and other terms are used for easy-care finishes. DP finished fabrics may still form creases while the product is being used but are designed to return to a smooth and crease-free configuration after washing and drying.

The chemistry of some common crosslinking agents is discussed in Chapter 1—Textile Chemicals. As shown in Figure 7-6, crosslinking agents have at least two functional groups which can react with hydroxyl groups on adjacent molecular chains in the amorphous regions of cellulose linking the chains to each other.

Preferably the crosslinking agent will have only two functional groups so that it can only crosslink the cellulose or form linear poly-

Figure 7-6. Schematic of crosslinking of cellulose

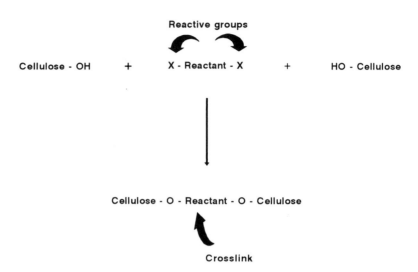

mers. Agents with two functional groups are often called "reactants" because they tend to be effective crosslinkers. Agents with more than two functional groups are called "aminoplast resins" because they can form three dimensional network polymers.

The effect achieved by crosslinking cellulose depends on the length of the crosslinks that are formed. The crosslinks must be taut in order to be most effective in producing crease resistance and crease recovery. Fabrics crosslinked while in the dry unswollen state resist swelling in water and creasing in the dry state because the crosslinks are short and taut. Crosslinking in commercial practice is usually done at high temperature on dry fabric to impart crease resistance and dimensional stability to the fabric.

The crosslinks in fibers crosslinked while wet and swollen become slack when the fiber is dried, and the amorphous regions collapse. Fabrics crosslinked while wet have crease resistance while wet but not in the dry state. These fabrics also absorb water and swell to a greater extent than fabrics crosslinked in the dry state. The properties of crosslinked cellulose can be optimized to some extent by controlling the amount of moisture in the fiber during crosslinking.

Since crosslinking affects the mobility of the molecular chains in the amorphous regions of the fiber, many properties of the fiber are affected. Furthermore, durable press resins are reactive substances and may themselves undergo changes as treated fabrics age. Some effects of application of durable press finishes are as follows:

- Flexibility, tensile strength, tear strength, and abrasion resistance of the fabric is usually decreased.
- Swelling in water is inhibited, and the fibers are less absorbent.
- Since dyes and other chemicals cannot penetrate crosslinked fibers easily, dyeing must usually be done before the crosslinking finish is applied. This is a particular problem in garment wet processing where it may be desirable to dye finished garments.
- On the positive side, crosslinking helps to trap dye molecules in the fiber and can thereby enhance the washfastness of the dye.
- Crosslinking resins sometimes cause a color change in dyed fabrics.
- Chlorine from bleaches may react with the resin causing discoloration or chemical damage to the cellulose. This problem is called "chlorine retention."
- Some dyes are sensitive to durable press resins and may change shade when the finish is applied.
- Some resins form decomposition products having a fishy odor.
- Light fastness of dyes may be decreased. This is believed to be caused by catalysts used in durable press formulations.
- Formaldehyde release in the finishing plant and from finished fabrics in retail stores may cause odor problems and is subject to regulation by the government.
- Durable press finishing may accentuate soil retention by the fabric.

Use of a softener in the durable press formulation partially overcomes the loss of strength and resistance to abrasion due to crosslinking. Strength problems are less severe in cellulosic/polyester blends than in 100% cellulosic fibers since polyester is unaffected by the finishing agents. Problems with odor, chlorine retention, lightfastness of dyes, and dye shade changes are usually minimized by judicious selection of the finish and dyes.

Formaldehyde release from durable-press finished fabrics has been greatly reduced as chemists have developed improved finishes, catalysts, and application methods. A formaldehyde-free crosslinking system based on esterification has also been developed. The system uses

Figure 7-7. Reaction of butane tetra carboxylic acid with cellulose (16)

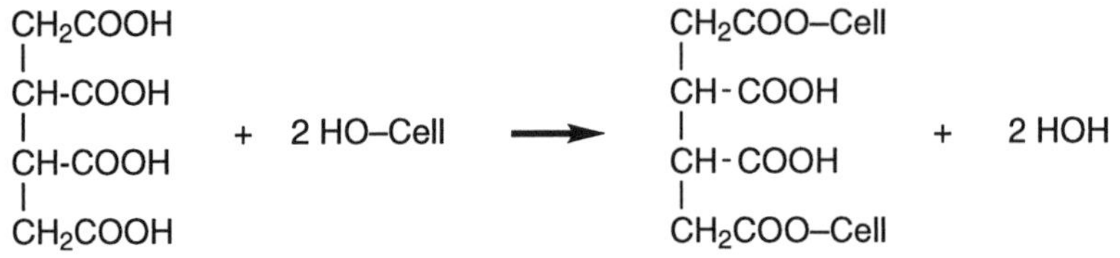

$$
\begin{array}{l}
\text{CH}_2\text{COOH} \\
\quad | \\
\text{CH-COOH} \\
\quad | \quad\quad + \;\; 2\,\text{HO–Cell} \;\longrightarrow\; \\
\text{CH-COOH} \\
\quad | \\
\text{CH}_2\text{COOH}
\end{array}
\qquad
\begin{array}{l}
\text{CH}_2\text{COO–Cell} \\
\quad | \\
\text{CH-COOH} \\
\quad | \quad\quad + \;\; 2\,\text{HOH} \\
\text{CH-COOH} \\
\quad | \\
\text{CH}_2\text{COO–Cell}
\end{array}
$$

polyfunctional carboxylic acids which form ester linkages with the hydroxyl groups of cellulose. As shown in Figure 7-7, butane tetracarboxylic acid (BTCA) is an example of such an agent. A key characteristic of the crosslinking agent is believed to be the capability to form an anhydride intermediate which in turn reacts with the alcoholic cellulose hydroxyl group. The catalyst system is also believed to be crucial in achieving the desired properties in materials crosslinked with BTCA. Phosphate-based catalysts are used.

Durable press performance of fabrics finished with BTCA is reportedly very good. High cost, durability to alkaline laundering, and adverse effects on sulfur dyes are some of the problems that have been cited for BTCA as a durable press agent.

Application of Durable Press Finishes

Following is a hypothetical formulation for durable press (DP) finishing.

Wetting agent	1%
Reactant (resin)	15%
Catalyst	3%
Softener	3%
Hand builder	3%
Water	75%

In practice, DP finish formulations vary greatly depending on the type of fabric being finished, the performance specifications for the fabric, and the type of finishing agent being used. Application of N-methylol reactants is catalyzed by acids. Although mineral acids will work, Lewis acids are the preferred catalysts for durable press finishing. Lewis acids require high temperature curing. Magnesium chloride is the most common Lewis acid catalyst for DP finishing. It is not a particularly active catalyst and does not affect shade, lightfastness of dyes, or fabric strength as much as other catalysts. Catalysis can be enhanced by using small amounts of more active catalysts along with magnesium chloride.

Durable press finishes are usually applied by a pad-dry-cure process. The fabric is framed to the required width during the drying stage. Curing is accomplished by heating the fabric to temperatures above 150°C for a minute or so.

Evaluation of Durable Press Finished Fabric

Durable press finishes must impart easy care, shrinkage resistance, and pleasing appearance characteristics to the fabric. Other desirable properties such as fabric strength, abrasion resistance, and absorbency must be maintained to an acceptable degree in the finished fabric. Standard methods have been published for evaluation of all of these properties.

Durable press performance is often evaluated by methods based on visual appearance. Standard methods are used to evaluate appearance of durable press fabrics and apparel after mechanical deformation (wrinkling) or repeated home laundering. Other standard methods are designed to evaluate the appearance of seams and creases in durable press items after laundering. These appearance methods compare the appearance of the laundered test item to that of a series of photographic or plastic replicas representing various grades of appearance. (14)

Wrinkle recovery of fabrics is measured using the recovery angle method. The method measures the ability of a fabric to recover from folding deformations. The test specimens are creased and compressed under controlled conditions. After being creased under a controlled load for the specified time, the angle of recovery from creasing is measured. (14)

Dimensional change means change in length or width of textile materials. A standard method for measuring dimensional changes during laundering subjects the item to standard procedures simulating home laundering and drying. The amount of change in dimensions is measured by using pairs of bench marks applied to the fabric before it is laundered. (14)

Flame Retardant Finishes

A limitation of many textile fibers, especially cellulosics, is their tendency to burn readily. Flammability of textile products is regu-

Figure 7-8. Mechanism of the combustion of cellulose

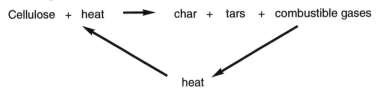

lated by federal and state governments. The federal Flammable Fabrics Act of 1953 requires virtually all textile products to meet minimum standards of flame retardancy. A series of amendments to the Flammable Fabrics Act of 1953, require children's sleepwear, carpets, and mattresses to meet stringent standards for resistance to burning.

Textile fibers vary greatly in flammability. All organic fibers burn if the conditions are severe enough. Cellulosic fibers ignite at relatively low temperature and burn rapidly. Polyamide and polyester fibers do not ignite easily because they melt and recede from a flame. However, in a blend with cellulosic fibers which prevent them from receding from the flame, they burn vigorously. Often a blend of cellulose with a synthetic fiber will burn more readily than a fabric made from either of these individual fibers types. Acrylic fibers are difficult to ignite but burn rapidly with much evolution of heat after ignition takes place. Wool has a high ignition temperature and low heat of combustion making it naturally flame retardant. Aramid and modacrylic fibers are very flame retardant, and most of their uses are the result of their outstanding resistance to thermal decomposition.

Three conditions must exist for textile materials to support combustion. There must be a source of ignition, oxygen, and a fuel source (the textile material). Generally, not much can be done about sources of ignition and elimination of oxygen in the vicinity of textile materials so the propensity of the textile fiber to burn must be altered in order to make the material flame retardant. Figure 7-8 shows the mechanism of combustion of cellulose.

When the temperature of cellulose is raised to about 350°C by the ignition source, cellulose begins to decompose producing solid char, liquid products called tar, and a mixture of combustible gases. If the amount of heat produced by the burning gases is sufficient, further decomposition of cellulose takes place, and combustion is self-supporting. One of the tarry components of the decomposition of cellulose is levoglucosan. Upon further heating, levoglucosan decomposes to low molecular weight flammable gases.

Treatment of cellulose (and other fibers) with certain chemicals alters the mechanism of thermal decomposition so that combustion is not self-supporting. Therefore, when the ignition source is removed, the flame extinguishes.

Generally, flammability standards require that textile products be self-extinguishing under specified conditions. This means that the material must not support combustion for very long after the ignition source is removed even though it may continue to burn as long as an external ignition source is present.

Several chemical treatments have been used successfully as flame retardants on textile materials. However, inherently flame retardant fibers are used in lieu of chemical treatments in many applications requiring flame retardancy because of questions regarding threats of chemical flame retardant treatments to human health.

Flame retardant chemical treatments may be nondurable or durable. Nondurable treatments may be used where the treated material will not be exposed to water or where only temporary flame retardance is needed. Durable treatments are used where the fabric must be washed. Flammability standards for apparel and household textiles require that the treatments be durable to laundering.

Simple water soluble acidic ammonium phosphates, ammonium chloride, borax/boric acid mixtures and other inorganic salts function as non durable flame retardants. These chemicals are believed to inhibit the formation of levoglucosan when cellulose decomposes. Therefore, less volatile gases and more solid char are formed, and burning is impeded. Additionally, the borax/boric acid treatment may form a thin glassy coating on the fibers excluding the oxygen required for combustion of the fibers.

Durable flame retardant finishes based on the presence of both nitrogen and phosphorus are effective on cotton. Like the nondurable flame retardants, the durable N/P flame retardants are believed to inhibit the formation of volatile decomposition products when cellulose is pyrolyzed by preventing the formation of levoglucosan. The most common N/P flame retardant system uses tetrakis (hydroxymethyl) phosphonium chloride as the source of phosphorus.

$$[P(CH_2OH)_4]^+ \ Cl^-$$

THPC

The sulfate may be used in lieu of the chloride. In this case the material is referred to as THPS. THPC and THPS react with cellulose and are thus durable to washing. These substances also react with amino groups to form polymers within the fiber. Amino compounds commonly used as the nitrogen source in N/P flame retardant systems are methylolated urea and melamine.

Nitrogen/phosphorus flame retardant systems containing the nitrogen and phosphorus atoms in the same molecule have also been successful. The best known of these are the phosphonalkanoic amides.

$$(RO)_2POCH_2CH_2CONHCH_2OH \quad R = Alkyl\ group$$

Reaction of the compound with cellulose at the methylol group makes the finish durable to washing.

Antimony/halogen treatments also produce durable flame retardants. The fabric is treated with a mixture of antimony oxide, a chlorinated wax, and a binder chemical. Antimony/ halogen flame retardants are believed to function either by scavenging free radicals which propagate combustion or by a dehydration mechanism which promotes the formation of solid char during the thermal decomposition of cellulose.

Application of Flame Retardants

Flame retardant finishes are usually applied by a pad-dry-cure process. Some flame retardants for synthetic fibers have affinity for the fibers and can be applied by exhaust methods. These types of finishes may be applied in a batch process immediately after exhaust dyeing.

Evaluation of Fabric Flammability

Tests for flammability of textiles are designed to measure ease of ignition, rate of flame spread, extent of flame spread, rate of heat release, and extent of smoke generation.

The Flammable Fabrics Act of 1953 required most fabrics used in wearing apparel to pass a test wherein a 2 x 6 inch fabric sample mounted at an angle of 45° was exposed to a flame for 1 second. In order to pass the test, the sample could not ignite and spread up the length of the sample in less than 3.5 seconds for smooth fabrics or 4 seconds for napped fabrics. This test was intended mainly for fabrics not treated with flame retardants.

The 1967 amendment to the Flammable Fabrics Act of 1953 led to several flammability standards. The carpet and rug standard subjects 9 x 9 inch carpet specimens to the "pill" test. A methenamine tablet is placed in the center of the specimen and ignited. The tablet burns between 90 and 120 seconds. To pass the test the flame cannot spread more than 3 inches from the point at which the tablet was placed.

The Children's sleepwear standard subjects samples to a vertical flammability test which is more demanding than the 45° angle test. The 3.5 x 10 inch specimens are hung vertically in holders in a draft-free cabinet and exposed to a gas flame for 3 seconds. A test consisting of five specimens cannot have an average char length of more than 7 inches.

The mattress standard uses a "cigarette" test. The test is conducted by placing 9 lighted cigarettes at specified locations on the mattress surface. The test is also conducted with 9 cigarettes placed between two sheets on the mattress surface. The flame must not char the mattress for a distance of more than 2 inches from where any cigarette was placed.

The Limiting Oxygen Index (LOI or just OI) test was designed as a research tool but is used in flammability regulations. A sample mounted vertically in the test chamber is ignited at its upper end. The test chamber has a variable oxygen/nitrogen atmosphere. The LOI is the minimum concentration of oxygen that will just support combustion of the material. A low LOI means that the material burns readily. Materials with LOI greater than 21 are usually self-extinguishing in air.

Several smoke tests are used to measure the amount of smoke generated by burning materials. Most of these tests burn the material in a chamber and determine the smoke density by measuring the transmission of light through the smoke. One method burns the sample and collects the smoke on a filter for gravimetric measurement.

Water and Soil Repellent Finishes

Repellency is attained by limiting the wettability of fabrics. Wetting is governed by surface and interfacial tensions as discussed in Chapter 2. Thus, making the surface energy of a fabric such that a substance does not spread on the fabric makes the fabric resistant to that substance.

Coating of fabrics with a low surface energy film former such as polyvinyl chloride (PVC) or rubber makes the material completely waterproof. These impermeable types of coatings are sometimes used to make rainwear or other protective fabrics. Since these coated fabrics are also impervious to air, they may not be comfortable as wearing apparel.

Repellent finishes modify the surface of fibers and do not block the interstices. Therefore, the fabric remains porous to air and water vapor.

Some important types of water repellent finishes are wax emulsions, pyridinium compounds, N-methylol compounds, silicones, and fluorochemicals. These finishes may be used to impart water repellency to various natural and synthetic fibers.

Wax emulsion formulations usually contain a zirconium salt such as zirconium acetate in addition to the wax and emulsifying agents. Addition of film forming polymers or crosslinking reactants to wax emulsion formulations improves the durability of the wax emulsion water repellent finish.

Pyridinium-type water repellents consist of a long chain hydrocarbon group attached to a pyridinium ring.

$$C_{17}H_{35}\overset{\overset{O}{\|}}{C}-NH\cdot CH_2 N^+ \text{(pyridinium ring)} \quad Cl^-$$

The pyridinium compound reacts with cellulose leaving its hydrocarbon group attached to the fiber. The resulting fiber surface is more hydrophobic and water repellent.

The use of N-methylol compounds to impart water repellency is based on the reactions between N-methylol compounds and cellulose discussed earlier. N-methylol water repellents contain a long hydrocarbon group.

$$C_{17}H_{35}\overset{\overset{O}{\|}}{C}-NH-\overset{\overset{O}{\|}}{C}-NH-CH_2OH$$

The hydrocarbon group attaches to the fiber when the N-methylol group reacts with the cellulose hydroxyl group. A similar finish can be made by applying trimethylol melamine to the fabric and then reacting a long chain (fatty) alcohol or other hydrophobe with methy-lol groups on the melamine resin.

Polymerized siloxanes are good water repellents. Dimethyl poly-siloxane, methyl hydrogen polysiloxane, or a mixture of these two sub-stances is often used. The chemistry of these substances, which are also excellent fabric softeners, is discussed in Chapter 1—Textile Chemicals.

Fluorochemical finishes impart both water repellency and oil repel-lency to fabrics while the silicone and repellents based on hydrocar-bon hydrophobes provide only water repellency. The performance of fluorocarbon repellents results from the very low surface energy they produce. The surface of the fibers must be covered by the fluorocar-bon groups. Examples of fluorocarbon chemicals used as oil and water repellents are given in Chapter 1. Fabrics containing fluorocarbon fin-ishes are often referred to as being stain repellent or stain resistant.

Tests for Water Repellency

Tests for water repellency are generally of three types:

1. those that simulate rain by spraying water on the fabric,
2. those that simulate the penetration of water pressing against the fabric, and
3. those that measure the sorption of water by the immersed fabric.

Many variations of these tests have been devised, and standard meth-ods based on all three types have been published. (AATCC)

Test for Oil Repellency

The resistance of a textile fabric to wetting by oily liquids can be evaluated with a numbered series of test liquids which have a range of surface tensions. The fabric is given an oil repellency rating cor-responding to the liquid with the lowest surface tension which will not wet the fabric. A suitable series of test liquids is given in a pub-lished standard method for oil repellency. (14)

Soil Release Finishes

Soiling is mainly the result of adhesion and physical entrapment of particulate matter on fabrics. As textile products are laundered, physically entrapped particles are usually loosened and removed.

However, particulate matter mixed with oily soil adheres chemically to hydrophobic fibers like polyester making its removal more difficult. Soil release finishes make the surface of the fiber more hydrophilic so that adhesion between the fiber and hydrophobic soil is lowered.

Several approaches have been used to increase the hydrophilic nature of cellulose fibers. The surface of polyester can be modified by grafting on a substance having hydrophilic tails. Partial hydrolysis of the polyester surface forms hydrophilic carboxyl groups. One approach to improving the hydrophilicity and soil release capabilities of polyesters is the use of amphiphilic substances. These substances are either nonionic surfactants where the hydrophile-lipophile balance has been judiciously selected or block copolymers containing both hydrophobic and hydrophilic blocks. The hydrophobic part of the finish molecule has affinity for polyester and is sorbed into the fiber much like a disperse dye. The hydrophilic part does not have affinity for polyester and extends outward from the fiber surface making the surface more hydrophilic. High application temperature is required to achieve good penetration and bonding of these agents to polyester.

Soil release agents in durable press finishes are often anionic polymers, fluorocarbon polymers, or mixtures of the two. Copolymers of acrylic and methacrylic acid are effective as soil release agents when co-applied with durable press finishes or top-applied to durable press-finished fabrics. Soil release finishes for durable press fabrics are often not entirely satisfactory.

Softeners, Antistatic Agents, and Hand Builders

The way a fabric or garment feels to the touch is referred to as its "hand." Hand of fabrics is subjective to some extent and is often difficult to describe meaningfully with words. Nevertheless, hand is important, and hand modification is one of the most common goals of finishing of textiles.

Treatments which make the fabric more flexible and pliable impart the impression of softness. Softness generally comes from making the fibers themselves more flexible and from decreasing interfiber friction. Therefore, agents which plasticize fibers and lubricate the surface of fibers produce softness. Since softeners lubricate fibers, they may decrease yarn and fabric tensile strength by decreasing fiber cohesion. On the other hand, softeners usually improve abrasion resistance and tear strength of fabrics. Abrasion resistance is improved because of lubricity of the fabric surface or improved mobility of fibers in the softener-treated fabric. Tear strength is improved because of better mobility of fibers so that the load imparted by tearing action is better distributed over the individual fibers in the fabric.

Synthetic fibers such as nylon and polyester tend to accumulate static charge because they absorb little water. On the other hand, cellulosic fibers having higher moisture content tend to dissipate static charge. Surface active agents help to spread the small amount of moisture on the surface of fibers into a continuous film which can dissipate charge. Therefore, surfactants used as softeners are also effective as antistatic treatments. Cationic, anionic, and nonionic surfactants all exhibit some antistatic behavior. The durability of antistatic treatments is improved by using them along with N-methylol compounds which chemically bond them to the fibers.

Hand building is the opposite effect of softening. Hand builders add stiffness to the fibers and fabric. Agents which stiffen fibers, bind fibers together, or increase interfiber friction all produce stiffness. Hand builders usually increase tensile strength and abrasion resistance of fabrics but may decrease tear strength because of increased stiffness in the fabric.

Softeners

Softness of a fabric can be enhanced by either mechanical or chemical treatments. Mechanical softening was discussed along with other mechanical finishing processes. Softeners are among the most common textile chemicals. Softeners can be classified as anionic, cationic, or nonionic. These classes have different characteristics and each has its advantages in a particular case.

The hand imparted and the properties of a softener depend on the physical state of the softener, its chemical structure, and its behavior on the fabric. Low viscosity liquid softeners produce a flexible, silky hand while solid softeners provide lubrication but less pliability. Since hand is difficult to assess objectively, softener performance is usually based on human judgement.

Softeners are sometimes implicated in quality and environmental problems. The tendency of some softeners to develop a yellowish color when aged or heated can be undesirable especially in white fabrics. Volatile softeners may cause smoke problems in and around the textile manufacturing plant. Some softeners adversely affect light-fastness and crockfastness of dyes. Softeners may alter the shade of a dyed fabric. Odor problems on fabrics can be caused by softeners. Softeners which condense in dryers and vents can drip on fabrics, producing spots.

Anionic softeners are usually surfactants. The chemistry of these agents is discussed in Chapter 1. Most anionic softeners are either sulfates or sulfonates. The hydrophobic group may be a fatty alcohol, fatty ester, fatty amide, or another substance. The number of available substances of this type is very large.

Anionic surfactants provide good lubrication and improve the performance of fabrics in napping and other raising treatments. Anionic softeners are good foaming agents and have good rewetting characteristics. Most anionic softeners do not yellow.

Anionics provide less softness than cationic and nonionic softeners as a general rule. They have limited durability to laundering and drycleaning. Anionic surfactants do not have inherent affinity for most fibers and do not exhaust onto fabrics in batch processes. Therefore, they are most suitable for application by padding.

Like anionic softeners, cationic softeners are surfactants and their chemistry is discussed in Chapter 1. The positively charged group in a cationic softener molecule contains a nitrogen atom. The nitrogen may be in the form of a primary, secondary, or tertiary amine which becomes positively charged in acidic medium. Quaternary ammonium salts are charged at all pH values making them useful in alkaline medium as well as acidic medium. Quaternary ammonium surfactants function as germicides and antistats as well as softeners.

Cationic softeners are effective at very low add-on levels. They have inherent affinity for most fibers making them applicable using exhaust application procedures. Cationic surfactants are common in home laundry products.

Cationic softeners may affect shade and fastness properties of some dyes. Some have a tendency to yellow upon ageing. Use of cationic softeners may reduce water sorbancy and wettability of fabrics. Cationic surfactants sometimes aggravate soiling tendency of fabrics and inhibit soil removal.

Ethyoxylated materials, silicones, and hydrocarbon waxes comprise the nonionic softener classification. The ethoxylated types are nonionic surfactants, and their chemistry is discussed in Chapter 1—Textile Chemicals. The silicones are polymers and their chemistry is also discussed in Chapter 1.

Ethoxylated fatty acids, alcohols, amides, and amines can be ethoxylated to produce a wide variety of products which may be either solids or liquids.

Silicone softeners produce a slick soft hand. They are common on white fabrics and are good sewing lubricants. Silicones are stable to heat and light. Amino functional silicone products improve DP performance of cotton making them useful as garment finishes.

Since silicones function as water repellents as well as softeners, they are not useful where water sorbancy is required. Silicones are more expensive than fatty softeners.

Polyethylene emulsions are common softeners and sewing lubricants. Polyethylene softeners contain carboxyl groups formed by oxidation of the polymer. Many grades are available. Polyethylene softeners form a hard waxy coating on fibers and reduce interfiber friction. They are effective in preventing needle cutting in sewing.

Handbuilding

Treatment of fabrics with firming or stiffening agents makes sewing easier and adds consumer appeal to certain types of fabrics such as work denim. Handbuilding finishes may be either temporary or durable. A temporary handbuilder may be added to improve the sewing characteristics of a fabric or to add weight and make the fabric appear more substantial to the consumer. A temporary handbuilder is washed out after a few laundry cycles, and the garment becomes soft and more comfortable to wear. Starch, modified starch, or polyvinyl alcohol are the most common finishes for temporary handbuilding. The structure and properties of these water soluble polymers are discussed in Chapter 1. Since these chemicals are soluble or dispersible in water, they are applied by padding from aqueous solutions followed by drying. Curing of temporary handbuilders is not required since no chemical reactions are involved in their application. These temporary handbuilders function by binding together the fibers comprising the yarn and fabric and by forming films which coat the yarns and fabric.

The N-methylol, thermosetting compounds are used as durable handbuilders. Urea/formaldehyde and melamine/formaldehyde resins are commonly used handbuilders. They are applied by a pad-dry-cure process. These substances are potential crosslinkers for cellulose but function mainly by polymerization in the fiber during the curing stage of their application. The structure and properties of these N-methylol compounds is discussed in Chapter 1.

Various acrylic and other vinyl polymers can also be used as durable handbuilders. These polymers function by much the same mechanism as starch and polyvinyl alcohol. However, unlike starch and polyvinyl alcohol, these polymers are insoluble in water and durable to washing. The structure and properties of these polymers are discussed in Chapter 1.

Anti-Microbial Finishes

Growth of bacteria and fungi in textile fabrics is usually undesirable. Laundering with hot water and use of disinfectants such as chlorine or peroxygen bleaches destroys many microorganisms in textile products. Chemicals which prevent growth of bacteria and fungi are referred to as anti-microbial agents. Many chemicals are effective anti-microbial agents for fabrics used in environments where growth of micro-organisms must be prevented. Quaternary ammonium surfactants and antibiotics function as anti-microbial agents. Many chlorinated organic compounds and organometallic compounds containing copper, silver, iron, manganese, or zinc also make textile materials resist growth of microorganisms. However, many of these agents are also toxic to higher organisms and may resist degradation in the environment for long periods of time. Chlorinated organic compounds are also effective in inhibiting attack of insects on natural fibers composed of protein and cellulose.

Bibliography

1. Carty, P. and M.S. Byrne, The Chemical and Mechanical Finishing of Textile Materials, 2nd Ed., Newcastle upon Tyne Polytechnic Products Ltd., Newcastle upon Tyne, 1987.
2. Corbman, B.P., Textiles: Fiber to Fabric, McGraw-Hill Book Company, New York, NY, 1975.
3. Datye, K.V. and A.A. Vaidya, Chemical Processing of Synthetic Fibers and Blends, John Wiley and Sons, New York, NY, 1984.
4. Gunter, S., Creating Surface Effects on Knit Fabrics by Calendering, Embossing, Schreinering, Knitting Times, April 23, 1979, 18–25.
5. Hall, A.J., A Handbook of Textile Finishing, The National Trade

Press Ltd., London, 1957.

6. Hall, D.M. and W.S. Perkins, Preparation, Dyeing, and Finishing of Textiles: Lecture and Study Aids, Auburn University, Auburn, AL, 1977.

7. Herard, R.S., Equipment Developments for Napping, Shearing, Sueding, Sanding Circular Knits, Knitting Times, April 23, 1979, 12–17.

8. Hollen, N., Jane Saddler, Anna L. Langford, and Sara J. Kadolph, Textiles, 6th Ed., Macmillan Publishing Company, New York, NY, 1988.

9. Lewin, M., and S.B. Sello, Editors, Handbook of Fiber Science and Technology: Volume II—Functional Finishes, Part A, Marcel Dekker, Inc., New York, NY, 1983.

10. Lewin, M. and S.B. Sello, Editors, Handbook of Fiber Science and Technology: Volume II—Functional Finishes, Part B, Marcel Dekker, Inc., New York, NY, 1984.

11. Mark, H., Norman S. Wooding, and Sheldon M. Atlas, Editors, Chemical Aftertreatment of Textiles, John Wiley and Sons, New York, NY, 1971.

12. Marsh, J.T., An Introduction to Textile Finishing, Chapman and Hall Ltd., London, 1966.

13. Nettles, J.E., Handbook of Chemical Specialties, John Wiley and Sons, New York, NY, 1983.

14. Technical Manual of the American Association of Textile Chemists and Colorists, AATCC, Research Triangle Park, NC, published annually.

15. Trotman, E.R., Dyeing and Chemical Technology of Textile Fibres, 6th Ed., John Wiley and Sons, New York, NY, 1984.

16. Welsh, C.M., Durable Press Finishing without Formaldehyde, Textile Chemist and Colorist, 22, No. 5, 13–16, May, 1990.

Chapter 8

Textile Chemical Processes

This chapter discusses some principles of application of chemicals to textile materials. Chemical treatment of textile materials is done in batch, continuous, and semi-continuous process. The principles discussed below can be applied to various processes including slashing, preparation of materials for dyeing, dyeing, and chemical finishing.

A batch process treats a specific amount of material with chemical formulations for a specific length of time. Several different treatments may be done sequentially by draining and refilling the bath between treatments. The complete process may all be done in one machine, or the batch may be transferred from one machine to another for various steps in the process. Various types of equipment are available for batch wet processing of textile materials. Batch wet processing machines for fiber, yarn, fabric, and garments are discussed in Chapter 6, Dyeing and Printing Processes.

The amounts of chemicals used in formulations for batch processing may be based on either the amount of material being processed or the amount of formulation being used. The term "on weight of fiber (or fabric, or goods)" is used when the formulation is based on the amount of material being processed. This is usually expressed as a percentage and abbreviated "% owf" or "% owg." For example the amount of dye used in a formulation may be X% dye (owf). The term "on weight of bath (or solution)" is used when the formulation is based on the amount of bath being used. Amounts of chemicals based on weight of solution are usually expressed as a percentage or as weight per volume (grams/liter, ounces/gallon).

Continuous processes treat materials by passing the material in a continuous strand through one or more processing steps arranged in tandem. Specific continuous wet processes for textile materials are described in Chapter 6—Dyeing and Printing Processes, Chapter 2—

Preparation for Dyeing and Finishing, and Chapter 7—Finishing. The amount of chemicals applied to the fabric (add-on) at the padder depends on the concentration of chemicals in the formulation and the "wet pickup." Wet pickup is the amount of formulation picked up by the fabric and is usually expressed as a percentage on weight of the dry fabric.

$$\text{Wet pickup (\%)} = \frac{\text{Weight of formulation picked up}}{\text{Weight of dry fabric}} \times 100$$

$$\text{Add-on (\%)} = \text{Concentration of formulation (\%)} \times \frac{\text{Wet pickup (\%)}}{100}$$

Therefore, the wet pickup must be controlled across the width and along the length of fabric in order to achieve uniform add-on of chemicals.

Applicators

Padder

Padding is the most common method for application of chemical formulations to textile materials in continuous processes. Padding consists of contacting the material with the formulation, usually by immersion, and squeezing the excess formulation out with squeeze rolls.

Various designs of padders are available. The shape and volume of the trough and the number and arrangement of guide rolls and squeeze rolls varies. Low volume in the padder trough minimizes tailing due to preferential pickup of water or chemicals by the fabric.

Wet pickup in the padder is affected by material characteristics, machine and process parameters, and formulation characteristics. These factors, some of which are also applicable to other types of applicators, are as follows:

Material characteristics

Fiber type—Hydrophilic fibers give higher wet pickup than hydrophobic fibers

Yarn and fabric construction—Low twist yarns give higher wet pickup than high twist yarns. Open end yarns give higher wet pickup than ring spun yarns.

Wettability of the material

Machine conditions

Pressure of squeeze rolls—Higher squeeze roll pressure extracts more formulation giving lower wet pickup.

Nature of roll covering

Hardness of squeeze roll covering—Hard rolls extract more formulation than soft rolls.

Speed of the machine—The length of time the fabric is in the nip of the squeeze rolls usually affects wet pickup more than length of time in the formulation. So faster line speed usually causes higher wet pickup.

Formulation Characteristics

Viscosity—Flow characteristics of the formulation greatly affect wet pickup. Higher viscosity usually gives higher wet pickup.

Surface tension—Wetting rate of the material can affect wet pickup so control of surface tension of the formulation is important.

Temperature—Viscosity and surface tension of the formulation and wettability of the material are affected by formulation temperature. Therefore, a change in temperature can either increase or decrease wet pickup in the padder.

Concentration—Since viscosity and surface tension depend on chemical concentrations in the formulation, concentration change in the formulation will affect wet pickup.

Kiss Rolls

Kiss rolls represent one of several methods that may be used to apply chemicals using a limited amount of water. Applying chemicals using less chemical formulation than the fabric needs to become completely "wet" is difficult because the formulation will preferentially wet the first area of the fabric with which it comes in contact resulting in nonuniform application of the formulation. However, limiting the amount of water added to the fabric can be beneficial so several "low-wet-pickup" application methods have been developed. Possible benefits of "low-wet-pickup" applicators include the following:

1. The amount of energy required to heat and dry the material is directly proportional to the amount of water that must be vaporized. Lowering the amount of water used reduces the energy requirements for heating and drying the material.

Figure 8-1.   Kiss roll applicator

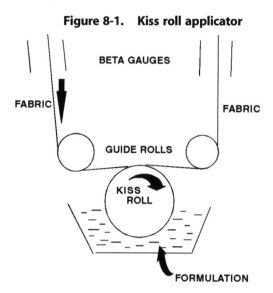

2. Some chemicals are utilized more efficiently when applied using a limited amount of water. This effect is usually related to location of chemicals and control of migration of chemicals during drying. Migration during drying can be controlled better if only a limited amount of water is used.

A schematic diagram of a kiss roll applicator is shown in Figure 8-1. The kiss roll picks up a thin film of chemical formulation from the trough in which it turns. The formulation is transferred from the kiss roll to the continuously moving fabric. The speed of the kiss roll relative to the fabric speed determines the wet pickup achieved. Moisture sensors such as ß-gauges measure the wet pickup and signal the drive to adjust the kiss roll speed to give the desired wet pickup. The flow characteristics of the chemical formulation are important with kiss roll applicators since the formulation must uniformly wet the kiss roll if uniform application of the chemical formulation is to be achieved.

Applicators similar in principle to the kiss roll applicator include engraved rolls and porous rolls. Both of these methods use rolls which transfer a limited amount of chemical formulation to fabrics which they contact. They differ from the kiss roll applicator in that their surface speed is the same as that of the fabric, and they have a squeeze roll which presses the fabric against the applicator roll to facilitate transfer of the formulation to the fabric.

Foam Applicators

Foam applicators limit the amount of water added to the fabric by replacing a portion of the water in the formulation with air. The chemical formulation is mixed with air in a foam generator to create a foam usually having very fine bubble size. Incorporation of air into the formulation creates a large volume which can be spread on the textile fabric more uniformly than can the unfoamed liquid.

The relative amounts of liquid and air in the foam are usually expressed as the "blow ratio" of the foam. Blow ratio is the reciprocal of the specific gravity of the foam. For example, if the foam weighs 0.1 g/ml, the blow ratio is said to be 10 to 1. For practical purposes, this means that a foam having a blow ratio of 10 to 1 is 90% air and 10% chemical formulation by volume.

Foams are inherently unstable and will separate into gaseous and liquid phases as the foam ages. The relative stability of a foamed formulation is important in foam application systems. Some methods require very stable foams while others require very unstable foams. The stability of the foam must be tailored for the particular application. Foam stability is expressed in terms of the half-life of the foam. The half-life of a foam is the length of time required for half of the liquid in the foam to drain out and become a separate liquid phase. Half-lives of foams used in textile applications range from a few seconds to many hours.

The two general types of foam applicators are called "open foam" and "closed foam" processes. An open foam process is one in which the foam leaves the generator and comes in contact with the atmosphere before being applied to the fabric. In a closed foam process the foam is trapped in the applicator under pressure up to the point at which it contacts the fabric being treated. Examples of these two types of applicators are shown in Figure 8-2.

Open foam applicators include knife coaters which spread the foam on the surface of the fabric and the horizontal pad which coats the fabric with foam and crushes the foam into the fabric as the fabric passes through the nip of the rolls. Wet pickup is determined mainly by the blow ratio of the foam. An open foam process requires a foam of relatively long half-life since the blow ratio must remain essentially constant at all times.

The closed foam applicator shown in the figure forces the foam under pressure through a slot which is sealed by the fabric passing

Figure 8-2.   Foam applicators

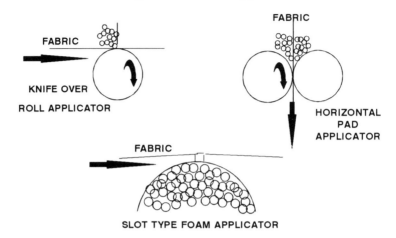

continuously across the slot. The wet pickup is determined by the feed rate of the foam generator and the speed of the fabric crossing the slot. Foam having a relatively short half-life is preferred because the foam should collapse upon contact with the fabric. The blow ratio and foam pressure affect the degree of penetration of formulation into the fabric.

Curved Blade Applicator

The curved blade applicator is shown in Figure 8-3. This applicator, which is designed for application of chemicals using limited amounts of water, meters formulation onto the fabric at a predetermined rate. Formulation is delivered to the curved blade through a

Figure 8-3.   Curved blade applicator

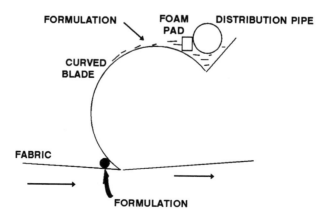

Figure 8-4. Vacuum extraction slot

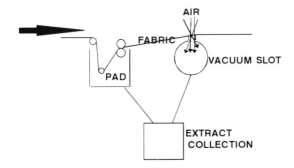

perforated distribution pipe. Formulation accumulates in the weir and overflows down the blade to be deposited on the fabric passing the tip of the blade. Wet pickup is determined by the relative rates of formulation feed and speed of fabric passing the blade. Flow characteristics of the formulation are critical since the blade must be completely wet by the formulation to prevent the occurrence of untreated spots on the fabric.

Vacuum Extraction Applicators

Vacuum extraction slots can be used to apply chemical formulations using limited amounts of water. However, the principle of vacuum extraction is "low leave-on" rather than "low add-on" which is the principle used in kiss roll, foam, and curved blade applicators. As shown in Figure 8-4, the fabric is saturated with formulation prior to its passage over the vacuum slot. The vacuum slot pulls air through the fabric extracting loosely bound formulation from the fabric. Vacuum chemical applicators are normally equipped with recovery units to collect the extract since recycle of the extracted chemicals is usually required to make the method economical.

The degree of extraction depends mostly on the type of fabric being processed and somewhat on the vacuum level applied, the viscosity of the formulation being extracted, and the speed of the fabric. Figure 8-5 shows the relationship between residual wet pickup and vacuum level applied for a polyester-cotton blend fabric. The degree of extraction with increasing vacuum level diminishes dramatically at vacuum levels higher than 10-15 inches of Hg. The extent of extraction of formulation is greater for hydrophobic fibers like polyester than for hydrophilic fibers like cotton.

Figure 8-5. Effect of vacuum level on residual wet pickup of polyester/cotton fabric

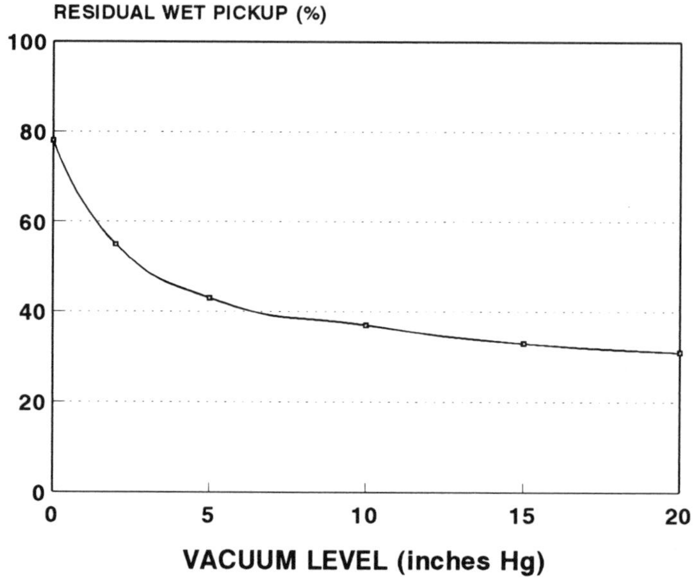

RESIDUAL WET PICKUP (%)

VACUUM LEVEL (inches Hg)

Vacuum extraction can be used simply for dewatering fabric prior to entry of the fabric into a thermal dryer, application of chemical formulations, or enhanced washing of fabrics. Vacuum-assisted washing is sometimes used in conjunction with spray systems to facilitate good exchange of washwater with contaminants in the fabric.

Dryers

Textile materials are usually wetted and dried several times in preparation, dyeing, and finishing processes. Moisture can be removed from textile materials to some extent by mechanical methods such as squeezing, centrifugal extraction, or vacuum extraction. These mechanical methods remove only the moisture which is very loosely bound to the textile material such as that which is located in the interstices between the yarns comprising the fabric. Water droplets trapped within the fibers and yarns and water molecules bound to the fibers by secondary forces such as hydrogen bonding are not removable by mechanical means and must be vaporized in order to be removed from the material during the drying process.

Vaporization of water requires a large amount of energy so good removal of loosely bound water using mechanical means usually is desirable to minimize cost of drying. Most drying processes for textile materials use thermal energy. The thermal energy heats water in the textile material. As the temperature of the water rises, water molecules begin to vaporize and escape into the atmosphere around the material. Mechanisms for heat transfer to textile materials are classified as follows:

Indirect
  Convection
  Conduction
  Irradiation

Direct
  Dielectric
    Microwave
    Radio Frequency

The indirect methods all rely on a heat source external to the material to be dried. In convection heating, hot air is circulated around the material to be dried. Super heated steam or other hot gases can be substituted for air in convection drying. In conduction heating, heat is transferred from a hot surface to the material to be dried by contact between the hot surface and the material being dried. Radiant drying, or drying by irradiation, uses a source with a high content of infrared waves. Water molecules absorb infrared energy causing the water to heat and vaporize. Dielectric heating is classified as direct heating because it is electric energy which vibrates the entire water molecule causing molecular friction and generating heat inside the wet textile material.

Both convection drying and conduction drying often use steam to deliver the energy to the point of drying. Steam is generated in a boiler usually by burning fuel. The mechanism of steam generation is illustrated in Figure 8-6. The temperature of water in the boiler rises 1°F for each BTU of energy input per pound of water. The heat in the water is called "sensible heat." When the water reaches its boiling point, further energy input causes vaporization of water molecules. A pound of water absorbs about 970 BTU's in changing phase from liquid to vapor. The heat absorbed during the phase change from liquid to vapor is called the heat of vaporization or the "latent heat." The latent heat in steam is the energy which is used to evaporate water in a drying process.

Figure 8-6.   Generation of steam

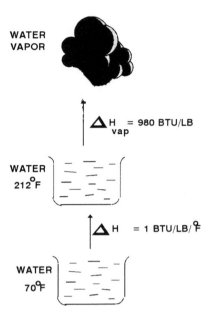

WATER
VAPOR

ΔH_{vap} = 980 BTU/LB

WATER
212°F

ΔH = 1 BTU/LB/°F

WATER
70°F

Convection Dryers

Air for convection drying can be heated using heat exchangers with steam as the heat transfer medium. Alternatively, air can be heated directly from a gas-fired burner.

Dyed yarn packages are often dried by convection. A common type of dryer for yarn packages is called the rapid dryer. The packages on the same perforated cores that were used for dyeing the yarn are placed in the dryer. Hot air is forced through the packages to vaporize the water. The moisture laden air is then passed through a condenser to lower its humidity. The dry air is then reheated in a heat exchanger before being recirculated through the wet yarn.

Continuous drying by convection is usually done in a tenter frame. Blowers impinge hot air on both the bottom and top of the fabric as the fabric passes through the tenter frame.

The tenter frame is equipped with devices to control the dimensions of the fabric both lengthwise and widthwise. Fabrics may be stretched in the lengthwise direction by applying tension to the fabric as it enters the dryer. Some fabrics, notably knits, must be allowed to relax and shrink in length in order to achieve the desired bulk and stretch characteristics. Overfeeding fabric onto the frame allows this shrinkage as drying occurs. Width control is achieved by hold-

Figure 8-7.   Mechanism of cylinder drying

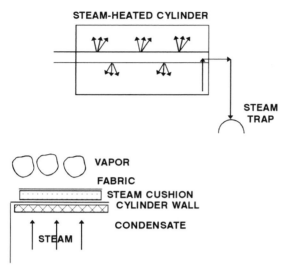

ing the fabric at the required width during drying. Tenter frames are equipped with an endless chain on each side which grips the fabric by both selvages as the fabric enters the frame. The distance between the chains can be increased or decreased along the length of the tenter frame to either stretch the fabric or allow it to shrink as drying proceeds. The gripping action of the chain can be either by pins or clips. In a pin tenter the fabric edges are simply pushed onto sharp pins protruding from the chain. The numerous small holes punched in the selvages by the pins may be undesirable in some cases. Clip tenters grip the fabric with metal clips closely spaced along the chain. Nonuniform heating where the clips grip the fabric can be a problem with clip tenters.

Tenter frames can be used for curing and heat setting of fabrics as well as for drying. In most instances, higher temperature is used for curing or heat setting than for drying. A tenter for high temperature applications may require a direct flame heat source rather than a steam-supplied heater exchanger to achieve the desired temperature.

Conduction Dryers

The best example of conduction drying in textiles is the use of steam-heated drying cylinders to dry materials in continuous processing ranges. The mechanism of cylinder drying is illustrated in Figure 8-7.

The events in the drying process are as follows:

1. Steam is generated in the boiler usually by burning fuel.
2. Steam is admitted to the cylinder through a rotating joint.
3. The cylinder wall condenses steam inside the cylinder.
4. Latent heat released by the condensing steam heats the cylinder wall.
5. Heat transfers through the cylinder wall heating the wet fabric.
6. Water in the fabric heats and vaporizes.
7. Heat transfer from the cylinder to the fabric cools the cylinder so the cylinder condenses more steam.
8. The hot condensate is siphoned from the bottom of the cylinder and returned to the boiler.

This exact same mechanism applies to heating of water in jacketed vessels or with closed heating coils.

Drying capacity of a continuous processing machine often determines the production rate of the machine. Therefore, maximizing the drying rate is often desirable and economically important. Several factors which affect the drying rate in a cylinder drying apparatus can be identified by studying the above description and the figure. These factors are as follows:

1. Cylinder dimensions (or number of cylinders)- The amount of heat transfer and therefore the drying rate depends on the length of time the material is in contact with the heated surface.
2. Steam pressure in the cylinders- Heat transfer rate is a function of cylinder surface temperature which in turn depends on steam pressure in the cylinders.
3. Conductivity of the cylinder wall- Rate of heat transfer depends on the thickness of the cylinder wall and its thermal conductivity. Since the walls of drying cylinders are thin, conductivity of the wall has only a small influence on drying rate.
4. Tension on the material being dried- Higher tension on the material increases contact of the material with the cylinder and increases heat transfer rate and drying rate.
5. Ventilation of the drying apparatus- Vaporization rate depends on the humidity of the surrounding atmosphere. Moisture laden air must be continuously replaced by dry air to keep the drying rate high.

6. The degree to which the material is dried can dramatically affect the drying rate and processing rate of a machine. When the fabric reaches its natural moisture regain, the remaining moisture is chemically bound, and each additional increment of moisture removal becomes more difficult. Therefore, drying materials more than is required can have a large effect on production from the machine.

Note that none of the items listed above will affect energy consumption much or at all. The amount of energy required to evaporate water is about the same regardless of the rate at which drying occurs.

Radiant Dryers

Infrared radiant dryers may be either gas-fired or electric. Gas-fired infrared dryers use burning gas to heat ceramic emitters which impinge the energy on the material passing between banks of the ceramic emitters. Electric infrared dryers use lamps as the infrared source. Predryers in continuous dyeing and finishing processes use infrared energy because the drying is uniform, and migration of chemicals is minimized. Infrared drying during application of coatings is also common. Since infrared waves travel in a straight line, the material must be in the path of the waves in order to absorb the energy and heat up. Therefore, the density of the material being dried affects the efficiency of IR drying. Reflectors are sometimes used to improve the efficiency of use of infrared energy in IR drying processes.

Dielectric Dryers

Most dielectric drying in textiles is done with radio frequency (RF) energy. Radio frequency is the portion of the electromagnetic spectrum between about 1 and 100 MHz. The fact that this range is used for radio communications accounts for the name radio frequency energy. A radio frequency drying oven uses high voltage and an oscillating electrical field. The material to be dried is exposed to the oscillating electrical field as illustrated in Figure 8-8.

The polarity of the electrodes changes at a rate equal to the frequency of the RF energy. Polar molecules, such as water, attempt to line up their poles with the electrical field. The oscillating polarity causes rapid movement of the water molecules. The friction between molecules caused by this motion generates heat in the material which causes the water to vaporize. RF drying is especially suitable for

Figure 8-8.   Schematic representation of dielectric heating mechanism

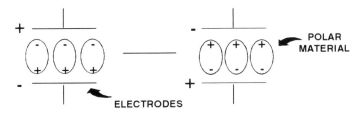

bulky materials such as yarn packages, skeins, and loose fiber. RF energy heats deep within the material and greatly accelerates drying of bulky materials which dry slowly in convection drying systems. Flat fabrics, nonwoven webs, and yarn sheets can be dried using RF energy with proper design of the electrode system.

Steamers

Steamers are commonly used in continuous wet processes to rapidly heat fabric to a temperature of about 100°C and maintain this temperature for the required processing time. A schematic diagram of a steamer is shown in Figure 6-10 on page 188. Steam is admitted from a boiler. The pressure in the steamer should be slightly higher than the pressure of the atmosphere outside the steamer to prevent entry of air into the steamer. Boiling water in the bottom of the steamer keeps the steam saturated with moisture. When cold wet fabric contacts steam, the steam condenses on the fabric transferring its heat to the fabric. If the steam is superheated (not saturated), condensation will not occur, and the steam may actually dry the fabric. Drying of the fabric in the steamer usually adversely affects quality of the material being processed. Air must be excluded from a steamer since it decreases the transfer of heat to the wet fabric. Air is excluded by maintaining a slight positive pressure in the steamer and by using caution with exhaust fans near the steamer.

Bibliography

1. Duckworth, C., Ed., Engineering in Textile Coloration, Dyers Company Publication Trust, West Yorkshire, England, 1983.
2. EPRI, Textile Industry: Profile and DSM Options, Electric Power Research Institute, Report CU-6789, July, 1990.

Index